MICHAEL LYNE

Sporting Artist

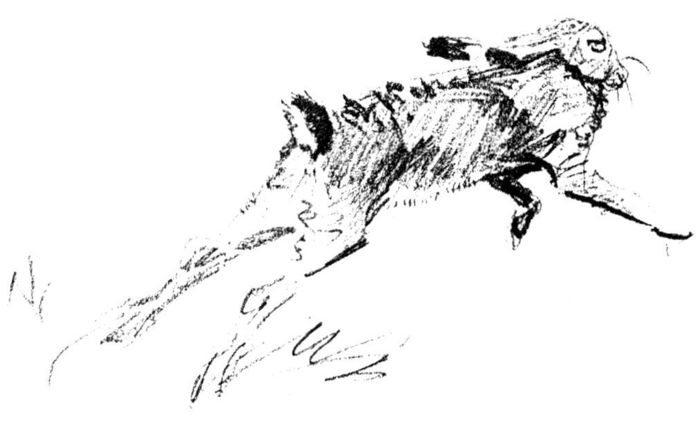

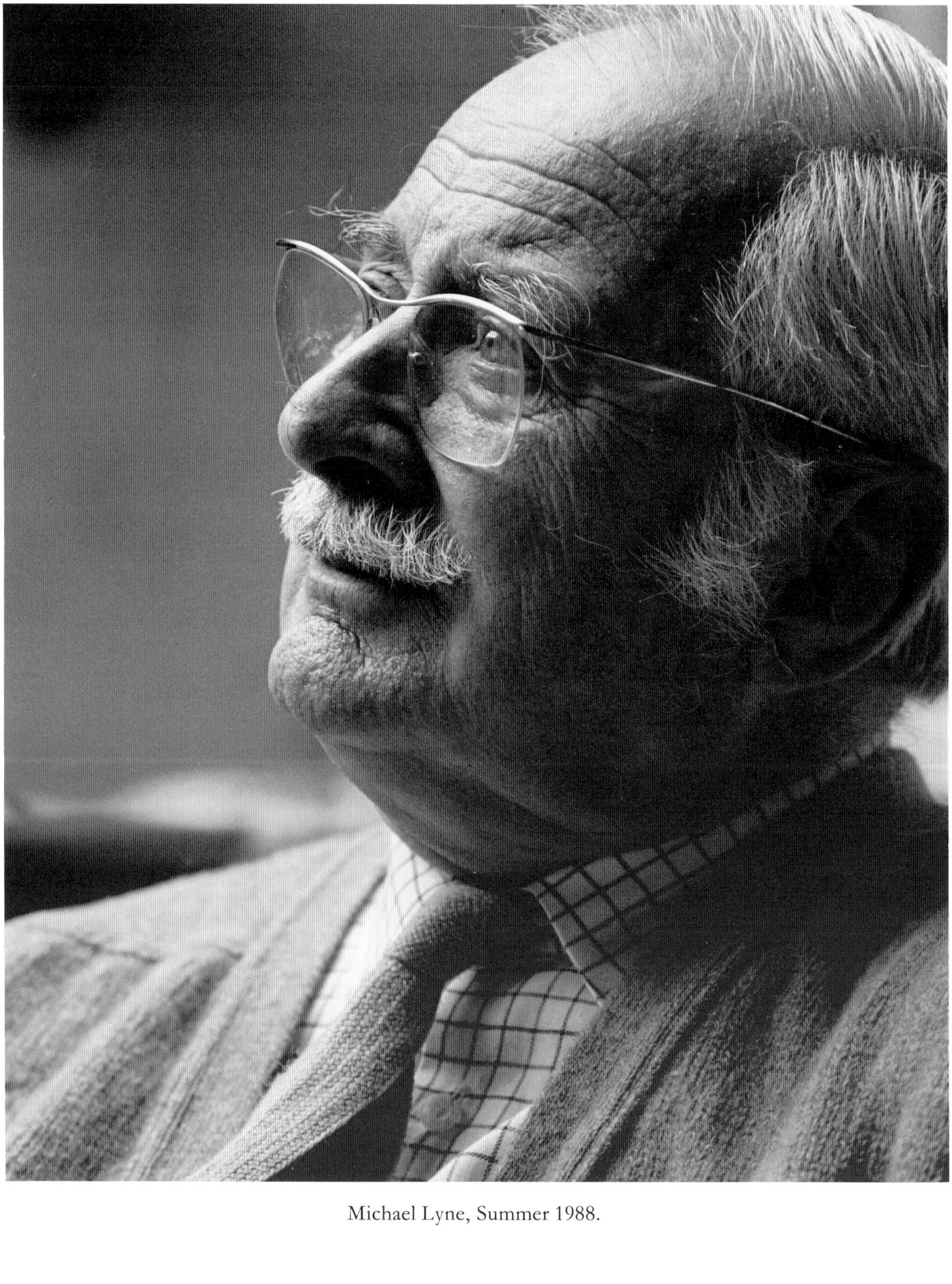

Michael Lyne, Summer 1988.

MICHAEL LYNE
Sporting Artist

John Yeates

Foreword by
Captain RE Wallace, MFH

THE
SPORTSMAN'S
PRESS
LONDON

Published by The Sportsman's Press 1992

TO JESSIE LYNE
WITHOUT WHOSE KNOWLEDGE, ENTHUSIASM AND HELP,
THIS BOOK WOULD NEVER HAVE BEEN WRITTEN

A catalogue record for this book
is available from the British Library

ISBN 0-948253-57 6

Printed in Great Britain by
BAS Printers Limited
Over Wallop, Hampshire

CONTENTS

LIST OF COLOUR PLATES

PLATE 9

Green Spring Valley Hounds, Maryland. J. Fife Symington MFH *and daughter*, 1952.
The Orange County, Virginia, running towards the Blue Ridge Mountains.

PLATE 10

1967 Grand National – The Twenty-Third Fence, 1967.
1965 Grand National – Canal Turn, 1965.

PLATE 11

Arabians Racing at Busetta Racecourse, Tripoli, 1968.
A Fall at the Third Fence: The Maryland Hunt Cup, 1966, 1966.

PLATE 12

The Huntsman, 1968.

PLATE 13

Going to a View Hallo, 1964.
VWH Crossing the River Thames at Kempsford, 1965.

PLATE 14

Ascot: The Parade Ring.
Ascot: The Start, 1964.

PLATE 15

The Last Ounce, 1969.
Photograph for Second and Third.

PLATE 16

Racehorses being exercised on Cleeve Hill, above Cheltenham, 1935.
The Cotswold Hunt, A Lawn Meet at Sudgrove House, 1975.

FOREWORD

by Captain R.E. Wallace, MFH

It was in 1935 that I was first aware of Michael, a neat, quiet figure who observed the scene with an obviously keen eye, as the Hawkstone otterhounds sought out and pursued the nomadic otter on the rivers of his native Herefordshire. The next autumn I was lucky enough to be hunting those wonderful Eton Beagles in that vale of Gloucestershire which lies between Tewkesbury and Winchcombe: Michael descended from his eyrie on Stanley Mount, where he met and courted the charming Jessie, to be a genuine helping hand to Bill Perkins and the young huntsman on those early morning expeditions. He caught the atmosphere in his little painting of a scene on the slopes of Dumbleton Hill (*see Plate 4*). Indeed his numerous watercolours of the Cotswold Hounds with Cyril Heber Percy, the North Cotswold and Bill Scott, and the Ledbury when Bob Champion was huntsman, are to some of us among the best of his work over the years. He had the knowledge of the chase which is essential and his colours of the winter scene were just right.

Michael and I had some affinity over hounds, and his breeding included the beagle crosses, produced before he helped set up the United Cotswold pack just before the war started. There are many tales of his hounds' exploits up in Dumfriesshire in the early days of the war, but I found him again when I returned to the Cotswold country, and then the Heythrop in 1948. An occasional glimpse was to be had of him, still observing a hunting day with that faintly quizzical look, but generally one did not realize he had been out until some masterpiece later appeared in a gallery or at an exhibition. Later personal acquaintance with the American foxhunting scene revealed the appreciation with which his work was widely received over there.

I fancy he found the London commercial pressures rather demanding in later life. His association with John and Judith Yeates gave him pleasure and he would have been delighted first with the exhibition at the Tryon Gallery, planned in his lifetime, but carried on in his honour and memory; and now this book, which must be commended to all who admire hounds, dogs and horses and Michael's interpretation of them. He and Jessie were great contributors to rural values.

ACKNOWLEDGMENTS

The author is grateful to the following:

For information: The Artist's family, particularly his sister, Mrs Mary Winnington Ingram and his children Edward and Diana; Sir Stephen Furness, Bart; Roy Heron; Peter Hunt and Caroline Yeates of the BFSS; Nigel Kearsley; Miss Daphne Moore; Major J.M.C.Parry, MFH; J. Fife Symington of Maryland, USA; Mrs Stella A. Walker; Captain R.E. Wallace, MFH.

For permission to use extracts from previously published work: The Editors of *Horse & Hound*, *The Field* and *Country Life;* Mrs Susan de Courcy Parry for permission to quote from the writings of her late husband (Dalesman); Miss Daphne Moore; Messrs J.A. Allen & Co. Ltd.

Help from fellow members of the Fine Art Trade: Tony Nevill, Frost and Reed; Claude Berry, Tryon Gallery; Turner Reuter Jnr, Red Fox Fine Art of the Commonwealth of Virginia. Also the Fine Art Trade Guild and Venture Prints for details of Limited Edition Prints. David Fuller and Michael Webb.

For permission to use photographs of paintings: The Lyne Trustees; Frost & Reed Ltd; N.M. Brown; Lance Dickerson; Bertram Firestone; The Misses Hepplewhite; Jim Meads; Paul Mellon; Jameina Lady Naylor-Leyland; Major J.M.C. Parry, MFH; Alan Heber Percy; J. Fife Symington; Arthur Vorys; Captain R.E. Wallace, MFH.

Last and Not Least: To my Wife for all her hard work in the preparation of the manuscript and artwork.

I thank God for instilling in me the love of animals and birds,
the quiet places, the simple and the grand things of beauty and
the compelling excitement of the chase

Michael Lyne: *A Parson's Son's Thanksgiving*

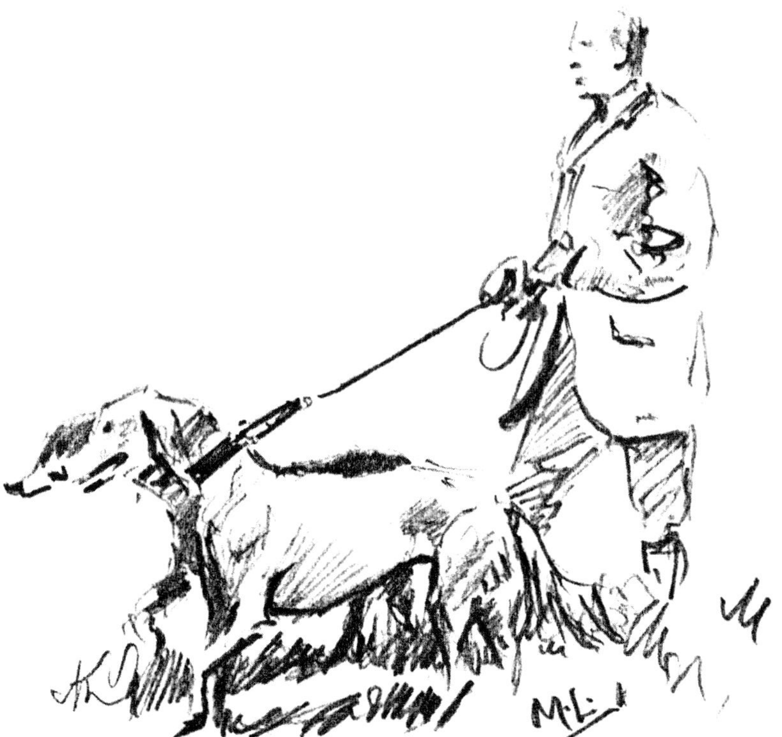

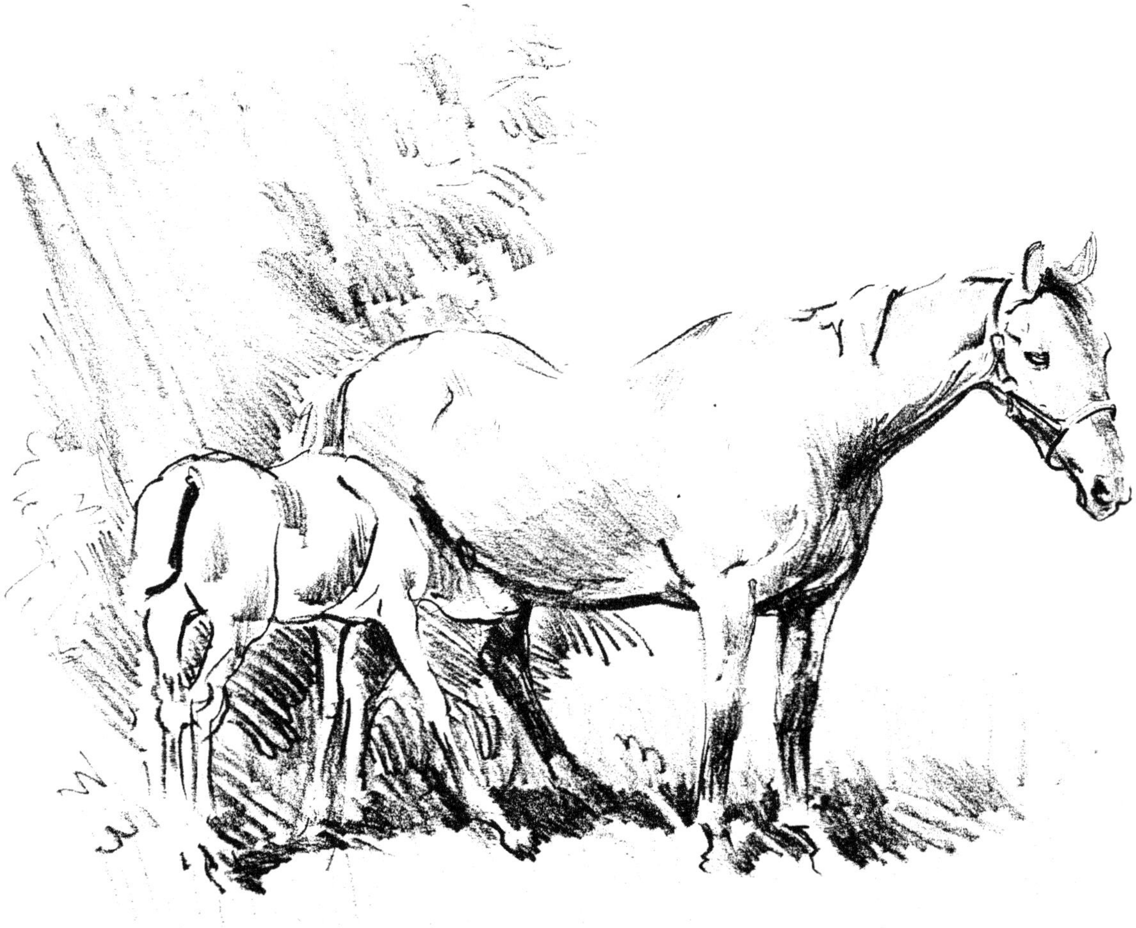

INTRODUCTION

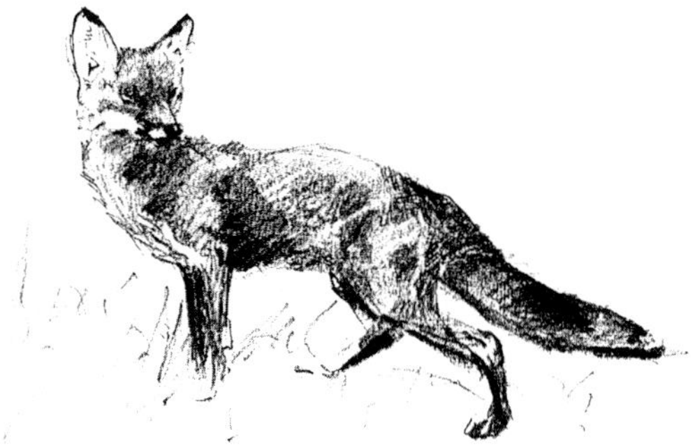

I was introduced to the Lynes and became Michael's agent in early 1980, having two years earlier started a small business in Somerset, the Heale Gallery, dealing in sporting and countryside pictures, on the basis of a countryman dealing with countrymen and sportsmen, and providing the traditional type of picture that had so much become a part of the English country home. I was, at the time, deeply involved in re-introducing Cecil Aldin's work to a new and younger public, being the first post-war dealer to handle a large volume of his pictures.

I was delighted to be invited, with my wife, to lunch at Dunfield, and most surprised when, over coffee, Michael asked me to act for him and sell his work, for though he wanted to reduce his painting commitments, he was deeply troubled that his public would soon forget him and his pictures. I accepted and soon the business association became a strong personal friendship, which only ended with Michael's death, but continues today with his widow, Jessie.

Michael wanted someone who was able to sell his work on a low key basis and provide a regular income, while at the same time protecting him from external pressures and commercial problems. It was an ideal arrangement and gave the Lynes the sense of security which might otherwise have been missing. Another aspect of the relationship which the Lynes greatly enjoyed, was the deep involvement of my wife. Michael had always enjoyed the total support of Jessie, and both enjoyed the family style of the business, the two wives becoming firm friends and working closely together.

In the early stages of preparing this manuscript, I intended to write a resumé of Michael Lyne as a man and as an artist, something which would do full justice to both him and his paintings. As work progressed, my feelings changed, I was aware of a man who, to his family, was a wise and loving father; to the sporting art world, an individualistic and idiosyncratic painter; and to the field sport fraternity, a dedicated foxhunter, beagler and coursing enthusiast, who, like us all, had faults, but was essentially both a modest and private person, entirely genuine in every respect. His circle of friends was small and reflected his sporting interests; artistically he was a loner and had no contact with other sporting artists, other than meeting Lionel Edwards and Tom Carr in the 1950s.

Many books will no doubt follow this volume and attempt, each in its turn, to be either analytical or critical; it is the purpose of this volume to be neither; rather to tell the story, just as it was, of the young man with the vision of our 'eternal heritage' and the talent and ability to present the vision in a fresh and compelling way for almost sixty years. During these years England was to change beyond recognition. The practice of field sports was no exception – and what was left in 1945 was to alter and be eroded by the growth of modern farming techniques and relentless urbanization of the countryside, nearly to a point where it could be said of foxhunting 'almost everything has changed'. Yet for Michael the end, in 1989, was the same as the beginning in 1930, his world seemed to be forever in a golden age, unaffected by the vicissitudes of a modern life; his talent still had the freshness and sanity of a much younger man though echoing an older, kinder England.

Dalesman, the late 'Bay' de Courcy-Parry, writing in 1938, drew to the attention of readers of the newly published *Horses, Hounds and Country* the timeless quality of Michael Lyne's work; 'In his pictures there is movement and life and in his backgrounds you see

The Belvoir at Goadby Gorse, 1987. Watercolour, 8 × 12 in (20 × 31 cm).

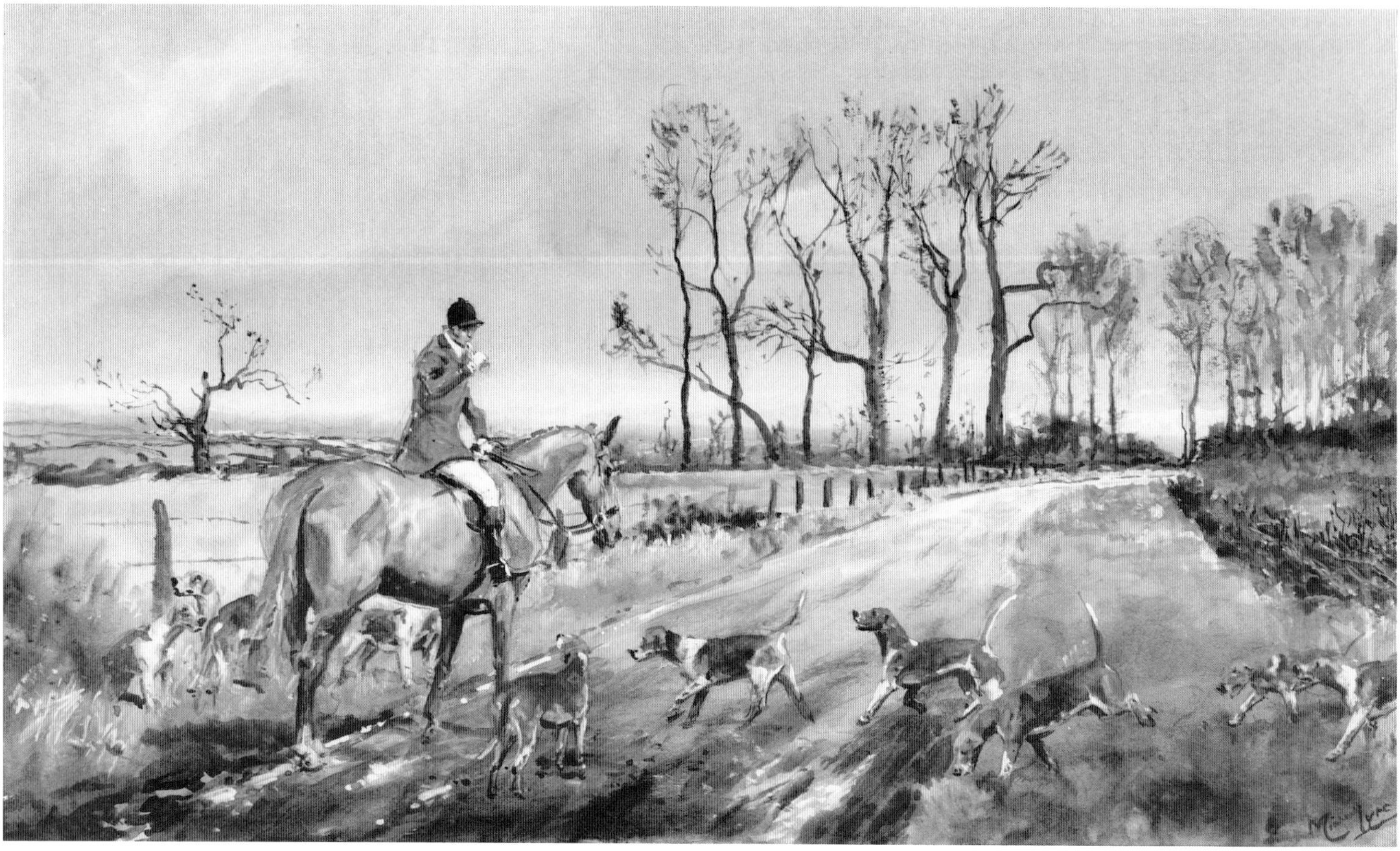

rolling to eternity, to the very dawn of time itself our eternal heritage, England.' With his customary shrewdness, Dalesman also spotted and commented on another facet of the twenty-six-year-old artist's work: 'The subject [hunting] has been ridden to uttermost endurance, then along comes Michael Lyne, with his pencil and his brush, with his vigour and his inimitable optimism and re-awakens all the old echoes again, captures the illusion, if illusion it be, or perhaps rather the enchantment, the magic, and imprisons it for evermore.'

Michael Lyne was a true countryman and a true gentleman, in addition to being a highly professional artist, and this fitted perfectly with his private and reticent character. He did not welcome investigation and analysis. Much that was written about him and his work would appear to be a pastiche of a perceptive and informed article written by the water-colour painter, Adrian Bury in 1965. Michael sought to redress the balance and produced two semi-autobiographical works: *A Parson's Son* (1974) and *The Michael Lyne Sketchbook* (1979). It is these, together with the much earlier *Horses, Hounds and Country* (1938) that reveal, to those who knew him well, the true nature, motivation and outlook of the man.

Michael Lyne fits into no accepted place in the history of English sporting art. Munnings and Edwards inspired him and provided the initial impetus for his art, but they were never imitated or copied, to think otherwise would be to do less than justice to Michael's ability and character. He was an honest man and never knowingly copied anyone or anything. To say that his work is a pastiche of Edwards or Munnings betrays a lack of understanding of his art; although he certainly felt that he followed too closely on their heels having worked in their shadow for most of his painting life.

In many ways Michael was a less sophisticated painter than Munnings and Edwards. He did not seek glamour and well-bred horses, his was a more earthy, intimate, visually experimental style of painting. There was also undoubtedly an influence from the photographers of *The Tatler* and the *Sporting and Dramatic News*, who had a vital, yet to be explored, impact on the foxhunting painters of the twentieth century: a point of reference used by most artists, including Lionel Edwards, and in the following generation, Malvern artist Eric Meade-King (1911–1987) and Peter Biegel (1913–1989) (who inherited Lionel Edwards' reference collection of old wide angle *Sporting and Dramatic* photographs) for the presentation of horses and figures in landscape.

A much more positive influence, in the post Second World War era, was that of Edward Seago, whom Michael had served with as a Camouflage Officer and whose oil paintings he greatly admired; particularly those of wide East Anglian landscapes with high driven skies and little foreground, executed in strong firm brushwork. Both the technique and presentation can clearly be seen in many of the Lyne oil paintings of the 1950s and 1960s and are shown to perfection in the high clear Cotswold skies of so many paintings.

It is interesting to consider the development of Michael Lyne's art. A gifted imaginative child, he was artistically untutored; though his mother was a well known floral artist and exhibited regularly, she never gave him any tuition in the art of watercolour painting. The only formal training he received was a short period at the Cheltenham School of Art, and until his death, his knowledge of the history of art was so limited, that other than the work of Stubbs and Landseer, he had little or no knowledge of European painters or painting. Michael read widely, but not on artistic matters. In addition to receiving no formal art education until his early twenties, Michael, other than in the pages of illustrated social and sporting magazines, would have had virtually no access to the work of living sporting painters other than one or two pictures in local Herefordshire houses, nor did he possess a library of illustrated sporting books until the late 1930s. Cheltenham and the Whitcombe Gallery would help rectify this deficiency, but it is a source of wonder to me that after a period of hibernation and gestation, Michael was able to produce, in 1934, watercolours such as those in the Heber Percy collection. These are full of knowledge of his subject, technically of a high quality, and carrying the authority of self-assurance. In his own words they were 'strong watercolours, combining the power of an oil painting with the delicacy of a watercolour', and indicating fully that the artist was a hunting man bound by the traditions and technicalities of his sport and well able to command the respect of his patrons. Also, Michael's positive and voluptuous sense of colour was very much in evidence, even in these early days.

It is also worthy of note that Michael did not meet Lionel Edwards until almost the end of the latter's long life (the mid-1950s) and then enquired of Edwards how he conceived his style of painting. Edwards referred to the pictures of Major Godfrey Douglas Giles (1857–1941), a painter almost unknown to Michael, depicting wide landscapes with a feeling of space and the excitement of the hunt. Certainly Michael felt that 'as regards the composition of a hunting picture, after much trial and error, it seems that there is no better way to paint a hunt scurry than in the style of Lionel Edwards'; it was these paintings which, Michael maintained, with their realism and excitement of the chase, influenced him to attempt to become a so-called sporting artist, though obviously he tried hard to improve on them.

The young Lyne succeeded in reconciling the conflicting interests of the artist and the sportsman, allowing himself little or no artistic licence, but giving a clear indication of what was happening and the distinctive atmosphere of the occasion (*see p. 69*). He had justified the expectations of 'those who give encouragement', the dedication of *Horses, Hounds and Country*. External influences were to be effective on two further occasions in Michael's life. The first in 1949, when he discovered the United States and subsequently oil painting. The second in 1967 when Stella A. Walker pleaded 'for sporting art to come out of the doldrums and for sporting artists to experiment'. Michael heeded this call and for the final years of his painting life, it was to provide the stimulus for his imaginative mind.

In his use of paint and brush, Michael was adventurous, the nearest sporting comparison being Gilbert Holiday (1879–1937), but Holiday did not paint in oils. In his early water-

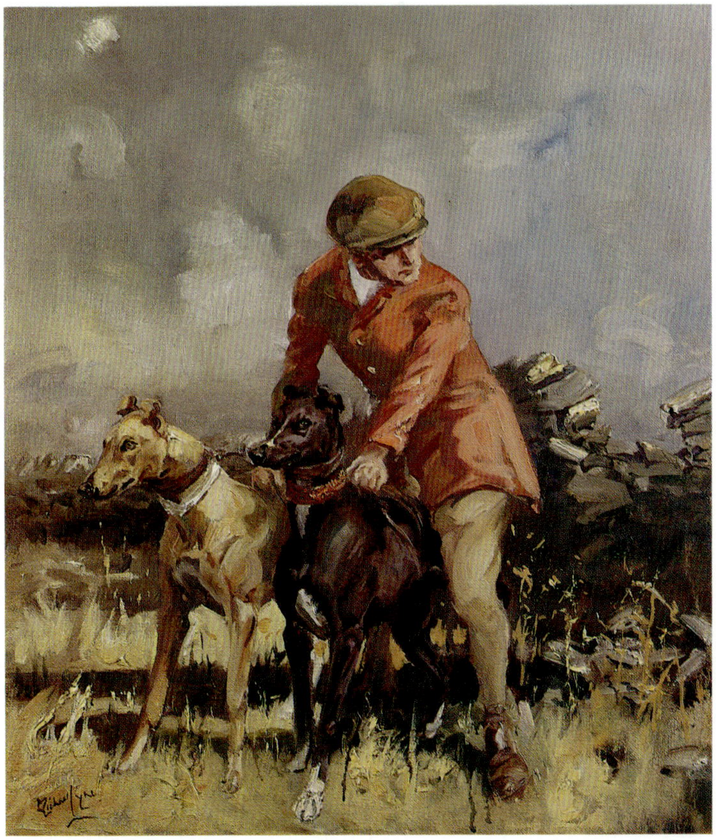

The Slipper, 1969. Signed, oil on canvas, 30 × 24 in (76 × 61 cm). The artist was a Steward of The National Coursing Club, the sport's ruling body.

PLATE 1

(*below*) *The White Pony* (or *Down from the Hill*), 1967. Signed, oil on canvas, 20 × 24 in (51 × 61 cm). Roddy, Colonel Harry Nicholl Gillie at the Black Corries, Argyllshire. Michael Lyne rated stalking the best of all field sports with its combination of skill, knowledge and dependence on the terrain.

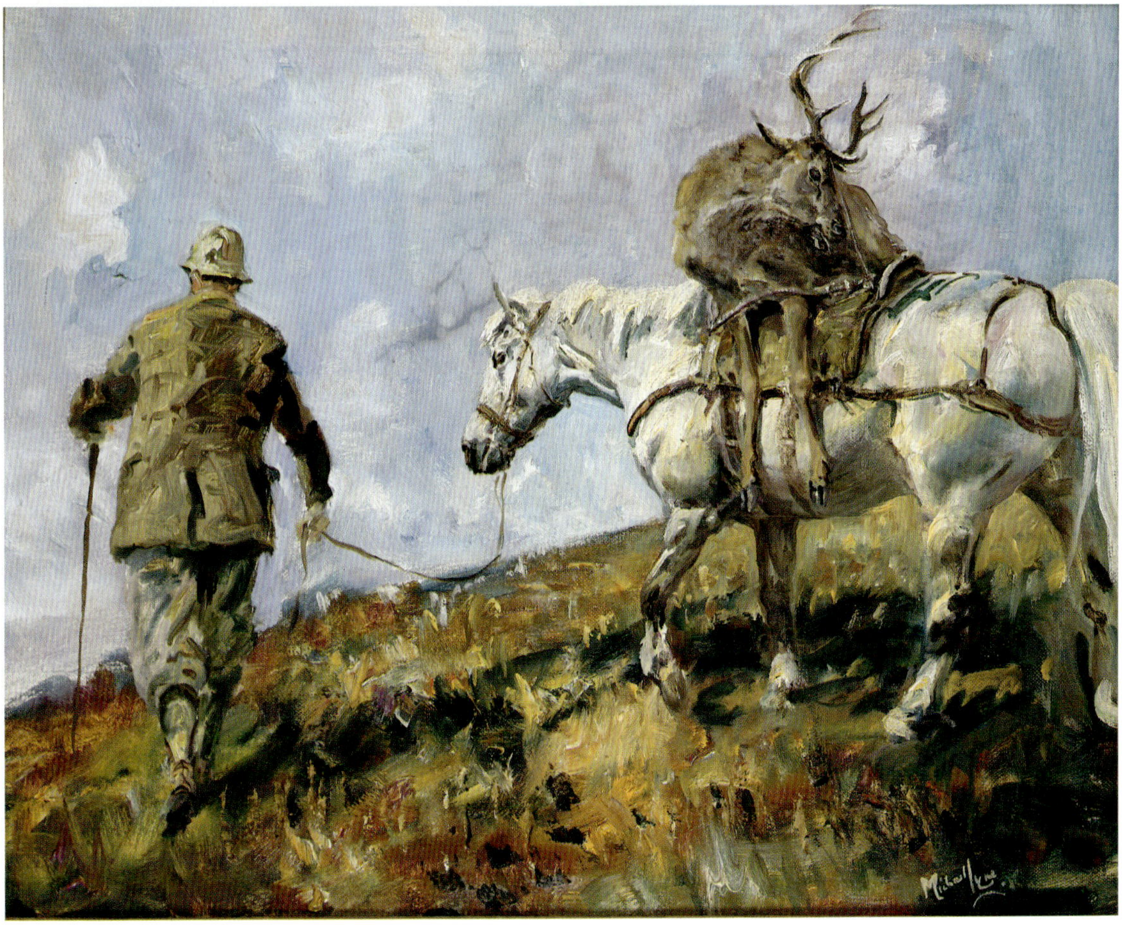

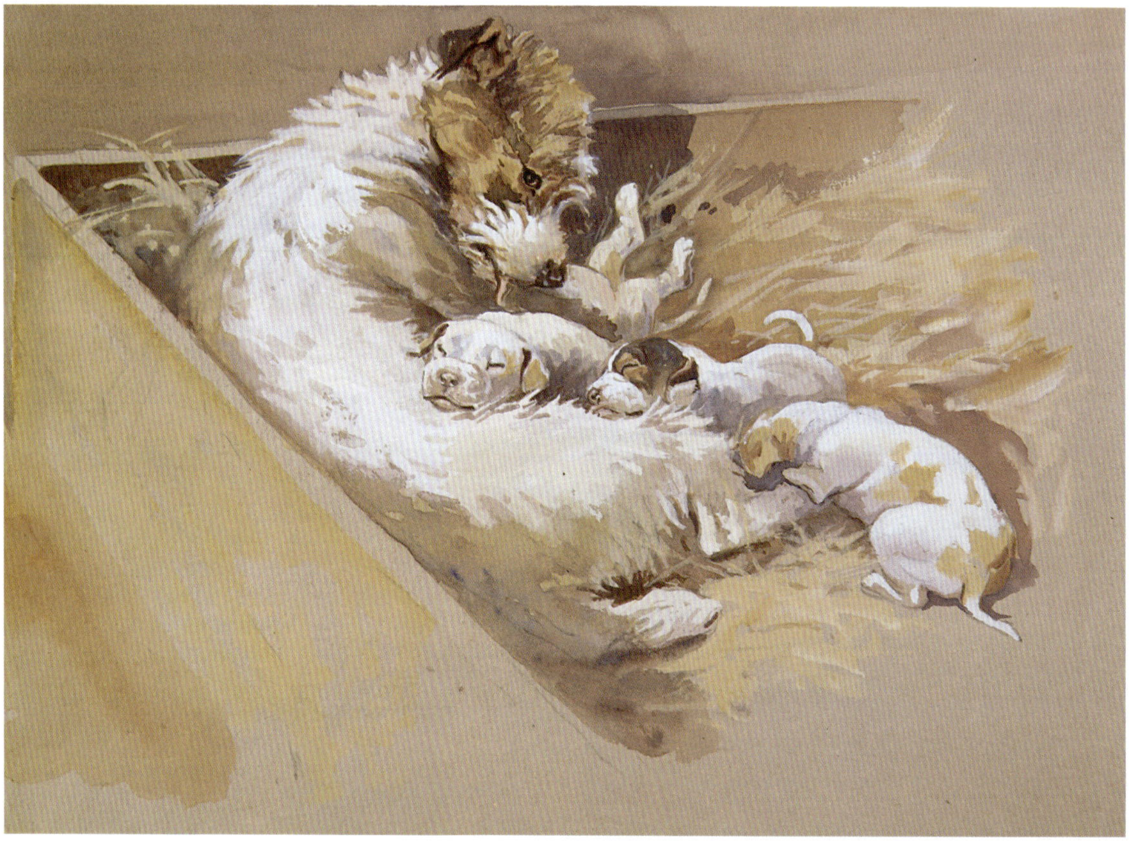

Lorna lying in a whelping box and four pups aged about three days, 1947. Unsigned, watercolour, 7 × 10 in (18 × 26 cm). Lorna was a rough-haired working terrier with some Sealyham blood bought from gypsies in the Doone Valley, Exmoor. She was mated with Pipewell Justice, a lemon and white beagle in 1946/7.

PLATE 2

The Pond at Dunfield: Winter, 1956. Signed and dated, oil on canvas, 16 × 20 in (41 × 51 cm). The wildfowl include scaup on the pond, Bahama pintail (*top right*), and (*from top left*), teal, Carolina, Chilean teal and Mandarin duck.

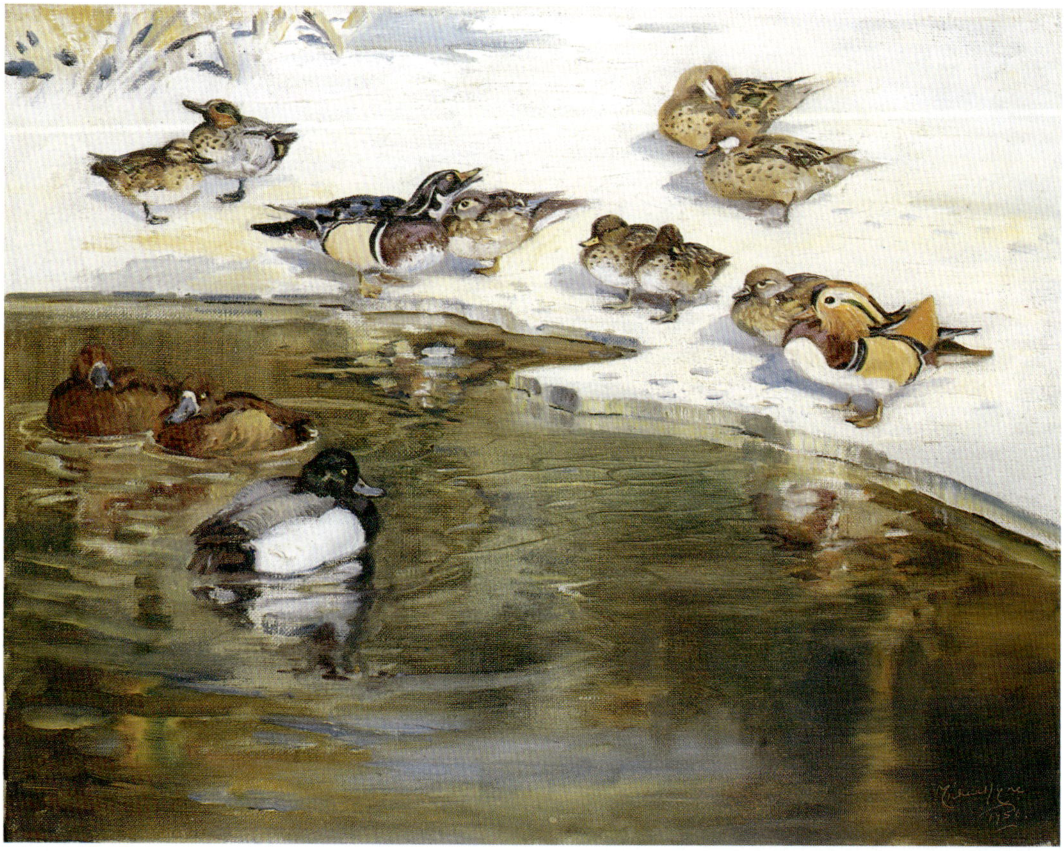

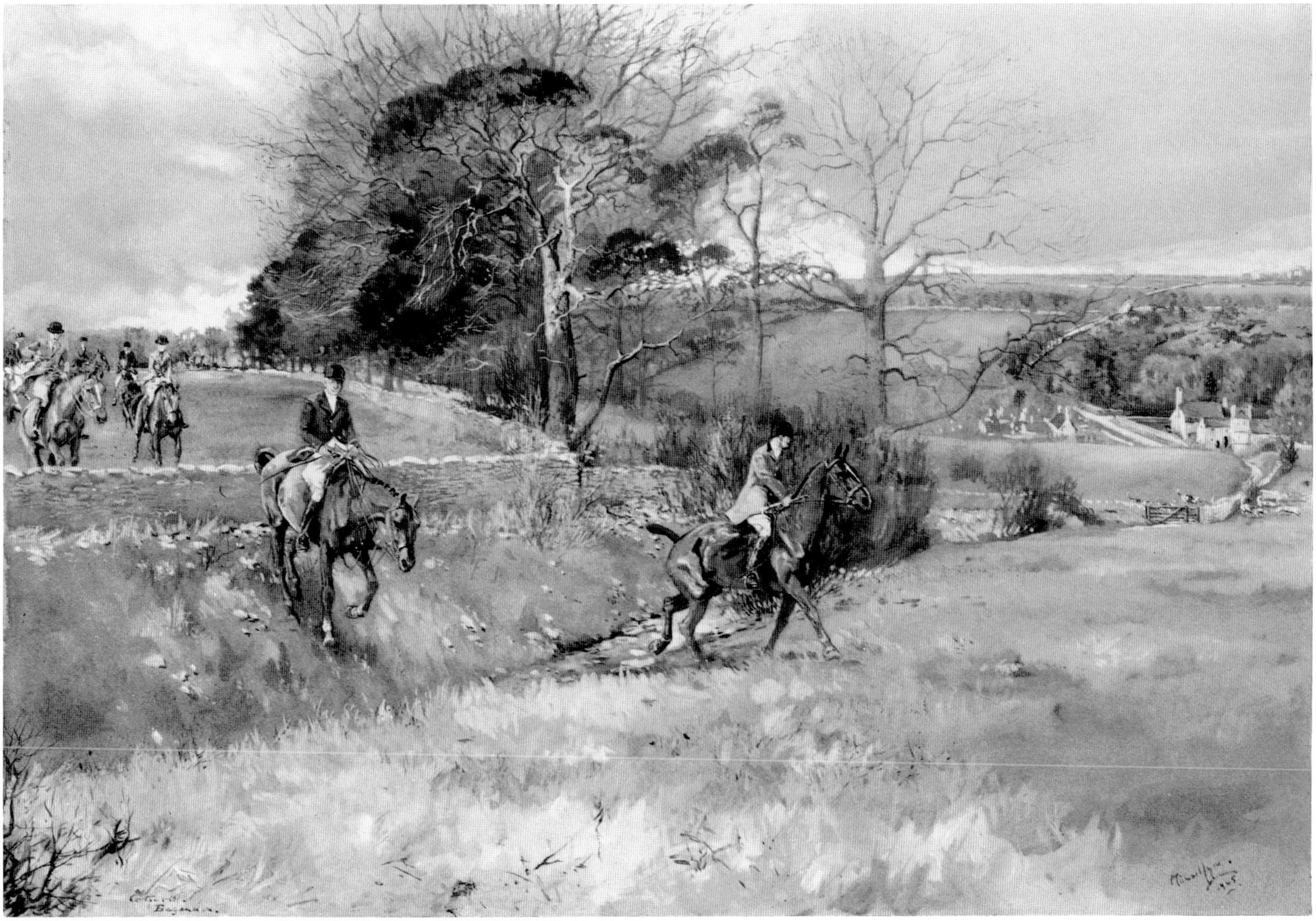

The Cotswold at Bagendon, 1945. Watercolour, 13 × 19 in (33 × 48 cm).
This painting was included in the Retrospective Exhibition at the Tryon Gallery in 1989.

colours, Michael painted in the consistency in which the paint came from the tube, using in addition white, so that the paint was used opaquely and the pictures can be more accurately described as gouache or watercolour with body. It is only in sketches that there is the usual translucency of watercolour on paper. Later he developed the vigourous brush stroke and palette knife works of the large oils of the mature period, and finally the more watery watercolour studies when he was preoccupied with effect and atmosphere, rather than detail, and the oils became rather stark and abrasive in style. However much Michael's methods and approach with paint and brush may have varied throughout his working life, his draughtmanship remained impeccably constant: pen and pencil were never idle and a stream of working sketches, finely observed drawings and book illustrations were

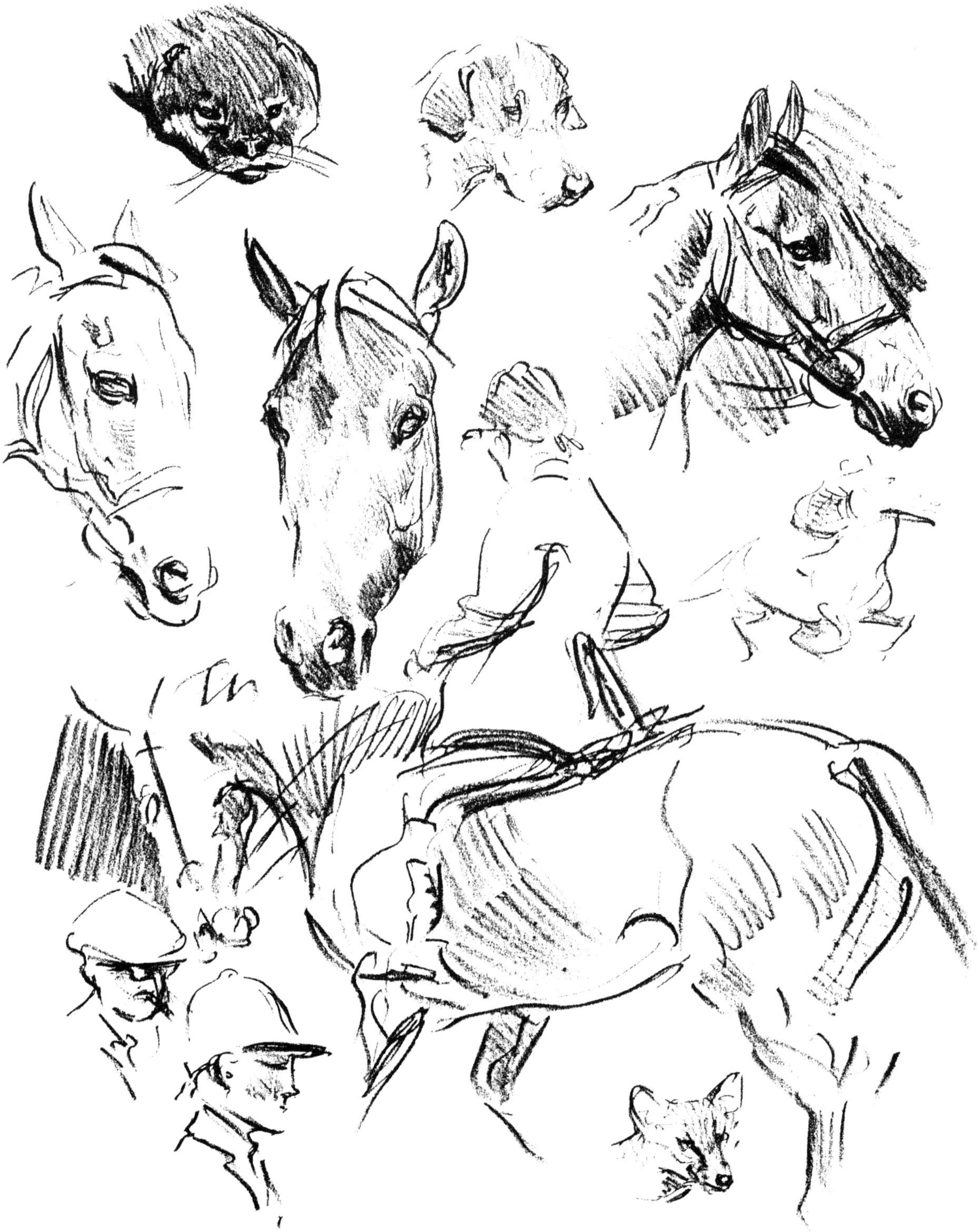

produced which are undoubtedly some of his finest works. These were supplemented at the end of his life, when it was no longer physically possible to go out on location and sketch, by a series of large charcoal working drawings in which it was possible to see Michael thinking aloud (*see p. 99*). Up to the very end, the pencil never stopped, and it is my view that Michael will be remembered as much for his draughtmanship as for his painting.

With Michael's death, not only a painting career of almost three score years ended, but also one of the greatest periods of English sporting art, for while he was only a junior contemporary of Munnings, Edwards, Snaffles, Stewart, Aldin and Holiday, it was he who carried on the great tradition and through his experimental approach to his later subject matter, has thrown out enough visual hints and challenges to serve as a point of departure to those who will follow after. It is sad that Michael had no gifts as a teacher and consequently no formal pupils – but he was a great encourager and advisor and many painters benefitted including Peter Curling, Nigel Kearsley, Louise Wood, Jean Walker and Ninetta Butterworth.

I will close on a personal note. Driving to Michael's funeral, together with my daughter, who whips in for a beagle pack, we turned east onto a minor road at the foot of Blunsdon Hill and half a mile or so further on we were both surprised to see a hare of immense proportions sitting upright in an open field gateway, solemnly watching the car pass by; in unison we both felt the urge to salute the animal. After the service I mentioned the encounter to Jessie Lyne, who smiled knowingly and commented that hares were never found in that area. An uncanny hunting coincidence or a final farewell? – Both my daughter and I prefer the latter explanation.

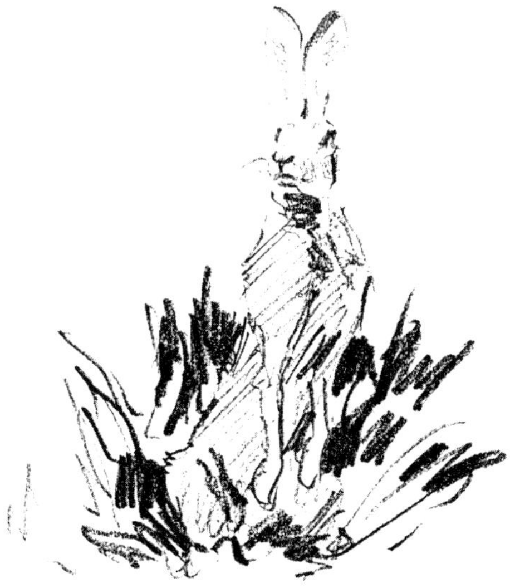

ONE

EARLY DAYS 1912–1932

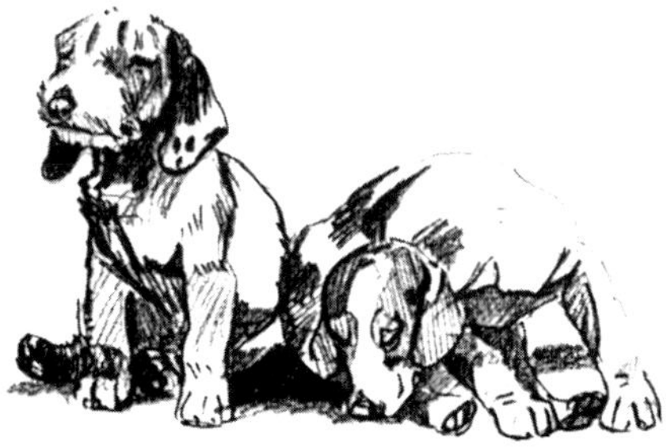

Breeding is of a particular interest to those professionally concerned with hounds and Thoroughbred racehorses, and it is also true that the child is the father of the man. Michael Lyne was born in 1912, the third and youngest son of the Reverend Arundell Lyne and Mrs Joan Lyne, in the small Herefordshire village of Upton Bishop near Ross-on-Wye, in the Welsh Marches. Charles Edward Michael Lyne inherited, in full measure, the artistic, practical, commercial and religious traits of his maternal ancestor, John Bacon, RA, (1740–1799) (see Appendix 1), together with the qualities brought into the family by his Jewish maternal great grandmother. In breeding and racing terms, this is exactly what so many strive to obtain – but so few achieve – one could in fact draw an analogy between our artist and those two great steeplechasers, Golden Miller and Arkle, each of whom was an unexpectedly brilliant progeny, from undistinguished breeding lines, inheriting through their dams outstanding qualities from far distant forebears.

Little is known of the Lynes other than they were an established clerical family from Liskeard, Cornwall, where they are well-represented amongst the tombstones of the parish churchyard. Richard Arundell Lyne (1870–1955) graduated from Selwyn College, Cambridge in 1892, after gaining some distinction in rowing, and trained for the ministry of the Church of England at Wells Theological College, Somerset. He was ordained deacon by the then Bishop of Hereford in 1894 and priest the following year; being given his title by the Rector of Ludlow where he served as curate for a number of years and commenced a ministry of over sixty years in the Diocese of Hereford. From Ludlow he moved to a succession of three small rural parishes. In 1905, whilst at Hoarwithy, he met the prosperous Bacon family from Burghclere, near Newbury, Berkshire, who had taken a large furnished house in the district for the summer. Unlike the Lynes, the Bacons were a well known and established family and traced their ancestry to the sculptor, John Bacon. The Bacons lived in some style at Burghclere; Francis Bacon was a successful architect of some substance and in addition to taking a moor in Scotland for the shooting, was also in the habit of moving to rural houses around England for the summer months, complete with family and servants. It was on such a jaunt that the Bacons moved to Herefordshire. Mr Lyne was attracted to the family who in true Trollopian fashion, considered him to be a suitable match for one of their elder daughters but in fact he was attracted to the youngest daughter, Cicely Joan, whom he married in 1906, having accepted the Vicarage

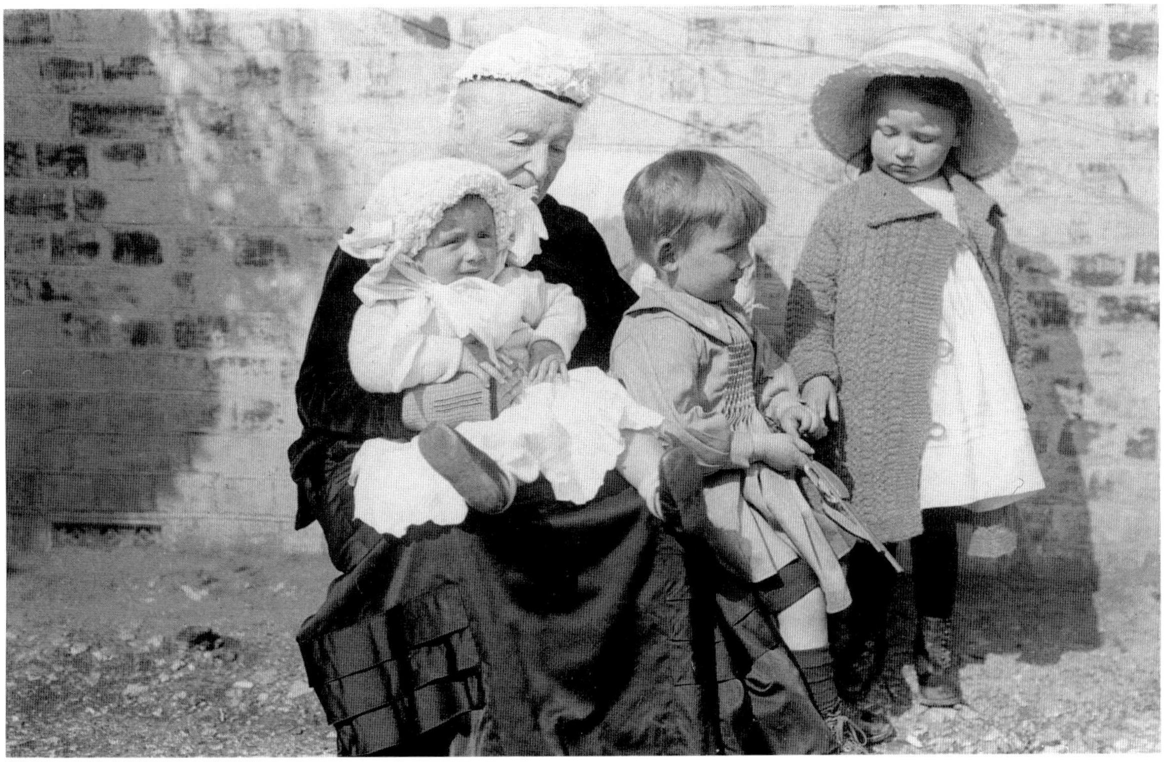

Taken about 1910, this photograph covers 180 years of family life. Mrs John Bacon, Michael's great grandmother, who was born in 1811, has John in her arms, with Richard and Mary standing. Mary, the last surviving Lyne child, now lives in Hampshire. It was from this great-grandmother that Michael inherited his powerful sense of colouring.

at Woolhope in anticipation of the event.The Lyne's first child, their daughter Mary was born at Woolhope, followed by a son, Richard. The family moved in 1910 to the Vicarage of Upton Bishop, Ross-on-Wye, where two further sons were born: John in 1911 and Michael a year later.

Towards the end of the First World War the four Lyne children, Mary, Richard, John and Michael, together with their nurse, spent a holiday with their maternal grandparents in Berkshire. During the course of the holiday Grandmother Bacon watched them closely and for each child made a character assessment, and forecast, with a considerable degree of accuracy, what their respective futures would be. Michael Lyne's assessment reads:

Very precocious, brilliant, imaginative.
Too fond of (gallery) praises.
He may become a great man or grow more
normal as he develops.
Strong in health. Excitable
Refined in features and figure.'

At home in the Upton Bishop Vicarage, the young Michael Lyne had left behind two small books: *The Lonely Dog* and *Mrs Bunny's Day Out* which he had dictated to his Mother and then illustrated. These, together with illustrated letters from school, are now treasured by the Lyne family.

Today the English country parson is with a few exceptions, almost a thing of the past; something one reads about on the pages of Trollope or sees in TV drama productions, when he was a gentleman graduate of Oxford, Cambridge or Trinity College, Dublin, looking after a large family and a small parish, on an even smaller income. Lyne's maximum income was £328 per annum plus his vicarage! Today the parish priest is far removed from his parson forebear. The amalgamation of parishes, lack of interest in organised religion, rising standards of living, the growth of the social services and steady drift to the towns have all undermined the place of the parson in rural society. The impact of modern life has been total: even on the Church of England. Richard Arundell Lyne, with the rest of his kind, represented the lost paternalism of a classical rural institution. He was a gentlemanly, kindly man, dedicated to the spiritual and moral welfare of his parishioners, tied to them by the structure of rural society and the working of his glebe land in time honoured tradition. At home he was the kind helpful father seeking to maintain his family and rear

Upton Bishop Vicarage, Ross-on-Wye, Herefordshire. Michael was born here in 1912; his father was Vicar from 1910–1925.

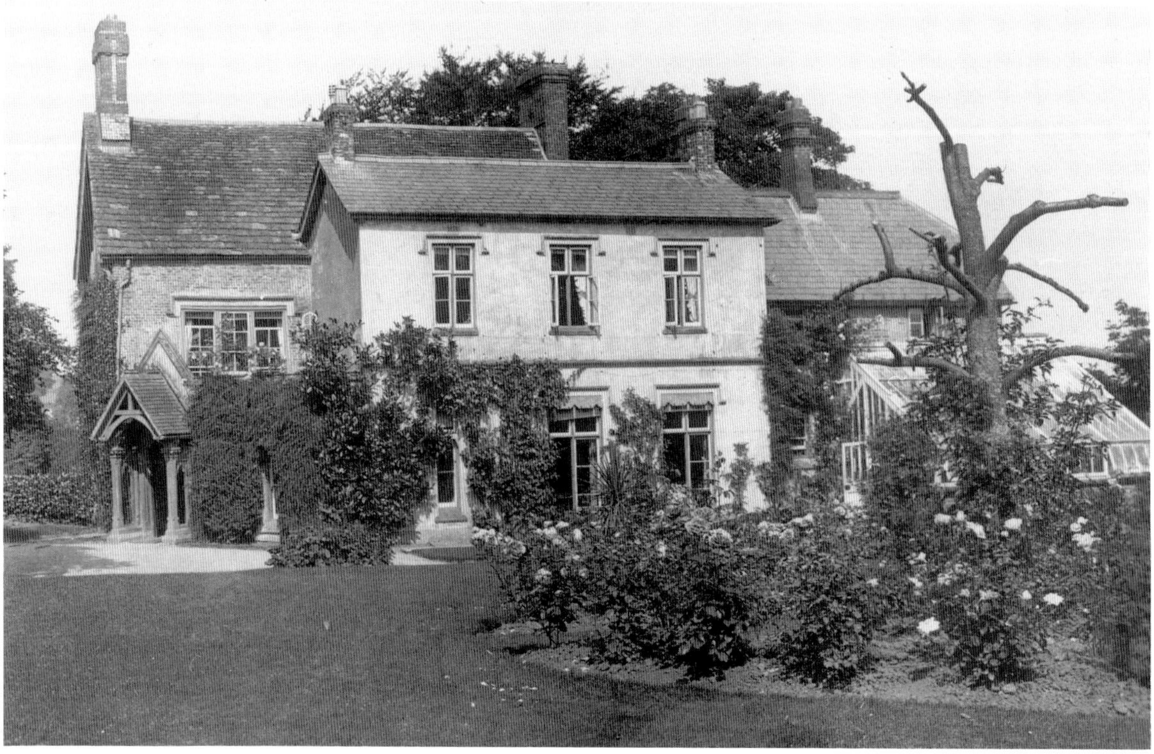

them as he himself had been reared; finding his relaxation in a close circle of friends and the care of his garden and greenhouse.

Society in the Welsh Marches had changed little over several hundred years: the First World War had come and gone, leaving deep and indelible marks, the country remained relatively untouched by the dramatic changes in urban society following the 1914–1918 War and the economic depression which followed. The old society and the old rural structures remained. Permanence was still the great feature of this countryside. Lyne spent the whole sixty years of his ministry in the Diocese of Hereford; local Masters of Foxhound and Harrier packs likewise served for long periods. Mr J.F. Twinberrow was Master of the North Ledbury from 1905 to 1931 and was followed first by his wife and then his daughter, Lady Waechter and her husband. Ray Thompson hunted the Wye Valley Otterhounds for twenty-five years and then proceeded to be Master of the Ross Harriers from 1940 to 1947. Farms remained within the same family for generations. The hurt of war had been great, every village war memorial testified to that, but rural life and society still remained.

In the pages of literature it is hunting writer Daphne Moore's brother, novelist John Moore, who, in his *Portrait of Elmbury* and *Brensham Village* gives a clear feeling and evocative account of the final score of years of this age, though in the Severn Valley – not the Wye Valley. What John Moore did for the Dalesman's 'Eternal Heritage, England', with his pen, his near contemporary, Michael Lyne, caught and perpetuated with his brush.

Upton Bishop Vicarage, now a private house due to parochial reorganisation, must have been identical with many more: over-large, inconvenient, with a large and well tended garden, farm buildings and a lot of glebe land. There were two maids to run the house and a gardener and a garden boy to look after the outside, plus a nanny (Annie Leighton – she spent seventy years with two generations of the family) to look after the children. The four children did everything together and in the words of the sole survivor Mary, had a 'wonderful childhood'. They became a completely self-contained unit, isolated not only by their rural location, but by the strict social code of the era. As Vicarage children, they would not mix with village children; likewise, unless invited, they would not mix with the families from the large houses. The village shop was well stocked and provided for all their needs: the nearest town was some miles distant and only accessible by pony cart, though Lyne had a motor car from 1910 onwards. The old house was full of stone passages, long corridors, in which to roller skate, and lots of stairs. The gardens and fields were to play in and the water supply failed in the summer. Adjoining the Vicarage was Upton Court, the home of the Powell family until 1967. They farmed, maintained a herd of pedigree Hereford cattle and hunted. Mr Powell was one of the two churchwardens of the parish and took a keen interest in the vicarage children.

The First World War had little direct effect on the Lyne family, Lyne being too old for service with the Royal Army Chaplains' Corps, and Michael only two years of age in 1914. But in common with every other family, the Lynes suffered the dreadful stress and shortage of food. One effect on the children was a shortage of children's parties, until they were much older, but the Sunday School treat was allowed and was something much to be looked forward to. Christmas saw a marked increase in family activity with the hand-making of presents for family and friends. Delivering the Parish Almanac was another job for the vicarage children, and made a useful objective in the daily walks with Nanny. The Almanac was in effect the Vicar's Christmas card to his parishioners and took the form of a large sheet of paper (to hang on the wall); in the middle it had a religious picture and was surrounded by all types of information: phases of the moon, first aid hints, and details of church services. Delivery was much enjoyed and the children found themselves in receipt of small gifts and sweets. Further Christmas bonuses included being allowed to decorate the church, under the watchful eye of the Sexton, and an annual visit to the Manor House, on Boxing Day, for tea.

Michael Lyne was always proud of his godfathers, both parishioners and friends of his father: one a Major, the other an Admiral. In time-honoured fashion, each would vie with the other as to who made the most spectacular entrance into church on Sundays, complete with family and servants. Michael was, like all younger brothers, always trying to keep up with his elder brothers and sister. As the youngest child and the one with artistic ability, he enjoyed a very special relationship with his mother which was to continue until her death in 1974. Again like younger children, being teased was also his lot – his small rather thick hands were referred to as 'mole paws'.

Unlike the other three Lyne children, Michael was educated at home until he was eleven, though he much resented having to take lessons and did not find it easy to make friends outside the family circle. In this sense Michael had a much lonelier childhood than his brothers and sister – suffering the restrictions of an isolated home and the strict social conventions of the time. It was inevitable that the gifted, precocious, imaginative child, should retreat into an escapist world of make-believe, though in typical fashion, this was very practical make-believe indeed.

It became his habit throughout his childhood to scribble drawings of animals, and the faster they moved the better young Lyne liked it. When he was very young, he had crazes for drawing different animals: he would insist on being told or reading about a different species of animal which he would illustrate and later draw in every conceivable position. For the duration of the craze (about a fortnight) he was, and lived, the part of the animal in his imagination, following as closely as possible the habits and characteristics of the creature concerned. Nanny Leighton's tolerance was severely exercised when, during a fox period, Michael obtained a fox brush from the kindly neighbour, Mr Powell of Upton Court and had it attached to the seat of his trousers, telling everyone in all seriousness that he was indeed a fox! Prior to going to Rossall his father gave Michael an inscribed copy of S.L. Bensusan's charming short novel, told in the first person, *The Life-Story of*

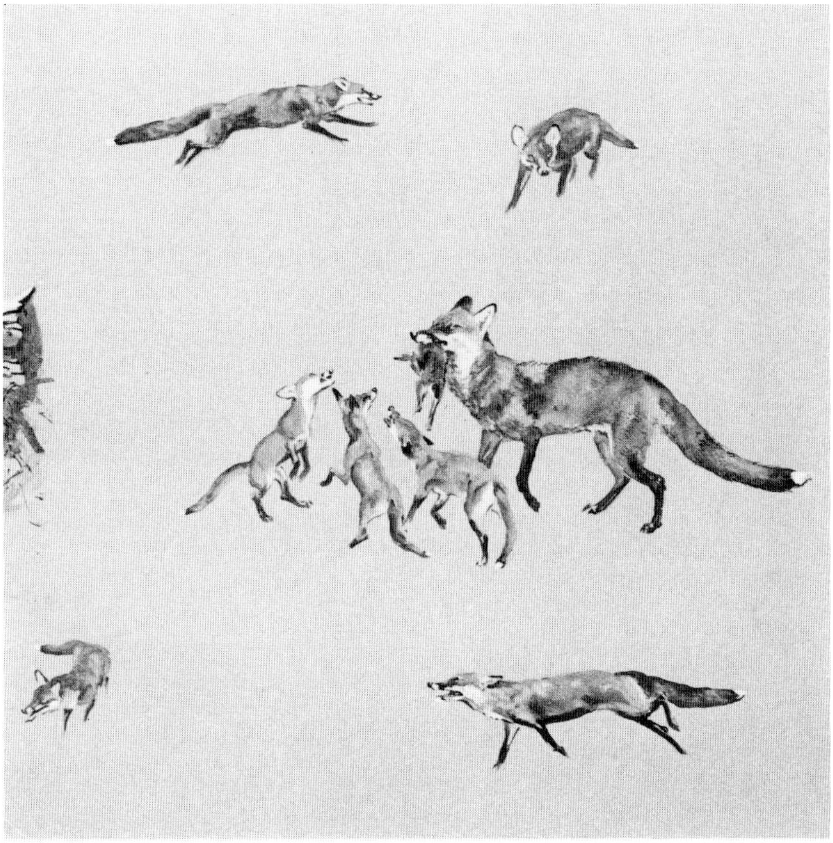

Studies of Foxes, 1982 (detail). Watercolour, 13 × 20 in (33 × 51 cm). Published by the Heale Gallery as a limited edition print.

the Foxhound. No doubt he appreciated his son's predilection.

Linders Wood, high above Ross-on-Wye, was where Michael saw his first hunted fox and forever became imbued with a love of the chase, although he always maintained that his first ever Meet was when he was aged two, and he was safely asleep in his pram. He subsequently went regularly to the Ross Harriers Meet at Crow Hill in the Upton Bishop parish. In later years, when he was home from school, he would attend all the local meets he could, with sketchbook and pencil in his hands, though at that stage his interest was much more in drawing animals.

In 1923 Michael followed his two elder brothers to Rossall School, a boy's public school on the shores of the Irish Sea at Fleetwood, Lancashire, founded in 1844 for the son's of clergy and others. Thus began one of the most miserable periods of the artist's life. Financial considerations in the form of reduced fees, would weigh heavily in Lyne's decision to send his youngest son to such a place, remote from home and family, but the remoteness and sense of isolation remained with Michael throughout his seven years at Rossall. After two years in the preparatory school where Michael first encountered salukis, the property of the headmaster, he passed into Mitre House, one of the ten houses of the senior school, under the supervision of H.V. Leonard, an OR who had lost an arm in the war, and the headmastership of the Revd E.J.W. Houghton DD, who had held the post since 1908. So isolated was the place that the family only visited Michael once throughout his seven years at the school. He deeply missed home, family and the three Sealyhams and mice looked after in his absence by elder sister Mary. It was inevitable that he should seek refuge in drawing, his letters home containing a maximum of sketches and a minimum of text. He was once caught by a master drawing during a history lesson, and was punished by being made to do some more in his own time, this was referred to at the time as 'Lyne's lines'. The spartan life of Rossall had little appeal, particularly as Michael had only an average ability at games: he found that a much more convivial way of passing time was to walk the mongrel belonging to the school tuck shop. Once established in the senior school, Michael started to assert his own individuality by not only drawing animals, but also modelling animals in Barbola paste on pipe cleaner skeletons, which he then hand

Rossall School, Fleetwood, Lancashire, in 1929, etched by Wallace Hester. Michael attended this school for the sons of clergy and others from 1925 to 1930.

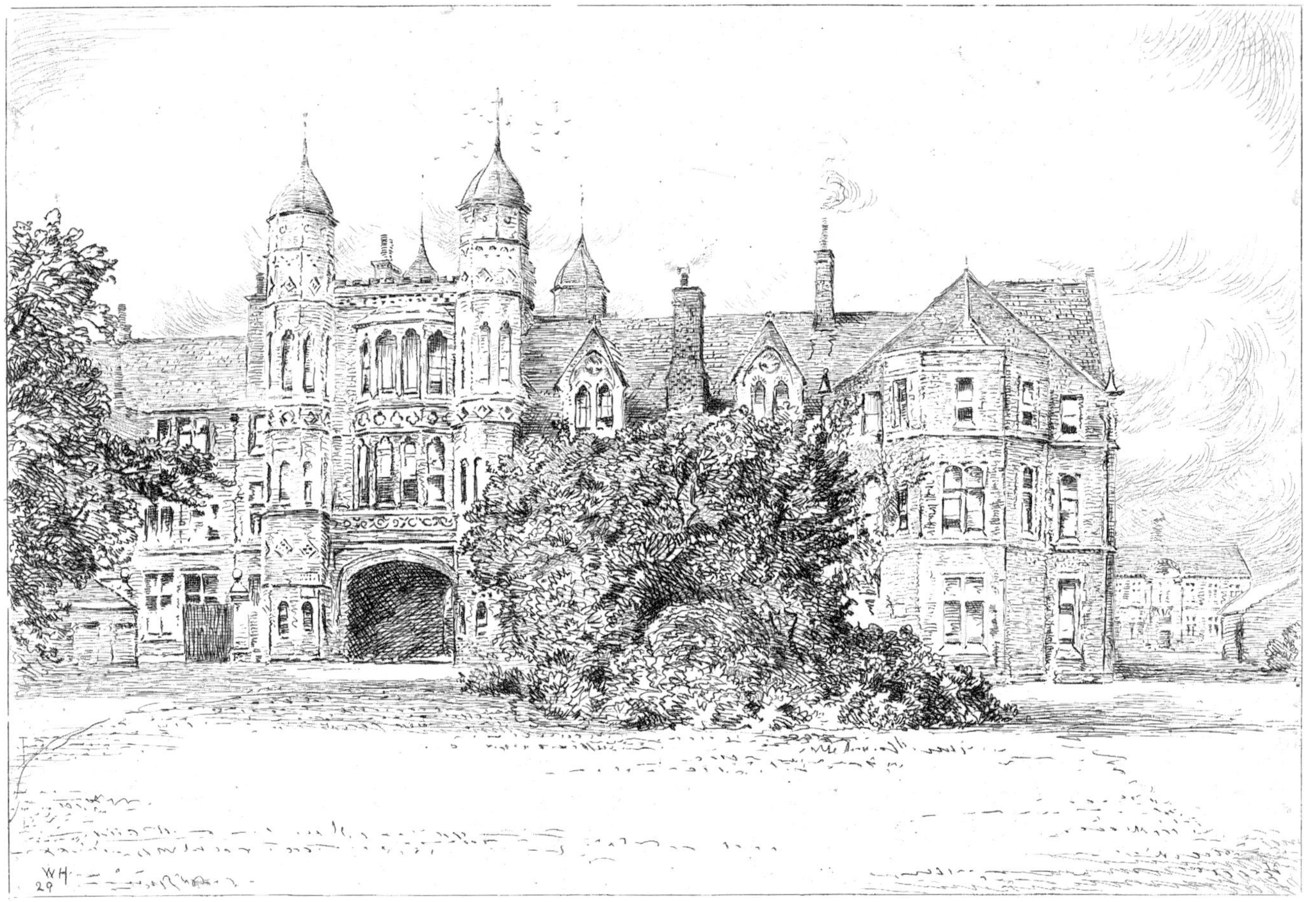

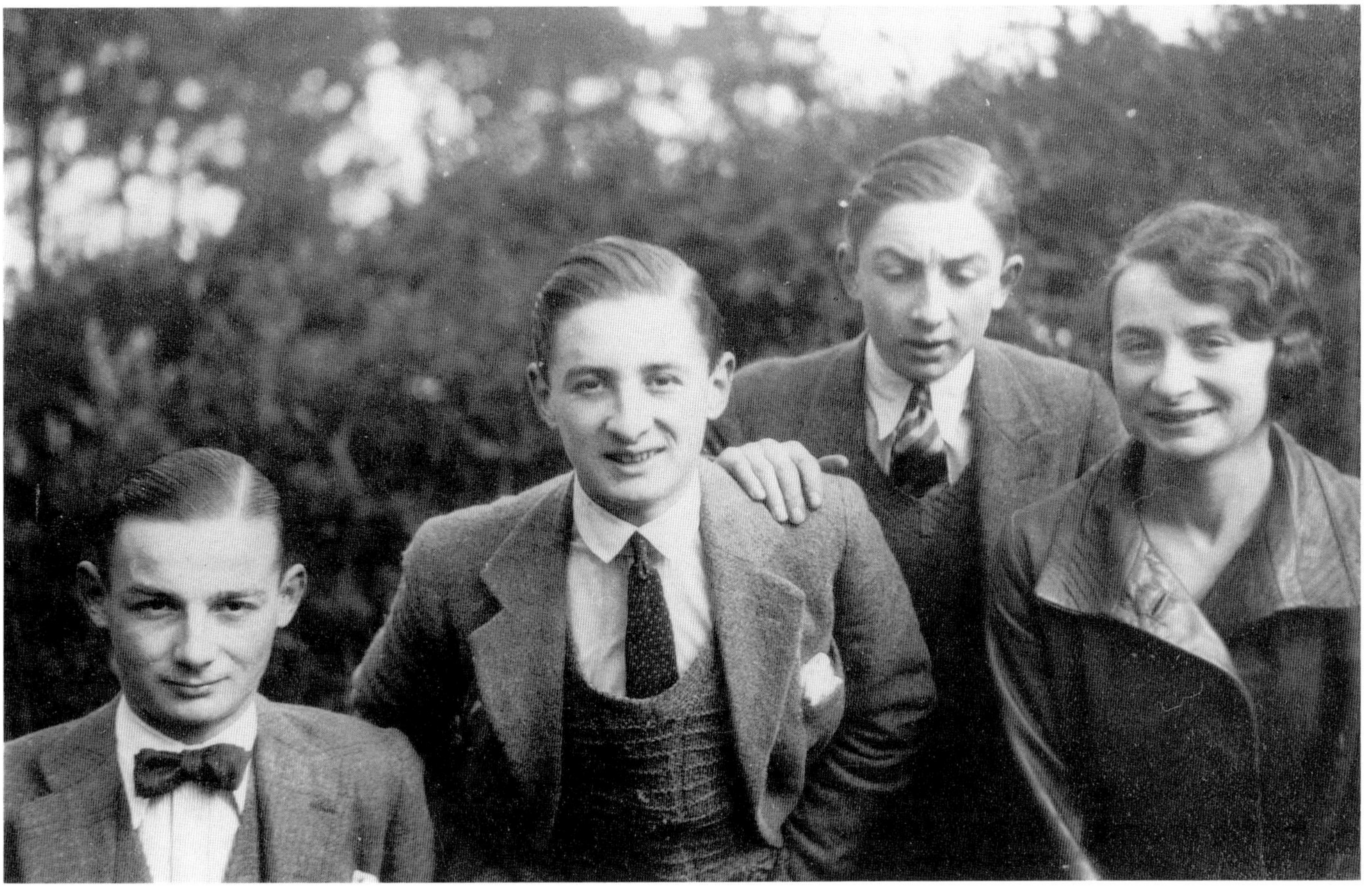

The four Lyne children about 1928. From left to right: Richard, John, Michael and Mary.

painted. Such activities took place in one of the school studies. Rossall in common with many other minor public schools operated a system of dormitories for sleeping, but boys of the senior school paired off to share studies for private work. Michael Lyne shared with Phillip Johnson for five years, and found in this fellow 'country boy' from Leicestershire, a sympathetic and understanding companion; not least he allowed Michael to decorate their study with hunting photographs from the pages of the *Sporting and Dramatic News*, *The Field* and *The Tatler*, and tolerated the ever present modelling materials and models.

A welcome bonus was provided when he broke a collar bone during a school rugger match. It was badly set in the school sanatorium and Michael was brought home to Herefordshire by his elder brother Richard, to have the collar bone reset in Worcester.

During 1925 Lyne had accepted the living of Bredenbury, near Bromyard, and moved there with his family to a large neat stone parsonage beside a small neat stone church. The village, astride the main Worcester to Aberystwyth road, gave easy access to Worcester, which would now be used for such necessities as visits to dentists and hospitals. It was about this time that Michael, anxious to fill the remaining gap in his study walls, went shopping with his mother to find a suitable print. Enquiring in the most promising shop for sporting prints, possibly featuring the Prince of Wales, the assistant replied 'No, I am afraid not, but I believe there is to be a book published on him shortly'. Such was the attraction of the late Duke of Windsor, then at the height of his foxhunting career.

Possibly it was about this time that Michael became aware of the problems of being a parson's son; living as a member of a vicarage family, and attending a school with a large number of boys from a similar background, he would have accepted it as a fact of life. The subtle differences between children from a clerical family and those from the secular world had not yet been felt.

Such was the social attitude of the English towards their clergy that a degree of separation was always maintained between secular 'society' and clerical families – a situation exacerbated in many clerical families by the shortage of money. The son of the vicarage who rides to hounds, or is invited to shoot or fish on favoured waters, always looks upon his participation in rather a different light from those who would accept such activities

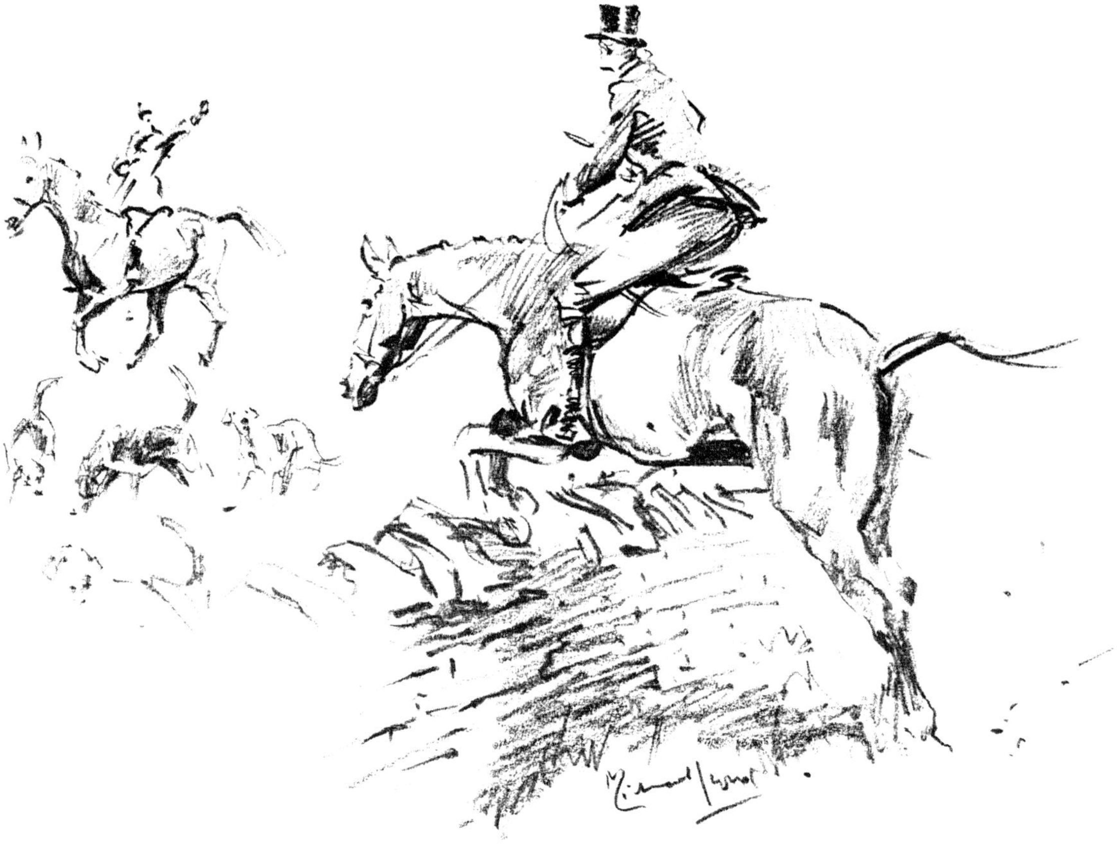

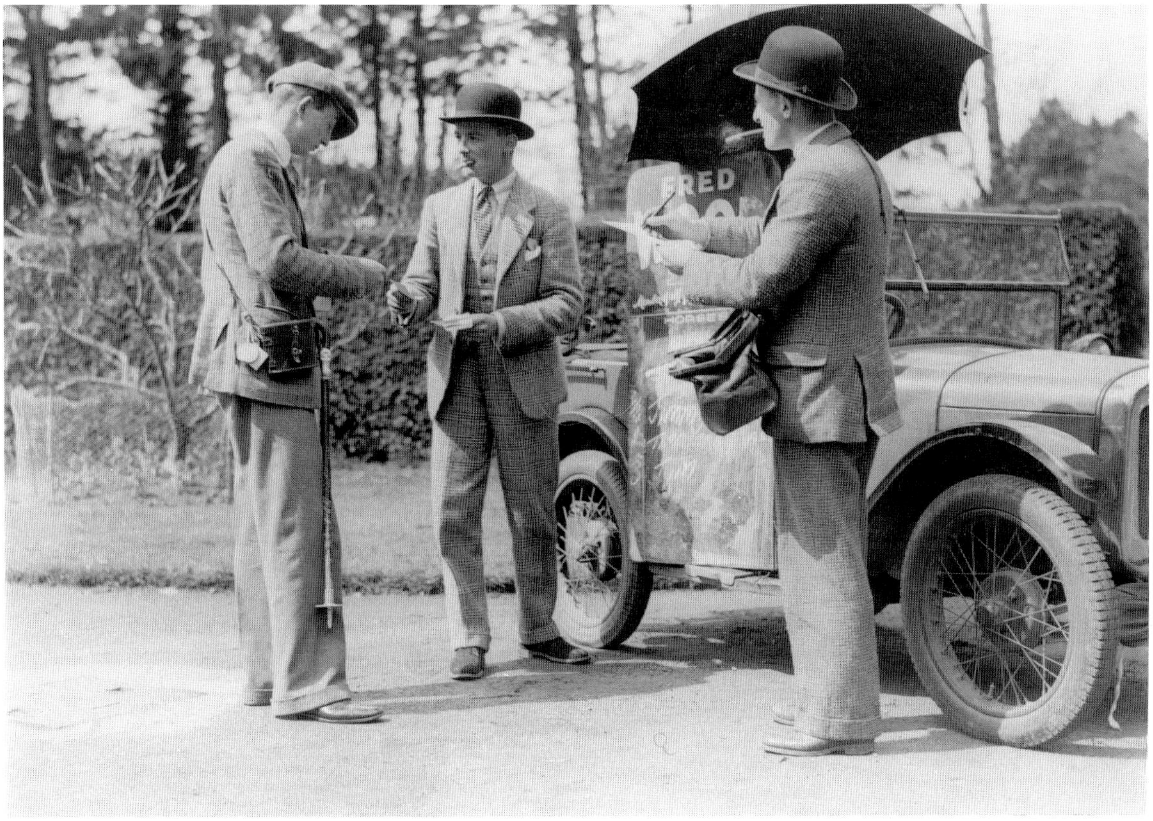

The Lynes at play, *c*1928. A mock race meeting (and party) in the parsonage grounds with *(from left to right)* Michael, Richard and John. The car was by courtesy of Mrs Joan Lyne, bookmaker's board by courtesy of a welching bookie at a local point-to-point.

as part of their normal daily round. It was no doubt with such feelings that the Lyne brothers took advantage of the permission to shoot over the extensive land of Bredenbury Court – the boys also added to the range of sport available by cultivating the local postman who delivered the mail by bicycle and always carried a ferret and purse nets!

Like so many English artists before him, Michael Lyne gladly acknowledged his debt to the paintings to be found in large houses: they provided an introduction to the works of two artists who were to influence him to become a sporting artist: Sir Alfred Munnings and Lionel Edwards.

In the late 1920s it was his mother's and maternal grandfather's view that Michael should follow an artistic career – but Michael was not convinced, preferring a veterinary career. His Housemaster very wisely advised that his love for animals might well be a disadvantage in the veterinary profession.

Leaving Rossall in 1930, poor examination results dictated that Michael be sent to a crammer to be prepared for the examinations of the Royal College of Veterinary Surgeons.

So in the late summer of that year, Michael found himself at the Vicarage at Easton, near Winchester, Hampshire, which the Vicar also ran as a crammer, to supplement his income.

The open chalk downs, the pleasant countryside and the brick and flint buildings of the Itchen Valley, provided a welcome contrast to the windswept Lancashire coast, although little, if any, progress was made on the academic front, but life was most enjoyable, walking his three Sealyhams and eventually carrying a gun to shoot rabbits. The vicar's wife may well have had a somewhat different view of Michael from that of her husband; for the Sealyhams, though rather hard of mouth, were expert in finding wounded game, and these, together with the rabbits, would find their way into the vicarage larder.

So the year in Hampshire passed and his father accepted that Michael would not be entering the veterinary profession and he was persuaded, with some guile on his son's part, to article Michael as a farm pupil in Worcestershire, near Malvern; Michael having learnt that some good hunting could be had with the North Ledbury. The season was all that it promised: the mainly broken coated Welsh hound pack gave wonderful sport, and the horse that Michael rode that season (1931–1932) proved more than adequate for the job.

During 1931 and 1932, whilst Michael Lyne was attempting to enter into animal-related professions, Britain was undergoing one of the worst economic and industrial recessions it had ever experienced, culminating in August 1931 with the then Labour Prime Minister, Ramsay MacDonald, undertaking to lead a coalition government. The impact was felt nationwide, even in the farming community, where failures became almost as common as within the manufacturing industries. Against such a background of stark gloom, it says

Otter Hounds drawn about 1984.

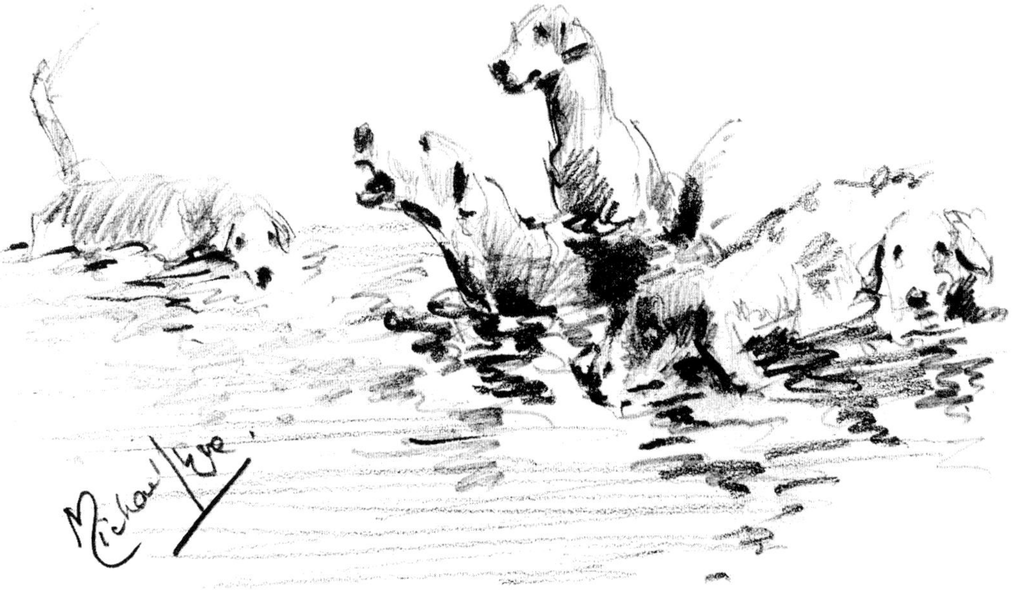

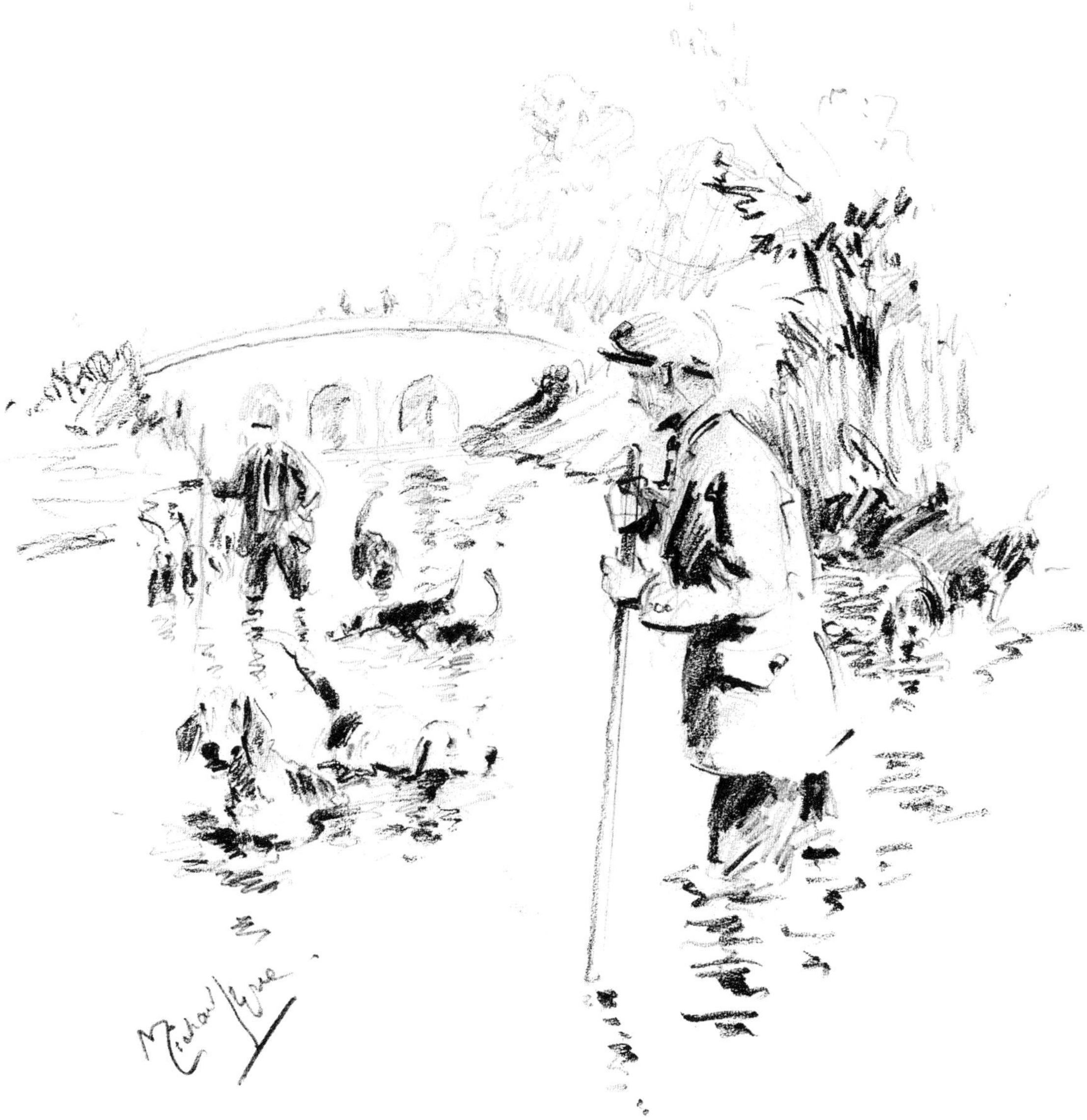

Otter hunting in the Wye Valley. This was drawn about 1984 from memory some fifty years after the event and shows the Hawkstone otterhounds with Pip Stanier (Joint Master and Huntsman for some seasons. Honorary Secretary from 1930 to 1958) in the foreground – but the hunting cap would not have been worn!

much for Lyne, that he was able to bow to the inevitable that Michael would never make either a vet or a farmer, and that some other future should be considered for this personable public school educated youngest son. In the meantime he allowed him to spend an idyllic summer enjoying the delights of otter hunting with two local packs – the Hawkstone Otterhounds and the Wye Valley Otterhounds. The former hunted on the River Lugg, a tributary of the Wye running south from Leominster and joining the main river near

Hereford. The latter hunted on the River Wye itself. Whilst both enjoyed very good sport, the Hawkstone was particularly smart. The pack was run as a members' club and in consequence, election was required in order to become a hunt member. It had its own clubhouse where members were able to change into dry clothing whilst hunting. The Wye Valley, by comparison, was run on similar lines to many other subscriber packs and expected its huntsmen and members to stay wet. Good sport was the order of the day in both hunts, it being provided by Arthur Jones and subsequently the 10th Lord Coventry in the Hawkstone, and Ray Thompson in the Wye Valley. Thompson was an interesting personality – a hard man, he could hunt all day and drink most of the night, still in wet clothes. It was the nostalgia for those summer days which prompted Michael to write, during the dark days of the Second World War, a charming and evocative essay, 'Notches on a Hazel Rod'.

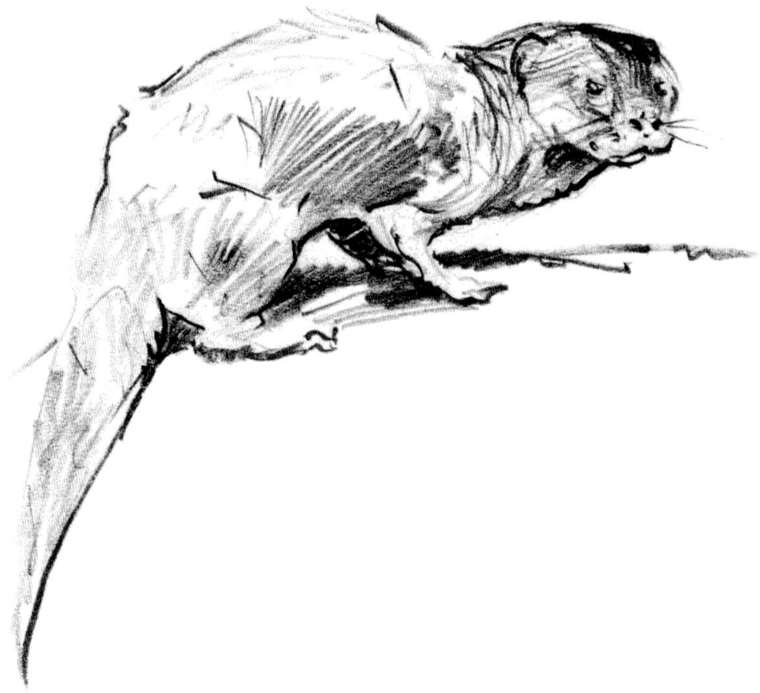

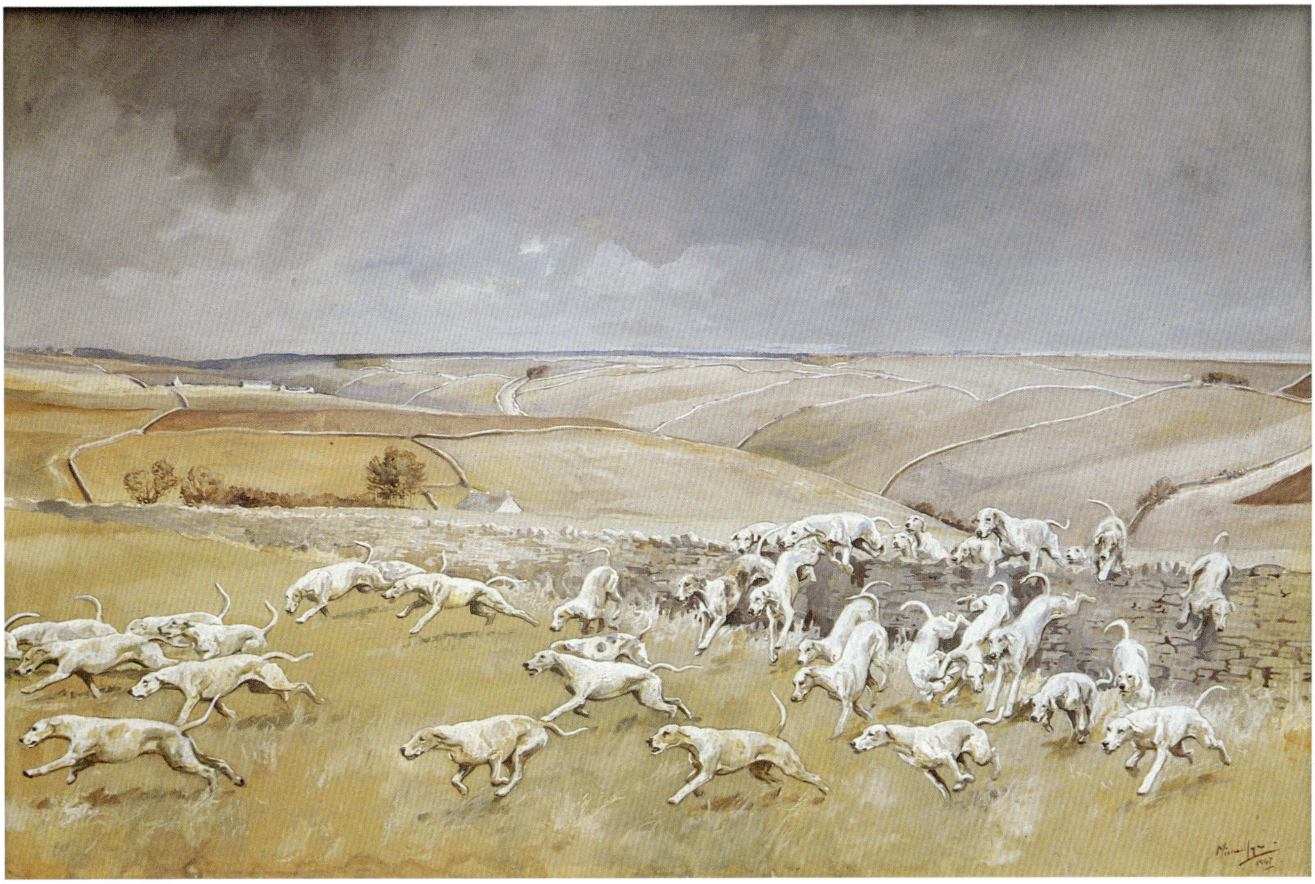

The Cotswold Hounds, 1947. Signed and dated watercolour, 13.5 × 20 in (34 × 51 cm). The painting above was commissioned by Colonel Cyril Heber Percy and shows the hounds running towards Lawrence Gorse by Shipton. The hounds were bred mainly from Lady Curre and Brecon stock and Michael Lyne was requested to show at least fifteen couple. No two hounds are in the same position.

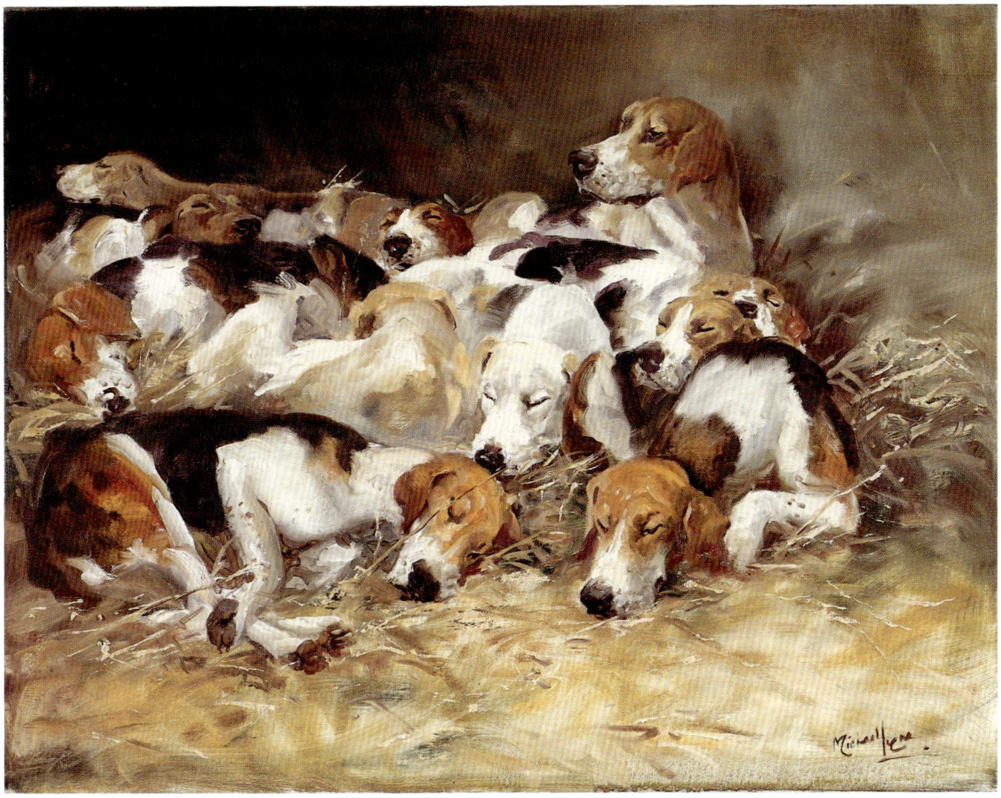

PLATE 3

(*right*) *Rest for the Weary*, 1974. Signed, oil on canvas, 24 × 30 in (61 × 76 cm). One of the series of paintings inspired by Stella A. Walker's call, in 1967, for a more imaginative approach to sporting paintings.

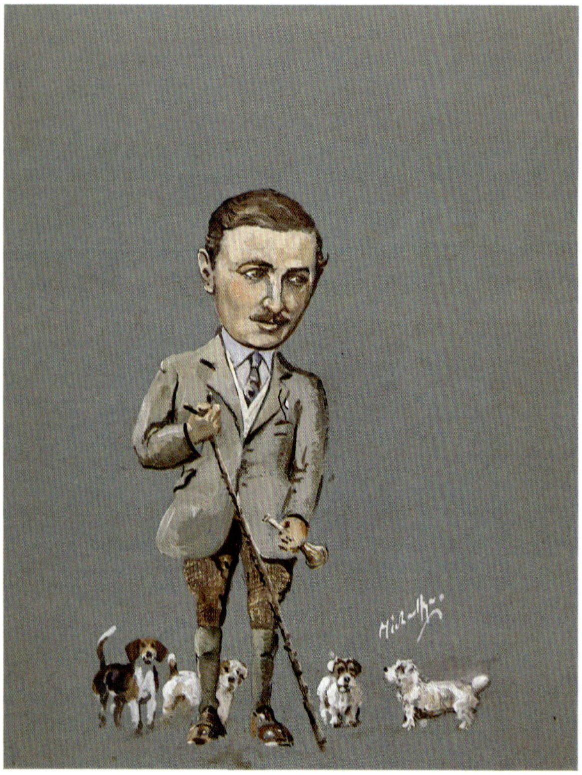

Michael Lyne with his pack: Mr Lyne's, 1937. Signed, watercolour, 12 × 8 in (30 × 20 cm). In this caricature, Michael depicts Cautious, the black and tan beagle bitch given to him by Captain Ronnie Wallace and his Sealyhams: Bonzo, Dolly and Bonnet.

PLATE 4

(*below*) *Eton College Hounds at Dumbleton Hill, September 1936*. Signed and dated watercolour, 11 × 15 in (28 × 38 cm). This was painted when Michael Lyne lived on Stanley Mount, shown in the background. Amongst the group are W. Perkins, M. Lyne, Eustace Pelly, Mark Mainwaring and Captain R. E. Wallace.

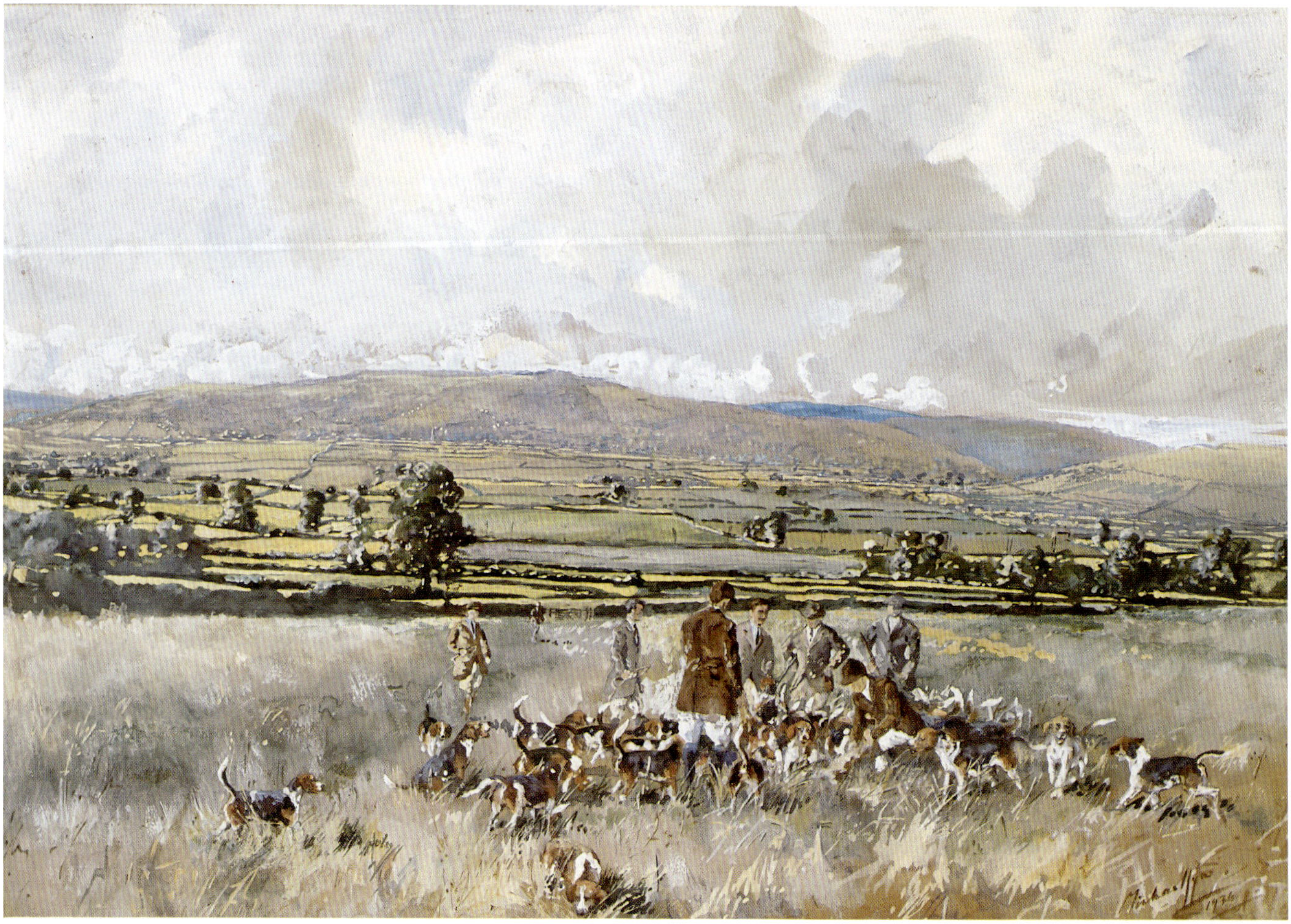

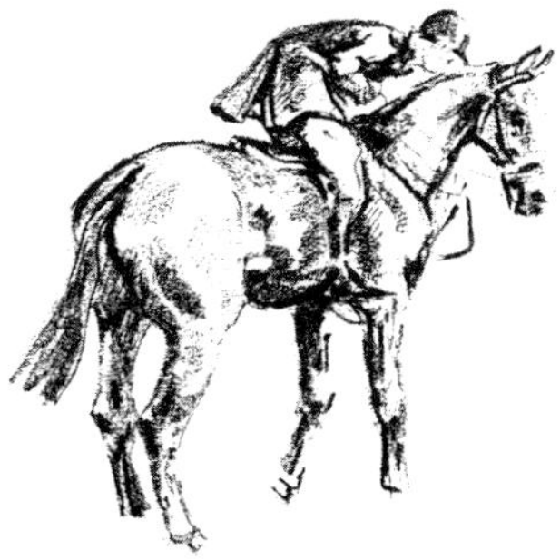

TWO

A GOOD START 1932 – 1939

The pleasant languorous summer was over all too quickly and in the autumn of 1932 Michael took a decision which was to set him firmly on the road to becoming a sporting artist. He accepted the post of secretary to his mentor, Sir Jocelyn Lucas, Bart (1880–1980). Michael Lyne had become acquainted with Sir Jocelyn whilst at Rossall, through their mutual interest in terrier breeding and field sports. Sir Jocelyn was at that time living at Winchcombe, Gloucestershire, on the western edge of the Cotswolds, and enjoying his final days as a bachelor, following service with the Royal Warwickshire Regiment. He was breeding Sealyhams and hunting a famous bobbery pack of Sealyhams, Jack Russells, beagle and basset hounds. In 1933 he married and was destined to become the Conservative Member of Parliament for Portsmouth South from 1939 to 1966, and a leading figure in the world of politics and dog breeding.

It is difficult to know how Michael coped with his secretarial duties, given his well-known aversion to paperwork, but he certainly enjoyed the opportunities which existed to participate in field sports, and to become, amongst other things, an official of the Evesham Vale Coursing Club, his first experience of coursing under rules. What was most significant about the appointment was that it became the penultimate link in the chain which determined that Michael Lyne should become a sporting artist and writer. It was Sir Jocelyn, an urbane and wise outsider, who was to give him the final push.

Michael's first positive move was to enrol at Cheltenham School of Art under the direction of the watercolour painter, Gerald Gardiner (born 1902), who at that time was living at the nearby village of Up Hatherley. It was he who taught Michael colour values and the importance of light and shade and reflected light. Ten years later this knowledge was amplified while working with Edward Seago on camouflage projects: Michael had a great admiration for Seago and learnt much from him during the dark days of the Second World War. In Gardiner's view, recognizing considerable inherited talent, the best way for Michael to learn art was to paint prolifically and benefit from the ability to recognize his own shortcomings. In the following two years, Michael became something of a recluse, such was his desire to paint continuously and develop his ability as a serious sporting artist. During this period of gestation, Michael found that his work had become of a quality acceptable to the well known Cheltenham firm of art dealers and print sellers, Arthur Whitcombe

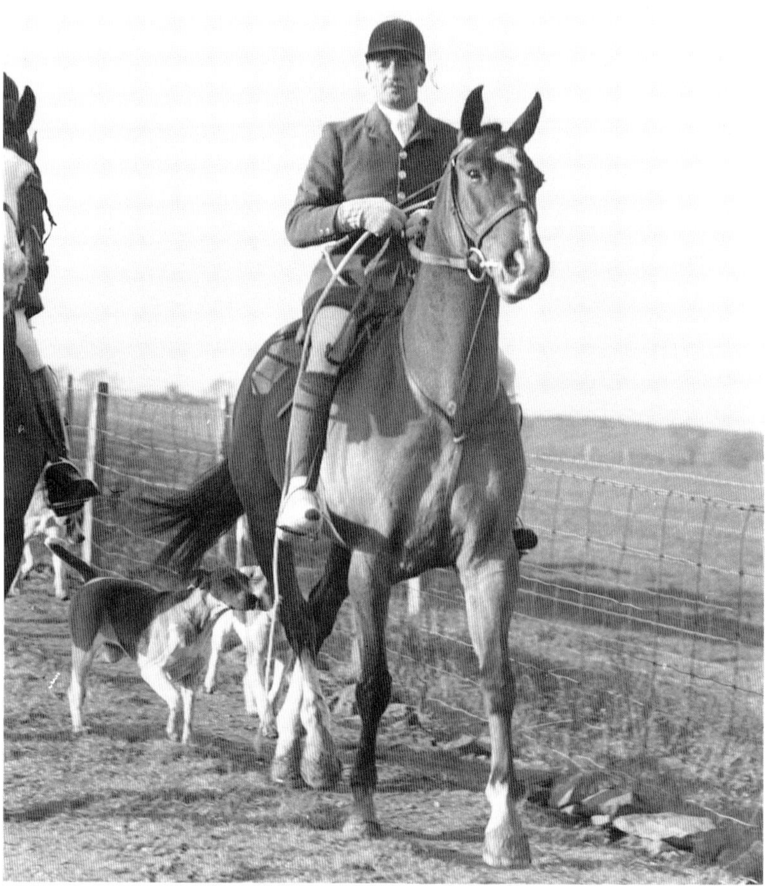

Lt Col Cyril Heber Percy, Joint Master and Huntsman of the Cottesmore 1946-1958, near Tilton-on-the-Hill, 1956. Whilst Master of the Cotswold in the mid to late 1930s he became Michael Lyne's first serious patron and was a life-long friend. Michael illustrated all Cyril Heber Percy's books and the family still have a fine collection of the artist's work.

& Co. of the Promenade. They began to show and sell Michael's watercolours, and during a visit to Cheltenham, the then Secretary of the Ledbury Hunt and former Master of the South Hereford, Captain H.A. Clive, noticed Michael's work in Whitcombe's gallery, and commissioned a series of pictures of the Ledbury, despite Michael arriving a day late for a luncheon invitation to discuss the proposed commission.

In later life, Michael had a low view of the quality of these works, but was forever grateful to Captain Clive for providing the opportunity that convinced him beyond all doubt that the advice he had received and the practical help of the then owner of Whitcombe's, Mr Rutland, was correct, and that he should become a professional painter. The final link in the chain had been forged, the decision made, and made to such effect that within a comparatively short period of time Michael had secured the important patronage of Lt Col Cyril Heber Percy (1905–1988), the then newly installed Master of the Cotswold, who purchased the first of many Lynes in his collection during 1934, the year of his appointment. Michael's debt to all these people is reflected in the dedication of his first book, *Horses, Hounds and Country* which is 'to those who gave encouragement'.

Looking at the paintings in the Heber Percy collection, one is immediately impressed by the precociousness of the watercolours. For a young and relatively inexperienced artist, the works show a deep understanding of the subject matter, a keen sense of detail, vibrant colour, and the ability to make a pleasing composition of horses and hounds, whether in action or repose. Also, even at this very early stage, the use of vignettes as an art form was well established in Michael's repertoire, with whole sheets of fox and hound studies. Given Michael's lack of access to original modern sporting paintings other than two in Welsh Marches houses, the technical achievement was very considerable, even allowing for the help which Gerald Gardiner must have given. A much more readily available source of inspiration were the reproductions of sporting paintings by Munnings and Edwards which regularly appeared on the covers and pages of *The Tatler* and *Sporting and Dramatic News*, together with a large selection of foxhunting photographs. It was these, in Michael's words, which with their realism and excitement of the chase, influenced him to attempt to become a sporting artist.

Family and friends provided the encouragement, Sir Alfred Munnings and Lionel Edwards provided the impetus for his art, but they were never imitated or copied, even in those early days. From the beginning Michael Lyne's art was both individualistic and idiosyncratic, with highly disciplined powers of observation and memory, the legacy of his childhood days at Upton Bishop and Bredenbury.

Also during 1934, Michael held his first public exhibition. At that time Sir James Croft was Master of the North Herefordshire and was living at the Hunt Kennels in Bodenham, not at Croft Castle. He allowed Michael to exhibit his paintings in an empty loose-box on the day of the Hunt's Puppy Show. One purchaser recalls that he acquired 'quite a

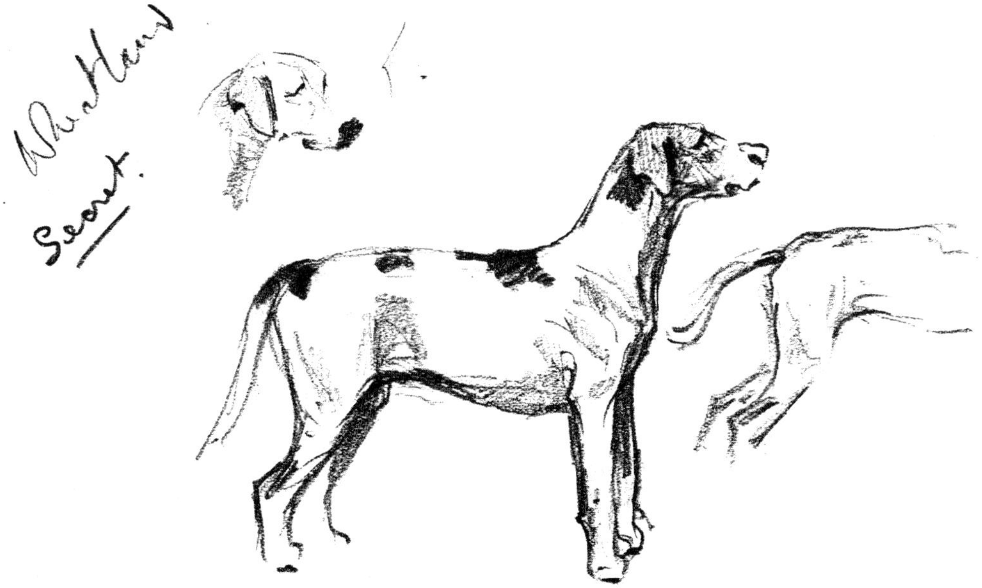

nice watercolour of hounds running, no horses, for thirty shillings' (£1.50) at this event.

Mr Rutland, the owner of Arthur Whitcombe & Co. of Cheltenham, was also very active on the young artist's behalf, by both showing his work and introducing it to a wider public, including London publishing houses, though, strangely, he never held an exhibition of Michael's works.

During 1936, through Rutland, Michael was commissioned by The Medici Society to produce the artwork for prints of *The Devon and Somerset Staghounds* and *The Ledbury,* and also by *Country Life*, the then market leaders in finely produced books on equestrian and field sport subjects, to illustrate Lt Col S.G. Goldschmidt's *Skilled Horsemanship*. This commission required a watercolour frontispiece and a series of sixteen full page pencil drawings of such diverse subjects as 'Polo demands co-ordination of hand and leg' to 'Well mannered hacks' (*see pp. 72 and 121*). The book was published in May 1937. This was followed later in 1937 by another *Country Life* publication *Rhymes of an Irish Huntsman* by Stanislaus Lynch, a young Irish foxhunter and poet, to which Michael contributed eight coloured and fifteen black and white illustrations following his first visit to Ireland. One review of this book observed 'Mr Lyne can draw a horse and can infuse into his drawing life and action, which is something that not every sporting artist can achieve.' Praise indeed for an emerging artist.

Another regular commission at that time was a Christmas card for the Cotswold Hunt, produced in return for flesh for Michael's pack of hounds. This was an admirable arrangement, for not only did it ensure a regular supply of feed for hounds, but it also added to Michael's knowledge of animal anatomy. Long hours in the flesh house, skinning and dissecting carcasses for beagle feed were not wasted. Like George Stubbs before him, Michael Lyne learnt his anatomy the hard way.

Since his move to the Cotswolds, Michael had hunted terriers. Initially with Sir Jocelyn Lucas' bobbery pack, then with his own private pack of Sealyhams. In Michael's own words, 'a pack which hunts anything from field mice bolted from their holes by bumble bees, to collies which have come a courting.' The three Sealyhams were Bonzo and her daughters Bonnet and Bester. Bonzo had won prizes on the show bench and appeared in the centrefold of the old *Morning Post* (later absorbed into the *Daily Telegraph*), in a photograph taken by the artist's mother, Mrs Joan Lyne, which had won first prize in a photographic competition organized by the newspaper. The pack was completed by the addition of the Beagle bitch, Cautious.

Cautious, who provided a turning point in Michael's life, was the gift of Captain R.E. Wallace, when he was Master of the Eton College Beagles. She was the means of both introducing Michael to beagling and later of providing him with his own pack, a wife and their first home. It was also the start of a friendship which lasted throughout the whole of Michael's life and one which he valued above all others. Ronnie Wallace was, to Michael, not only a brilliant huntsman, houndsman and Master, but one who totally recognized the importance of foxhunting as part of our English Heritage, and worked ceaselessly for it at national and international level. Both became eminent in their own fields and always found much to enjoy in each other's company.

In 1936 Ronnie Wallace was at Eton and Master of the College Beagles. During the summer holidays his parents had taken a house on the north-west edge of the Cotswolds, overlooking Tewkesbury Vale, and it was here that the young Master had brought his hounds for kennelling, and for hunting. Michael hunted with the Eton College and much enjoyed the sport and the company of the young Master, who gave Michael the rather thickset black and tan bitch, Cautious, for hunting rabbits. She quickly grew out of this and with her lovely double note, was a first-class hare hound. Later Michael was to breed with Cautious, using one of his Sealyham terriers to produce the Seagle, Constant, who had the useful quality of recognizing the scent of a tiring hare and driving on to be with the leading couples. The beagle/Sealyham cross was one much favoured by Michael, and

Cautious, a black and tan bitch, was Michael Lyne's first beagle. She was given to him in 1936 by Ronnie Wallace, then Master of the Eton College Hounds. This watercolour dates from 1937.

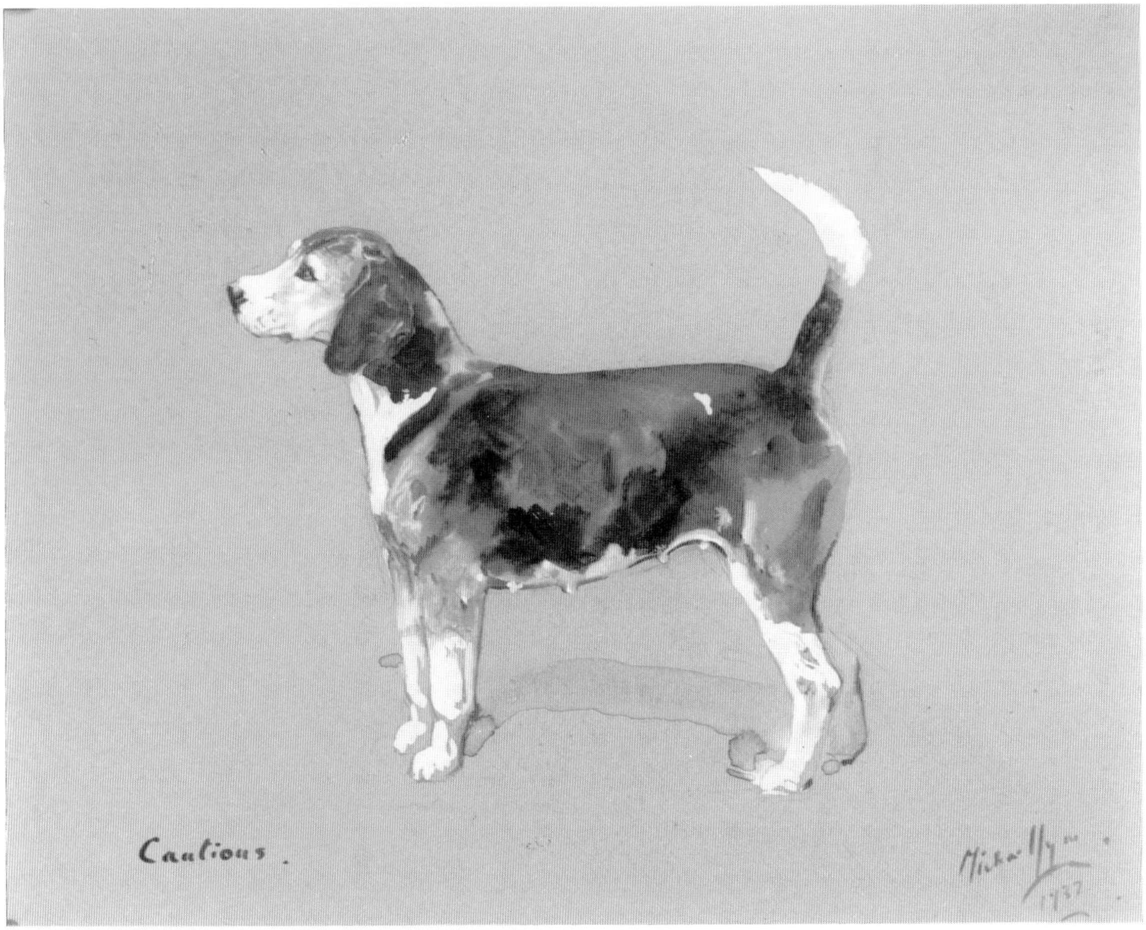

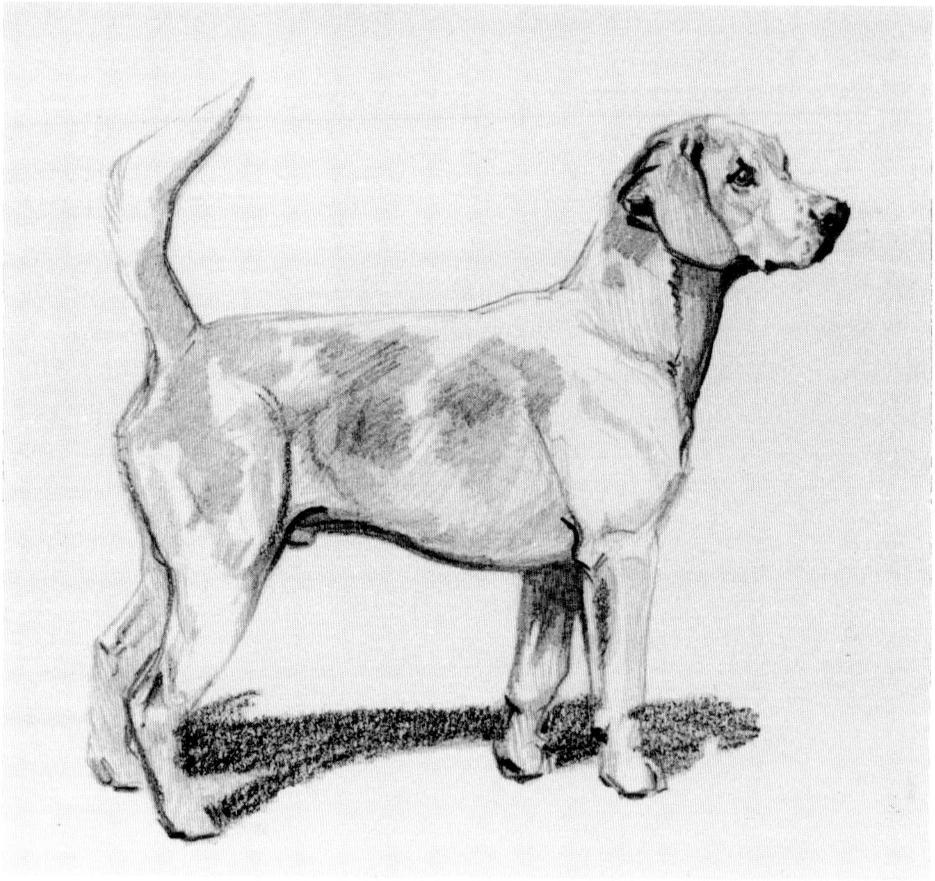

A pencil drawing from *From Litter to Later On*, published in 1973. It shows Pipewell Justice, a lemon and white beagle, 'a gay little hound', who was mated with Lorna, a rough haired working terrier with Sealyham blood in an effort to produce another seagle whelp in 1947. None of the seagles produced and hunted before the war had survived.

Mr Lyne's Beagles contained a couple or so, until a recognized pack of beagles was established, shortly before the outbreak of the Second World War.

Also during 1936, an event took place which Michael always recalled with a certain amount of dry humour. He had been commissioned to produce a painting of the Derby, and having been driven to Epsom on Derby Day by his brother John, they had made their way to the grandstand in search of a vantage point from which to view the race. They spent some time looking around, decided that their interest would be best served by gaining access to one of the private boxes, and successfully gate-crashed an aristocratic party, only to be discovered and courteously ejected whilst the horses were crossing the heath for the Off. In a final attempt to find an acceptable view, they walked slowly down the corridor at the rear of the private boxes and chose a door. Opening it, they could not believe their luck. The box appeared to be empty and offered a superb view of Epsom Downs: it was only as the horses climbed to Tattenham Corner that they became aware of a small, fat, solitary old man, intently watching the race through his racing glasses. As soon as the winner had passed the post, the old man rose and left the box in silence, giving the brothers Lyne a slight smile as he passed. When, a few minutes later, the Lynes saw HH The Aga Khan leading Mahmoud, with Charlie Smirke up, into the unsaddling enclosure, they realized who the third occupant of the box had been.

Mr Lyne resigned his living at Bredenbury in 1936 and retired to a house at Ledbury, some twenty miles to the south and equidistant between Hereford, Worcester and Gloucester. Mary remained with her parents, whilst Michael and his two brothers followed their respective careers, though they returned home as often as possible, and acquired a reputation both for their high spirited behaviour and similarity of looks, often passing as triplets amongst those who did not know them. They were a familiar sight in their mother's open Austin Seven at many social and sporting events, and were gently tolerated by their father. Of the three brothers it was John who became the first to own a motor car, and ultimately became the proud possessor of a large Lagonda sports car and the natural source of transport for his artistic brother on his trips around hunting countries, until Michael purchased a second-hand Morris Ten shortly before the outbreak of war.

The Revd Arundell Lyne with his children in 1938. *Left to right*: Michael, Revd Arundell Lyne, Richard, Mary and John; Bonzo is in front. The three brothers were often mistaken for triplets at this time.

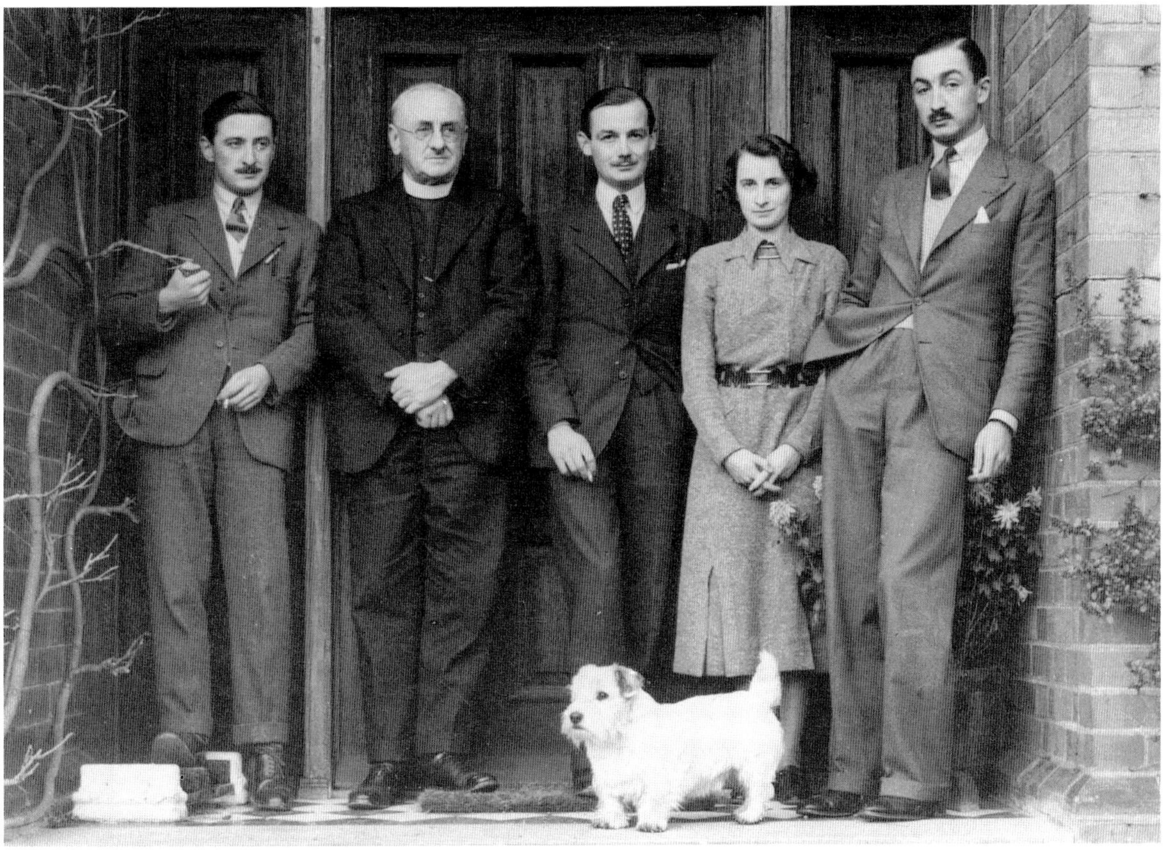

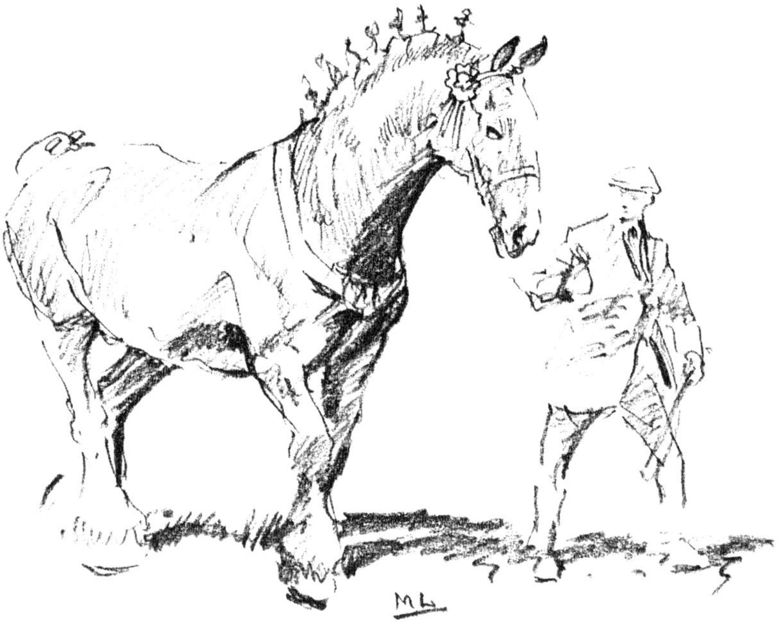

Michael's work continued to improve; the promises of two or three years previously began to mature and he developed a new air of authority and directness. He continued to immerse himself in hunting and the countryside, as it existed in the mid-1930s, little realising that what he was imbibing was soon to pass away forever. Yet for those who looked, small portents were beginning to appear; the improving economy and a desire for efficiency and speed brought new roads. New commercial and residential buildings appeared, often on green field sites on the edge of town, or worse still, ribbon development along the edge of roads, often joining up towns. Mechanisation increased in factories and on farms. Michael himself objected to the large number of car followers attracted to the Ledbury Hunt and the Devon and Somerset Stag Hounds. Urbanization had started, but it was, as yet, unorganised, and would need the awfulness of war and the upheaval of social change to give it the impetus which was to prove near fatal.

The year 1937 was taken up by preparations for Michael's first solo book *Horses, Hounds and Country*, and limited edition prints published by Eyre & Spottiswoode for the 1938 Christmas market. Also on sale at the same time was Lionel Edwards' latest offering *My Irish Sketchbook*. During the year London saw Michael's watercolours for the first time at a mixed exhibition of sporting paintings shown by the Renaissance Galleries, Lower Regent Street. Michael was reviewed as a young artist of much promise. His peers on that occasion included Charles Simpson, Alfred Haigh, Lionel Edwards, Cuthbert Bradley and Lucy Kemp-Welch. The exhibition induced a commission for four pictures of the Meynell Hunt at a fee of one hundred pounds. The *Daily Sketch* reported this success and also informed readers that 'the artist was under contract to carry on illustrating and had a workload up to 1940', adding for good measure 'a good start for a brilliant young man'. Michael Lyne was then twenty-five and already widely noticed for his illustrations in *Skilled Horsemanship*, and *Rhymes of an Irish Huntsman* both published earlier in the year.

Michael was feeling happy and confident, he was justifying the hopes of 'those who give encouragement', and was becoming financially independent. It was in this happy state that Mr Lyne's Beagles entered their final season as a private pack. By this time Michael had moved to Gretton Hill near Winchcombe, and was hunting a mixed pack of Stud Book beagles, Sealyhams and seagles (Sealyham/beagle cross). Dick Cheney had become joint master and Miss Jessie Taylor, daughter of a local farmer, was Whipper-In.

The country hunted was on the Gloucestershire/Worcestershire borders. The Vale country was between Teddington Hands on the Cheltenham/Evesham road, and Toddington near Winchcombe. The Hill country was the Cotswolds above Stanway. The area hunted was by permission of the Masters of the North Cotswold and Cotswold Hunts. Hunt uniform was a green coat with a tan collar. With Dick Cheney's help, a fine hare

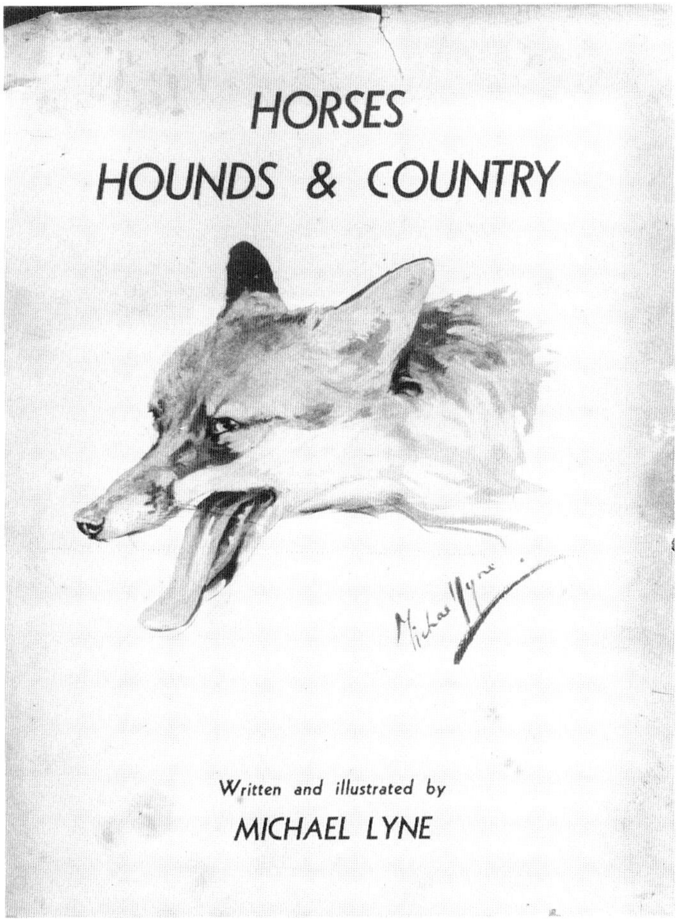

The dust wrapper for *Horse, Hounds and Country*, published in 1938.

hunting district was opened up and the pack started to attract embarrassingly large fields. In Michael's view, this was solely due to his policy of using only very old hounds. These were hounds drafted for reasons of their age and inability to run up with younger hounds. Without the anxiety of having to compete with younger hounds they took on a new lease of life and hunted together beautifully, and their combined wisdom and experience proved a very potent pack to hunt hare.

Another sporting artist, Thomas Ivester Lloyd (1873–1942) founded and hunted the Sherington Foot Beagles in Buckinghamshire, during the 1930s, and enjoyed much good sport. It would be interesting to learn if the two artist Master of Hounds ever met, though the writer very much doubts it. Michael, however, greatly admired Sir John Buchanan Jardine's magnum opus *Hounds of the World* which was illustrated by Ivester Lloyd, also Ivester Lloyd's own book *Hounds*.

The salad days of Mr Lyne's are recorded for posterity in the exquisitely written and decorated pages of Daphne Moore's *Hunting Diary*. Daphne Moore also came from the Three Counties and was born in Tewkesbury, Gloucestershire, where she and her writer brother, John, were roughly contemporary with Michael. It was Daphne, about to embark on a career as a sporting writer and commentator, whom Michael met otter hunting in Herefordshire. Two entries in her diary relate to Mr Lyne's. The first to a December meet at the Gretton Hill Kennels, where Miss Moore joined a very small and select field and five couple of hounds, which provided a copy book hunt; the hounds flying straight as an arrow after the first and only hare of the day. The second entry is for a month later, when Miss Moore enjoyed a great day's sport at the Tilesford Flying Club, Pershore, Worcestershire.

Michael had been invited to bring his hounds to hunt the notorious Aerodrome Hare which had been causing havoc on the runway for months, defying all attempts to dislodge her. Within ten minutes, hounds had put up the hare, and after almost an hour of classic hunting killed her, and found again, for a further two-and-a-half hours hunting. Miss Moore considered that this was a remarkable performance on the part of the Master and three-and-a-half couple.

Work was completed on the text and illustrations for *Horses, Hounds and Country* and six limited edition prints, early in 1938, but before the book was published, Michael had further paintings shown in the Renaissance Gallery, including two Irish subjects. He also enjoyed a highly successful first London Exhibition at Arthur Ackermann & Sons Gallery, 157 New Bond Street. *Horse and Hound* advised its readers that 'no hunting enthusiast should miss it, for every picture is a gem', the reviewer being particularly enthusiastic about the paintings of the Ledbury, the Heythrop and the United, then hunted by *Horse and Hound*'s 'Dalesmen', 'Bay' de Courcy Parry, who with his horse, Old Robert, was a favourite subject of the twenty-six-year-old artist.

Michael Lyne's first meeting with Dalesmen had taken place in 1926 when 'Bay' de

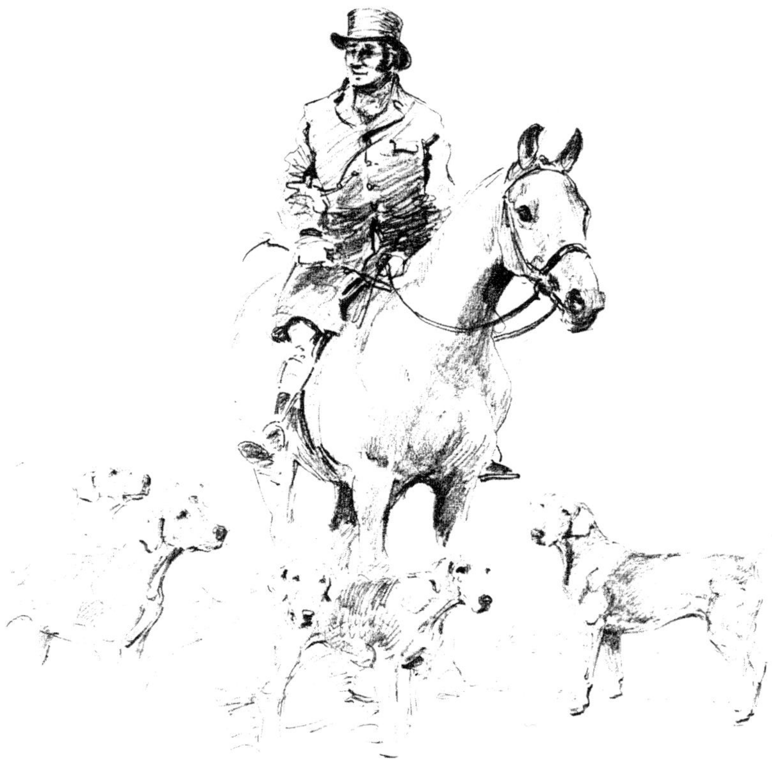

'Dalesman', Bay de Courcy Parry, the artist's hero and close friend. Michael drew him at the John Peel Day at Caldbeck, Cumbria in 1977, held to celebrate the 200th anniversary of Peel's christening. This illustration appears in *A Parson's Son.*

(*below*) Dalesman on his fine hunter Old Robert in the late 1930s outside the Anchor Inn, near Clun, Shropshire. This was Dalesman's home and headquarters when he hunted the United. This illustration appears in *Horses, Hounds and Country*.

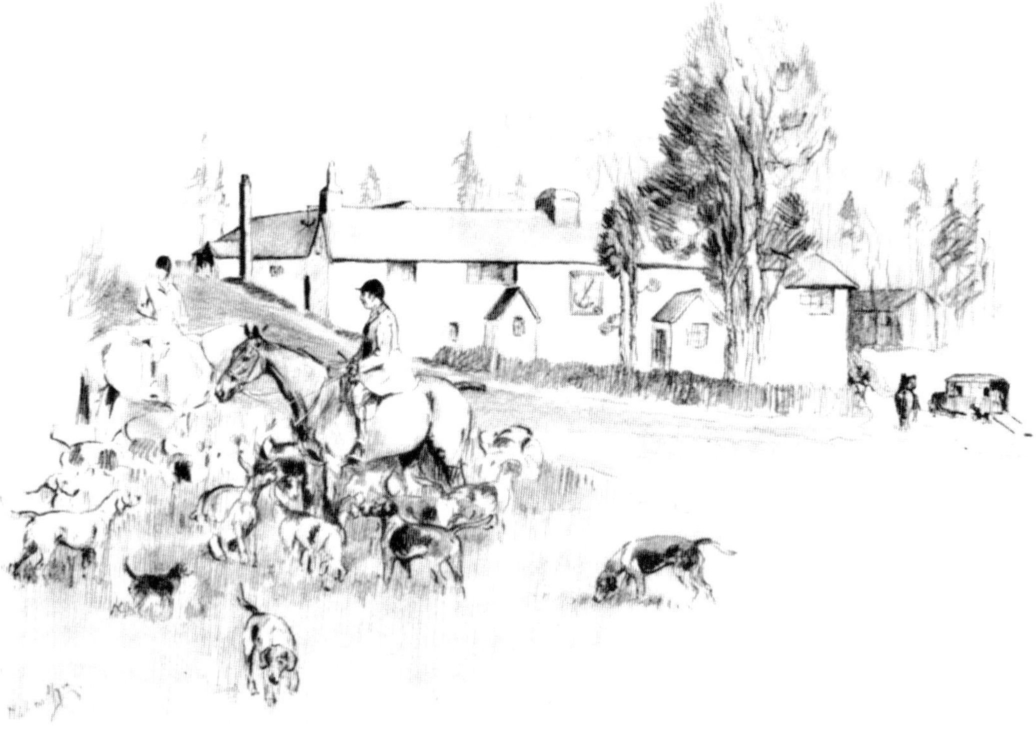

Courcy Parry was hunting the North Herefordshire and Michael was at Rossall. Michael was following on foot and, attempting to get a locked gate off its hinges to let Dalesmen onto the main road he failed, not having learnt the knack of putting one's back to the gate before trying to lift it. Twelve years later Michael could still remember the Master's hunting oaths when, with a beaten fox only a field or so in front of hounds, a wire fence with the slippery tarmac of the Bromyard to Leominster Road on the landing side making it folly to jump, he had to contend with a small, but well-meaning fourteen year old boy, attempting to open the gate. Dalesman flung himself from the horse, demonstrated how the job should be done, remounted and, without regaining his irons, was over the hedge on the far side of the road, his curses coming back above the cry of his hounds.

Dalesman willingly agreed to write the foreword to *Horses, Hounds and Country* for Michael, whom he well remembered, in his own words 'as a small and grubby lad attempting to help'. His first draft, typically, was in the form of a limerick:

There once was an artist called Michael
who followed the hounds on a cycle,
When he asked me to write a synopsis
about horses and foxes and copses,
I found it too irksome to taikle.

In its final form, the foreword was a classic of its kind, written with deep understanding and keen perception (see page 14).

'Bay' de Courcy Parry hunted the United from 1928 to 1939. He also hunted the Clun Forest Beagles and made the Anchor Inn, deep in the Kerry hills, his headquarters, kennelling hounds there during the summer and at Bishop's Castle in the winter. Dalesman, in fact, owned the Anchor, and although the story of its acquisition has been told many times, it is always worth re-telling, for it is so typical of the great huntsman. The United

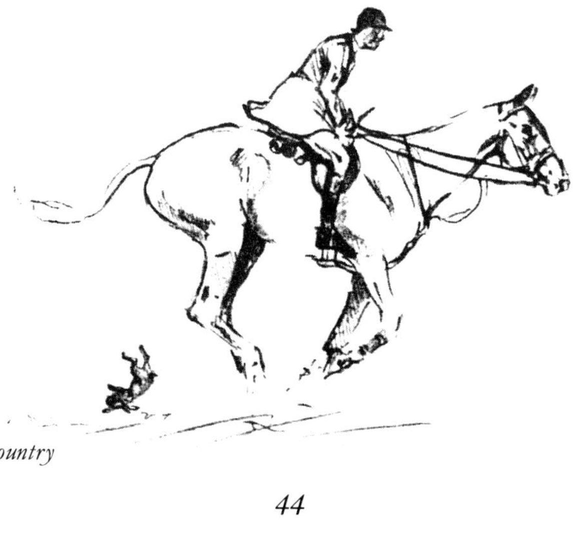

From *Horses, Hounds and Country*

was returning home in an exhausted state and reaching the inn found that it was closing time, so the only way to buy a drink was to buy the inn, this Dalesman did on the spot.

Michael's friendship with 'Bay' de Courcy Parry was to last until the latter's death in 1988 and, given the pair's love and understanding of hounds, it was always a source of much mutual pleasure.

When it was published in December 1938, *Horses, Hounds and Country* was very well received by the reviewers in both the sporting and national press, and that, at a time of year when with the pressures of Christmas, review space was at a premium in all publications however large or small. Of the many reviews, all were welcoming and laudatory ranging from 'the author carries conviction as a naturalist of perception and a lover of the land', to 'Mr Lyne brings to his work all the vigour of youth, allied with a superb technique and quick insight; his pictures are something more than mere records, they seem to breathe the spirit of all that is best in sport and nature'. One reviewer went as far as to comment, 'Mr Lyne draws well. He reminds one somewhat of Lionel Edwards, but works in more detail without overloading or obscuring his pictures.' Heady stuff indeed for a young artist in his mid-twenties.

While Michael was living the life of a sporting artist and writer in the Cotswolds, events in Europe were beginning to dictate a future that would change lifestyles and communities as nothing had before. Michael was fortunate in that he was able to enjoy and be completely influenced by what Dalesman so eloquently called 'our eternal heritage, England'. For Michael this heritage was a God-given gift which was to be enjoyed, and which would permeate his work until his death. Other facets of Michael's character were also contributing to the emerging artist's personality and visual understanding; his love for animals, his commitment as a naturalist, his remarkable powers of memory, his considerable inherited talent, and his natural sense of colour.

With the success of his first book guaranteed, Michael started to work on a sequel, *Hunting Here and There*, again to be published by Eyre & Spottiswoode. But fate was to take a cruel turn. The artwork and text were handed to the publishers shortly before the outbreak of the Second World War, subsequently to be destroyed by German bombs before it reached the printer, and lost forever. Roy Heron, the Cecil Aldin authority, comments that some of Aldin's original work was also destroyed by the Luftwaffe in Eyre & Spottiswoode's premises alongside the Thames. Possibly it was the same raid: Hitler has a lot to answer for!

The war was still a spectre of the future in the late summer months of 1938 for Michael, even though his elder brother, Richard, had joined the Territorial Army. Other matters were afoot. Michael was about to establish a recognized pack of beagles. Mr Lyne's Beagles were to be joined by the South Cotswold Beagles, until then hunted by Tom Mallinson, a Cotswold farmer, to form the United Cotswold Beagles. The joint masters of the new pack were Michael Lyne who carried the horn, Tom Mallinson and Dick Cheney and the

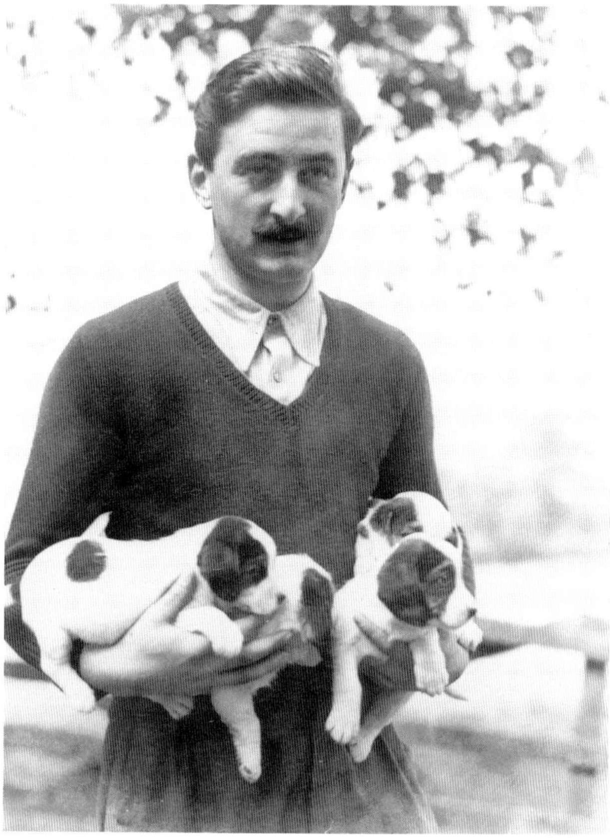

Michael Lyne with a beagle whelp in about 1938.

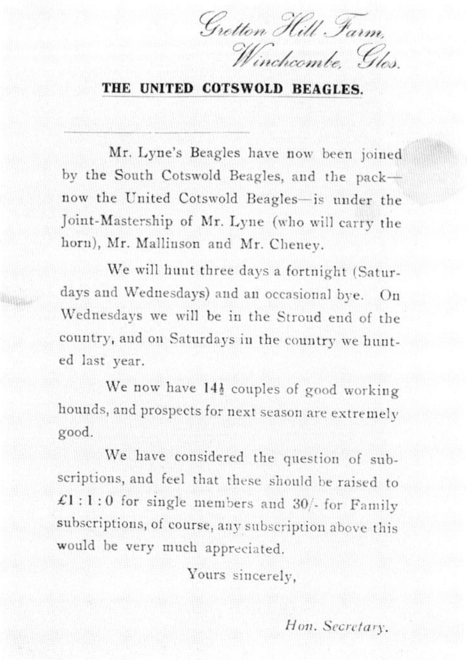

Gretton Hill Farm,
Winchcombe, Glos.

THE UNITED COTSWOLD BEAGLES.

Mr. Lyne's Beagles have now been joined by the South Cotswold Beagles, and the pack—now the United Cotswold Beagles—is under the Joint-Mastership of Mr. Lyne (who will carry the horn), Mr. Mallinson and Mr. Cheney.

We will hunt three days a fortnight (Saturdays and Wednesdays) and an occasional bye. On Wednesdays we will be in the Stroud end of the country, and on Saturdays in the country we hunted last year.

We now have 14½ couples of good working hounds, and prospects for next season are extremely good.

We have considered the question of subscriptions, and feel that these should be raised to £1 : 1 : 0 for single members and 30/- for Family subscriptions, of course, any subscription above this would be very much appreciated.

Yours sincerely,

Hon. Secretary.

United Cotswold Beagles: Notice to Mr Lyne's Subscribers, September 1938.

whipper-in was Miss Jessie Taylor. Their country was the Vale and Hill country, previously hunted, plus the old South Cotswold country around Stroud. With a combined total of fourteen-and-a-half couple of hounds, the prospects for the 1938–1939 season looked very promising indeed, with hunting on three days a fortnight, Saturdays and Wednesdays. Hounds hunted the North part of the country on Saturdays, and the South on Wednesdays. The season fully lived up to expectation and much good sport was had.

Ronnie Wallace's gift of Eton College Cautious started a life-long love affair with beagles. Michael rated them above all other hounds – to him they were the embodiment of all virtues, and to hunt them unparalleled joy; to look after, feed and exercise the best of fun, even if hard work at times.

As the season drew to a close, the dark menacing international clouds suddenly became intrusive, the three brothers returned to their parents' retirement home at Pye's Nest, Ledbury. Michael continued to work on his second book and prepared paintings for inclusion in a sporting art exhibition at Ackermann's. Again, good reviews were written, though

Captain 'Ronnie' Wallace, Joint Master and Huntsman of the Heythrop 1952–1977, in his first season with the Heythrop. He introduced Michael to beagles and became a life-long friend.

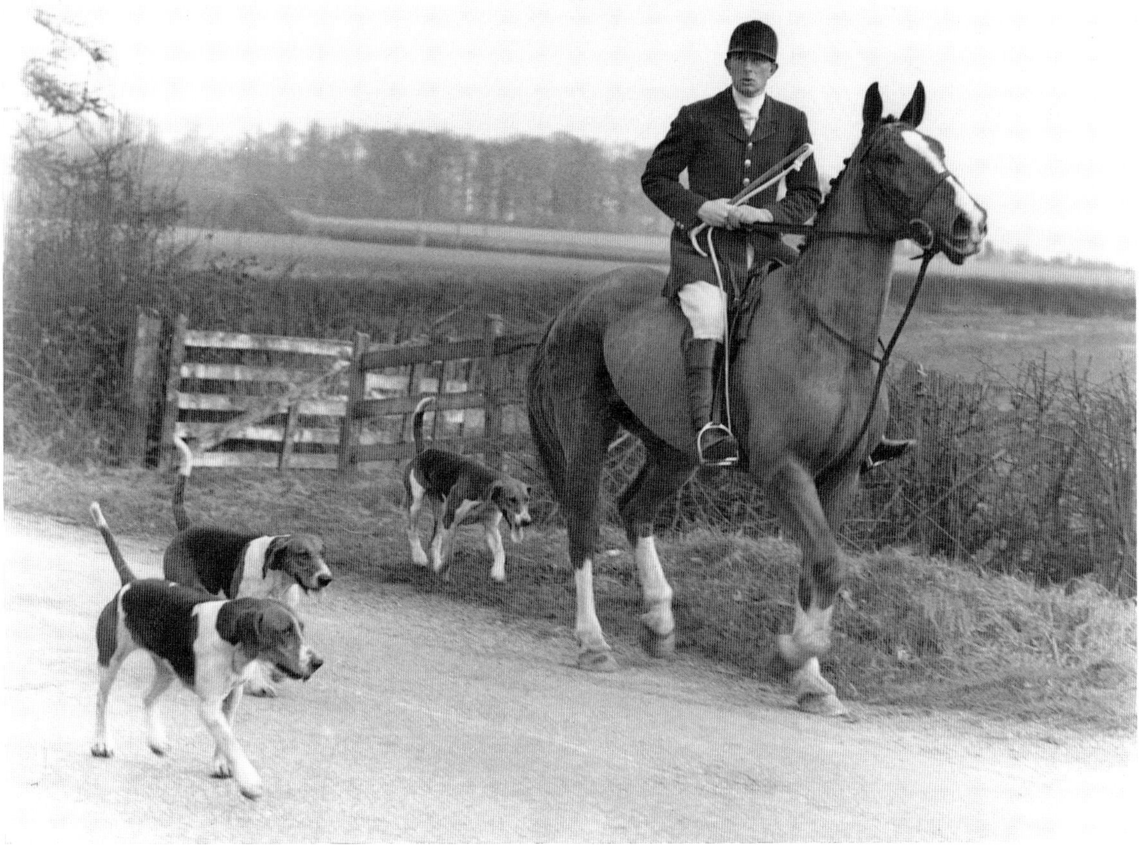

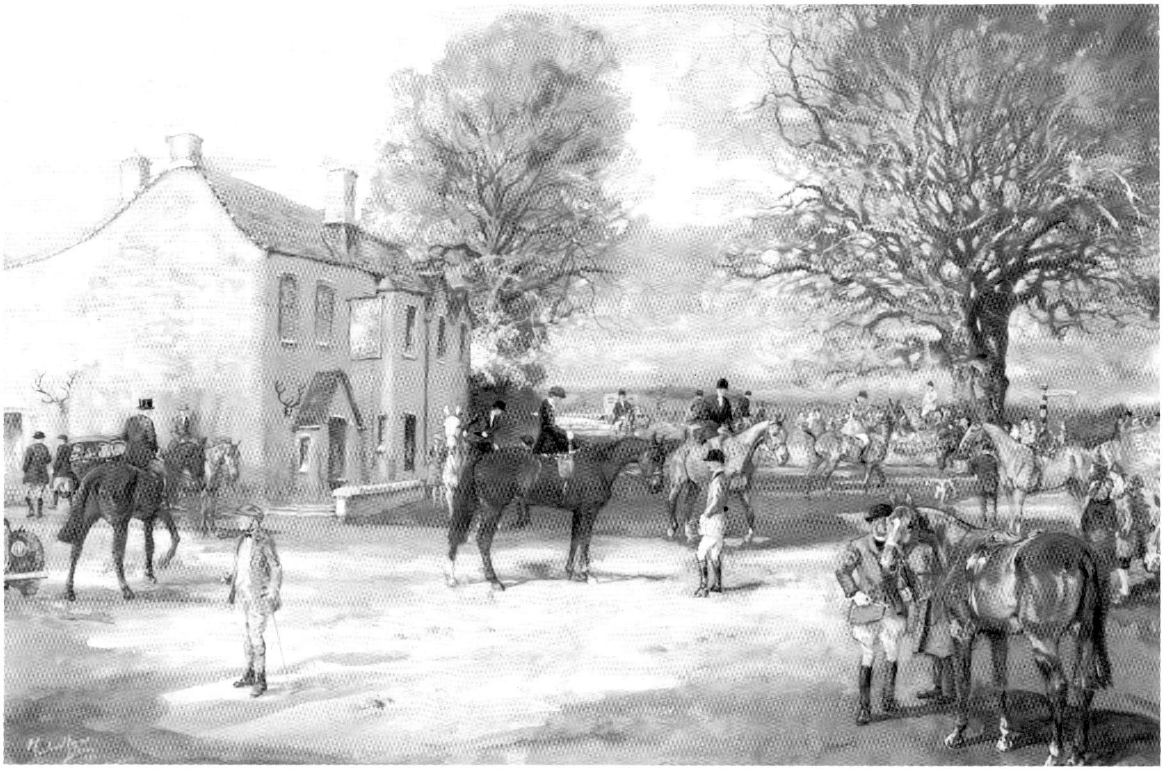

The Beaufort Meet at Hunter's Inn, Kingscote, Tetbury, 1947. Watercolour, 13 × 20 in (33 × 51 cm).

one critic complained that 'in some paintings, not content with what he has accomplished, he slap-dashes in the sky, thus distracting attention from the real matter in hand', and going on to compare this shortcoming with 'the good control of George Wright', another of Ackermann's artists.

The three brothers still continued to enjoy their high spirited approach to life, though Richard was somewhat inhibited by Territorial Army commitments. John's Lagonda was always at hand to provide transport supplemented, if necessary, by Michael's newly acquired Morris Ten. A final day's cubbing was enjoyed with the Wheatland, and then in Michael's own words, 'the War came and reality'. Michael and John each took the King's Shilling as privates in the Herefordshire regiment.

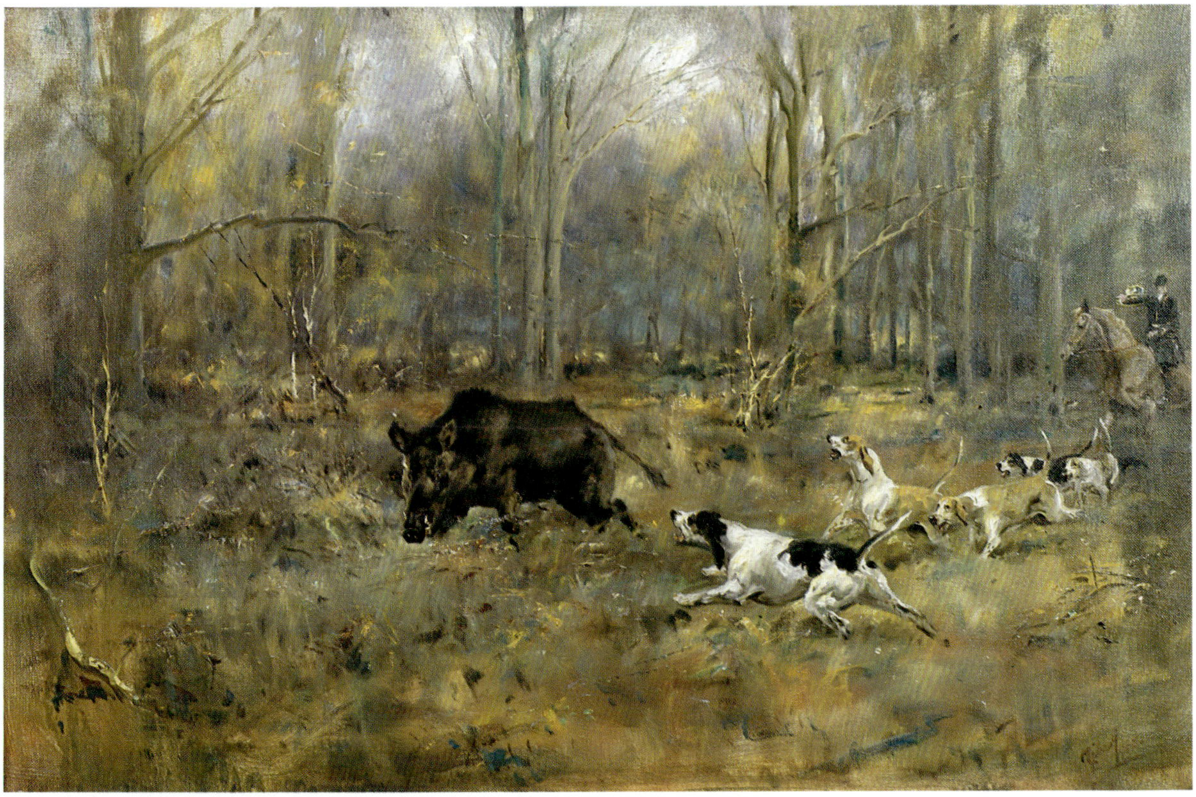

PLATE 5

Boar Hunting in the Ardennes, 1973. Signed, oil on canvas, 24 × 36 in (61 × 92 cm). The Ardennes visits with his friend John Treffry, MFH of the Cury, appealed to Michael Lyne's imagination and these paintings were kept in the Studio among treasures of the past. *(below) Madame de Rothschild's Staghounds, Forest of Compiègne, The End*, 1972. Signed, oil on canvas, 28 × 42 in (71 × 107 cm). Many may say the faces are blank and anonymous, but a member of the hunt, viewing the painting in 1989, could name all the figures from their attitude.

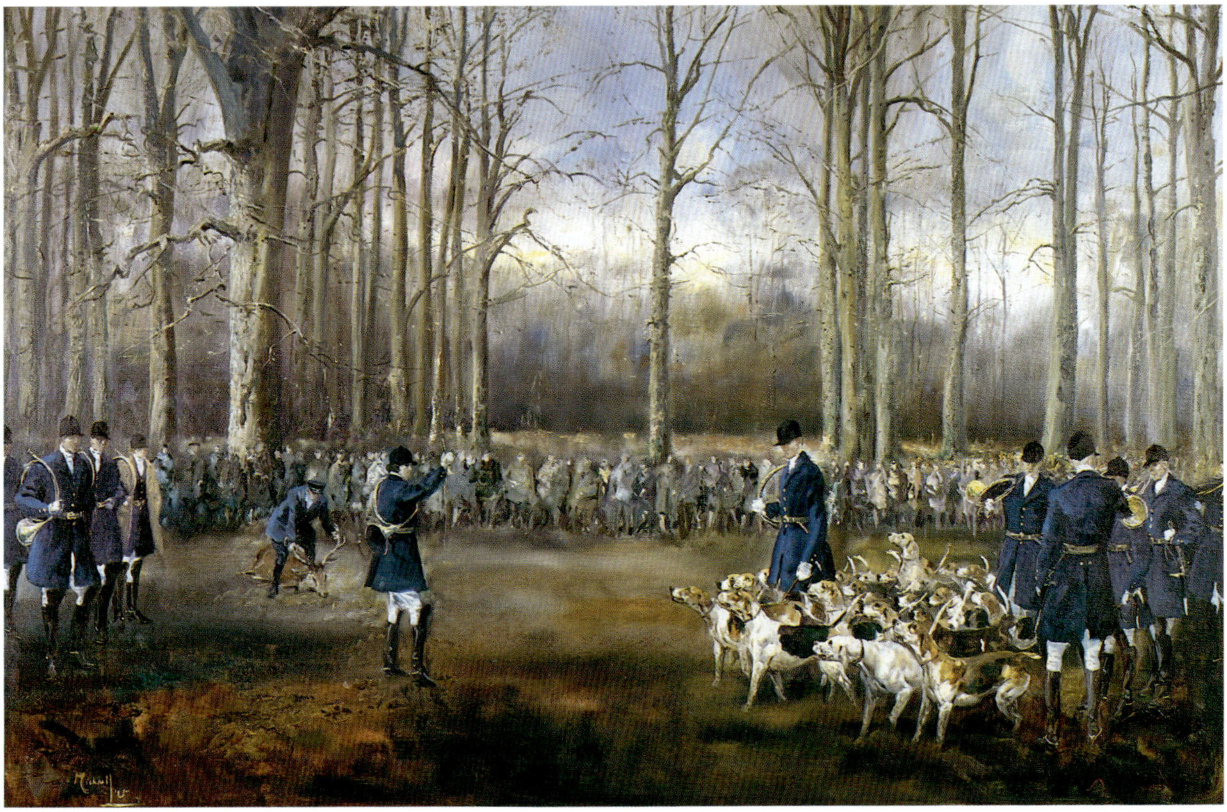

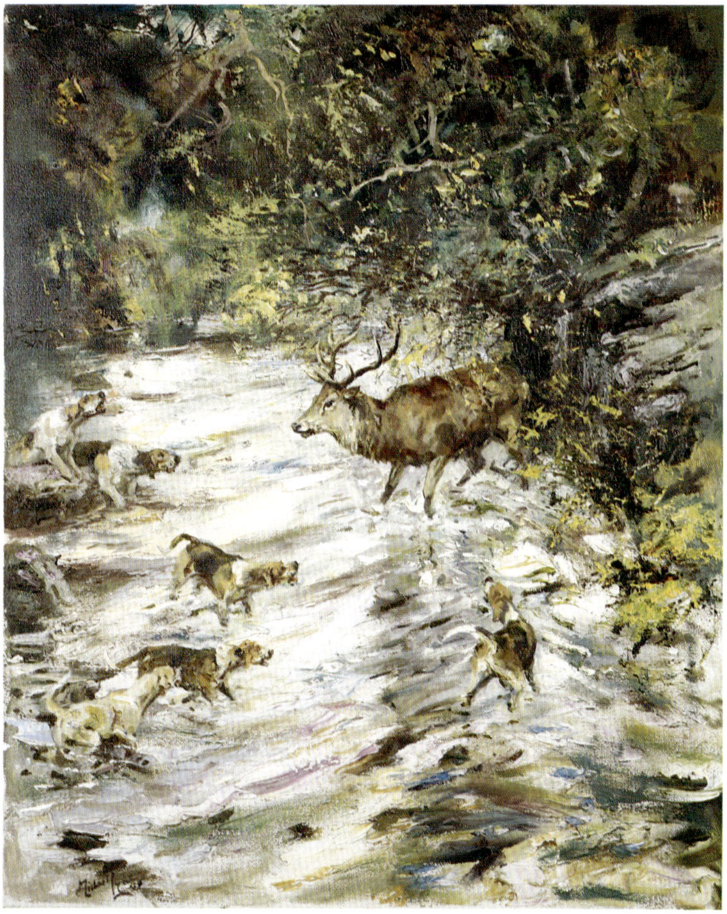

The Devon and Somerset Staghounds, Stag at bay on the River Barle, 1969. Signed, oil on canvas, 40 × 30 in (102 × 76 cm). Michael Lyne, like all other modern sporting artists, was drawn to Exmoor both to hunt and work.

PLATE 6

(*below*) *The West Waterford at the Vee Gap, Knockmealdown Mountains*, 1974. Signed, oil on canvas, 28 × 42 in (71 × 107 cm). Michael Lyne first worked on aerial views in the late 1930s and returned to them in the 1970s.

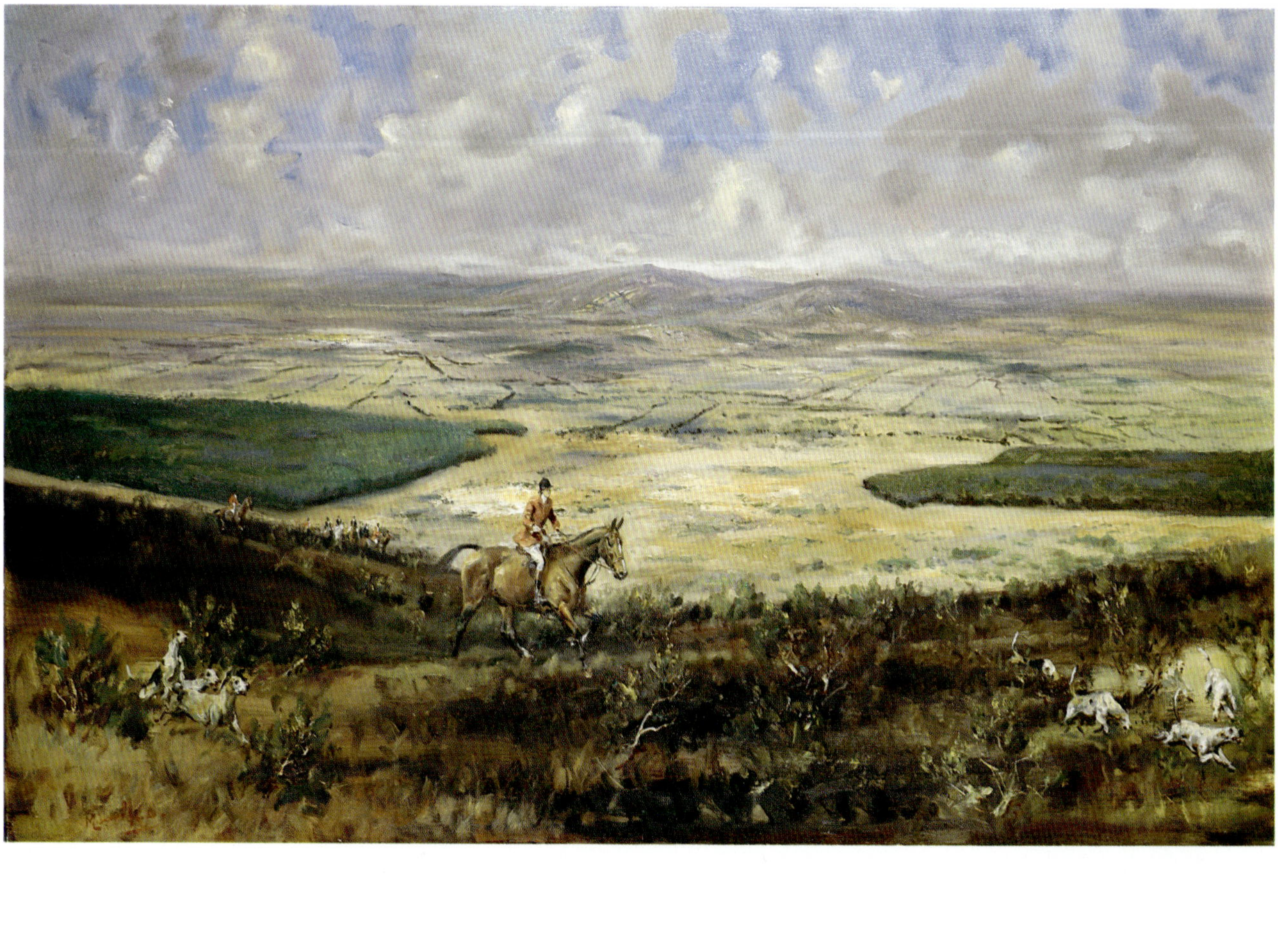

THREE

WARTIME INTERLUDE 1939 – 1945

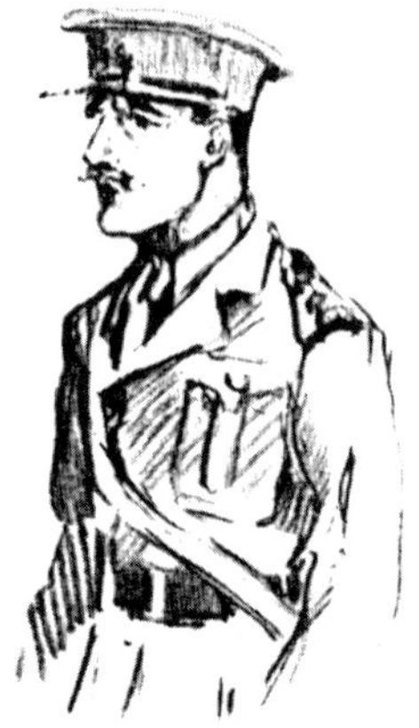

The Lyne brothers were all in the army; Dalesman, who had served as Captain in the Seaforth Highlanders in the First Word War, had rejoined as a private and was immediately sent to France with the BEF. Ronnie Wallace, Dick Cheney and Cyril Heber-Percy were also in the army. Sir Jocelyn Lucas who had recently been elected as Conservative Member of Parliament for Portsmouth South was serving in the Auxiliary Fire Service and was twice wounded in air raids.

Within a few months, hunting as such ceased to exist and was to be kept alive over the next six years by a few dedicated and older enthusiasts, and those in reserve occupations (excused military service) such as farmers. Although they did their best, some packs such as the Quarme Harriers of Somerset, were to be lost forever.

Michael was quickly sent on an Officers Training Course, and would shortly be commissioned, together with his brother John. On 6 December 1939 the engagement to be married was announced of Michael, to Jessie, daughter of Mr & Mrs F. Taylor of Gretton Hill, Winchcombe, Gloucestershire. Michael was to marry the girl who had whipped-in for him in happier days.

At the same time, *Horse and Hound* carried a report of 'A Capital Day's Hunting' enjoyed by the United Cotswold on 18 November, expressing regret at the absence of the popular Joint Masters, Michael Lyne and Dick Cheney. However, in April 1940, *Horse and Hound* could report that Michael had managed to get home for three weekends, probably only 48–hour passes and hunt hounds, though it noted with sadness, that the sole remaining Joint Master, Tom Mallinson, had been very ill.

Michael was commissioned in the Royal Engineers as a Camouflage Officer, and later transferred to a Surrey Regiment, the Queen's Royal Regiment as Regimental Camouflage Officer, working with the painter Edward Seago (1910–1974) whose work he greatly admired. A friend of that period, Major John Parry, MFH, now a Joint Master of the Belvoir, recalls that, 'at the Regimental depot in Guildford we had a very fierce Regimental Colonel who was a sportsman at heart. He had a habit of suddenly saying "Where's Nora", and unless one sprang to attention and said "There Sir", one was in trouble.' Major Parry also recalls that one day the Colonel suddenly said to Michael, 'How many soldiers are there here?' and Michael replied 'Twelve and a half couple, Sir'. From that moment he could do no wrong. Strange things were happening in the army at that time. Some one hundred and fifty miles away, in Warwick, a young classical scholar, Enoch Powell, then a lance corporal in the Royal Warwickshire Regiment, was working in the regimental kitchen and on being asked by a visiting brigadier on a tour of inspection how he liked kitchen work, Powell replied with a classical Greek quip. The Brigadier understood it and Lance Corporal Powell was soon posted to Aldershot for training as an intelligence officer, subsequently to become the youngest brigadier in the British Army, and later the distinguished Conservative Member of Parliament. When, in Northern France, a colonel queried why one of his majors had raised his hat to a newly promoted lance corporal, (Dalesman), he was advised by the major, 'One always raises one's hat to a Master of Hounds!'

In the early summer of 1940, Michael was at Seaford, Sussex, waiting to be drafted to France to join the hard pressed BEF. In early May he was granted a short embarkation leave (twelve hours) and immediately telegraphed his fiancee, 'Come down and marry me, but may have gone.'

The couple were married in Seaford Parish Church by Special Licence of the Archbishop of Canterbury. Michael's father travelled from Ledbury to assist in the ceremony. Michael arrived at the church on the only form of transport available, a very ancient ladies bicycle known to the foxhunting members of the officers' mess as the 'Bitch Bike'. The evacuation of the BEF from Dunkirk commenced shortly after the ceremony was over and Michael's draft was cancelled, giving the couple time for a short honeymoon in a Seaford guest house, away from the curious eyes of senior officers' wives who lived in the larger hotels.

After the honeymoon, Michael's regiment moved to Devon and then to Winchester for further training, and he found himself close to the crammers he had been at a decade previously. Rather than roaming the countryside with his terriers and shotgun as had been his custom then, he found as a member of the officers' mess, easy access to the superb fly-fishing which the area offered, receiving tuition from a fellow officer on the Itchin, where he spent many happy hours.

Winchester also had another benefit, for it was to there that *The Field* had been evacuated, and this gave Michael a ready entree to the editorial office. The editor was delighted to receive such offerings as a series of illustrated articles on 'First steps in Beagling' and illustrations for general use. Such commissions helped to ameliorate the loss during the blitz of the manuscript and illustrations of Michael's second book *Hunting Here and There*. Early in November 1940, *The Field* carried an article illustrated by Michael on 'A day with the United Cotswold Beagles' from which the reader learnt that the pack was surviving through the efforts of Group Captain Murlis Green and that a good day's sport had been had at the opening meet of the 1940–1941 season, though it had been marred by a speeding car ploughing through the middle of the pack when they were running back over a road. Fortunately only one hound, Striver, was hit and though badly cut, recovered.

In addition to his army duties, writing and fishing, Michael also exercised a certain amount of time and effort keeping his wife Jessie hidden in Winchester, contrary to Army Orders which would allow a stay of forty-eight hours only. During the summer they spent a long leave at the Lynes' family home in Ledbury, prior to Michael joining the newly formed Reconnaissance Corps at Lockerbie in the Scottish Lowlands, where, in 1942, the Lyne's son, Edward, was born. Sir Jocelyn Lucas and Dalesman were his godfathers.

The world of armoured warfare contained many equestrian personalities including Michael's new Commanding Officer at the Reconnaissance Training Centre, Colonel 'Bill' Whitbread, the founder of the Badminton Horse Trials and father of sponsorship in National Hunt Racing through the medium of the Whitbread Gold Trophy. Another personality was General Evelyn Fanshaw, Commanding Officer Armoured Training and RAC Training Establishments and later of the Hunters Improvement Society.

At Lockerbie Michael found several fellow officers from field sports backgrounds including two future MFHs, John Parry of the Belvoir and John Treffry of the Cury, and was able to enjoy beagling, fishing and shooting in rare off duty periods. Subsequently the training centre transferred to Catterick and the adjutant, Major John Parry, recalls that

Hounds Unattended, 1941. This was drawn for the first of a series of articles, 'First Steps in Beagling', written and illustrated by Michael Lyne for *The Field*, 1941 and subsequently included in the 1989 exhibition catalogue.

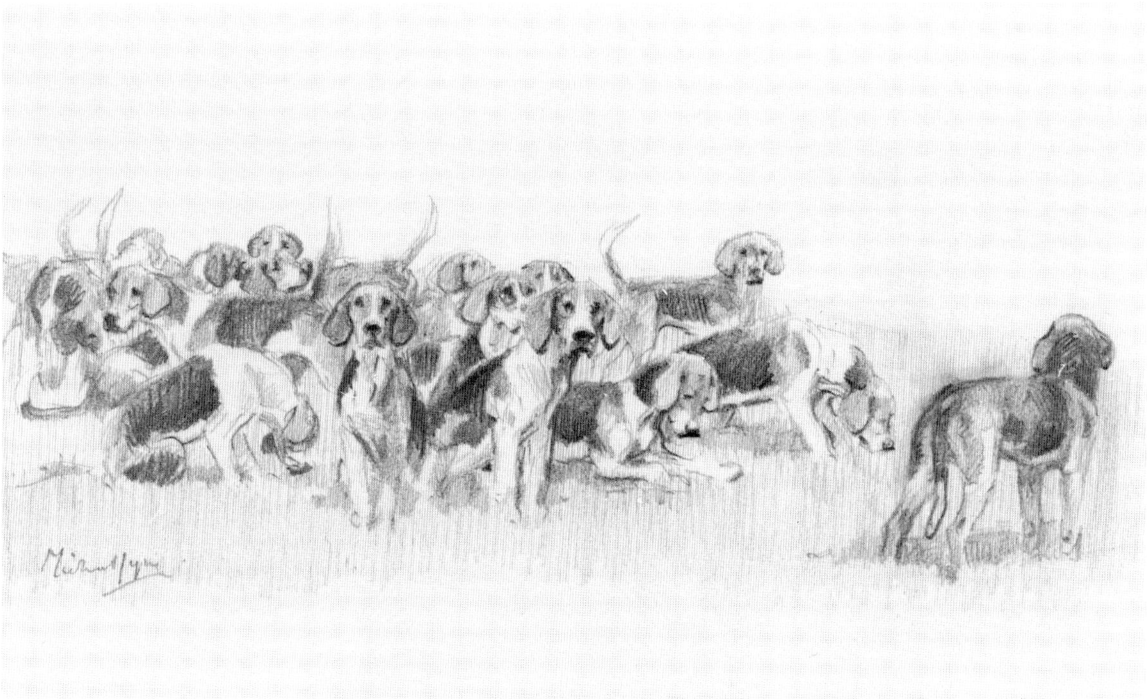

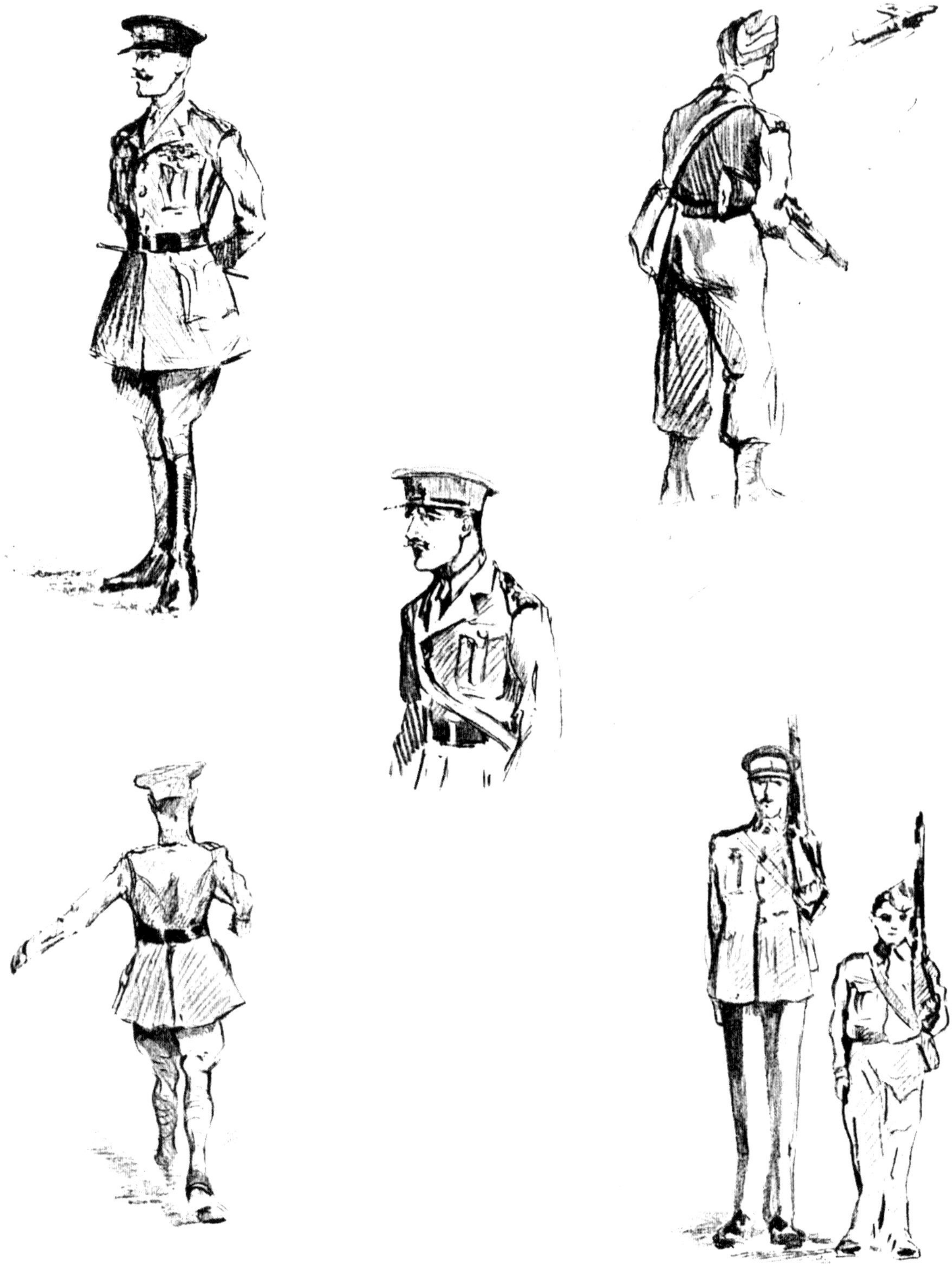

OCTU Personalities

he took over the remains of the Trinity Foot Beagles, Michael lending three or four couple of unentered United Cotswold Beagles, and with the assistance of Lieut Marriner as whipper-in, hunted the Yorkshire Dales near Catterick, for over two seasons. During this period several puppies were bred including United Cotswold Safeguard '44 by Trinity Foot Jupiter '35 out of Skegness Secret '42, who was subsequently widely used as a stallion hound and won on the flags, being second at Peterborough in 1950 and winning at Honiton in the same year.

Michael continued with his army duties and at the same time his talent was recognized by his regiment, in an unofficial capacity, who used him to produce designs and artwork for the regimental newsletter, Christmas cards and prints. Two such designs from 1943 were included in the retrospective exhibition held in London during April 1989.

Subsequently Michael was posted as a captain to Italy, spending eighteen months on the Bay of Naples. All that remains of this enforced exile is a delightful and unusual sketch-book in the family's possession, containing light and colourful watercolours of bullocks, attractive girls, officers' mess mule racing and hot rocky landscapes.

Reconnaissance Regiment: Gun Carrier with officer imagining a huntsman and hounds crossing in front of him. This was a watercolour for a Christmas card for the Reconnaissance Training Centre, Lockerbie.

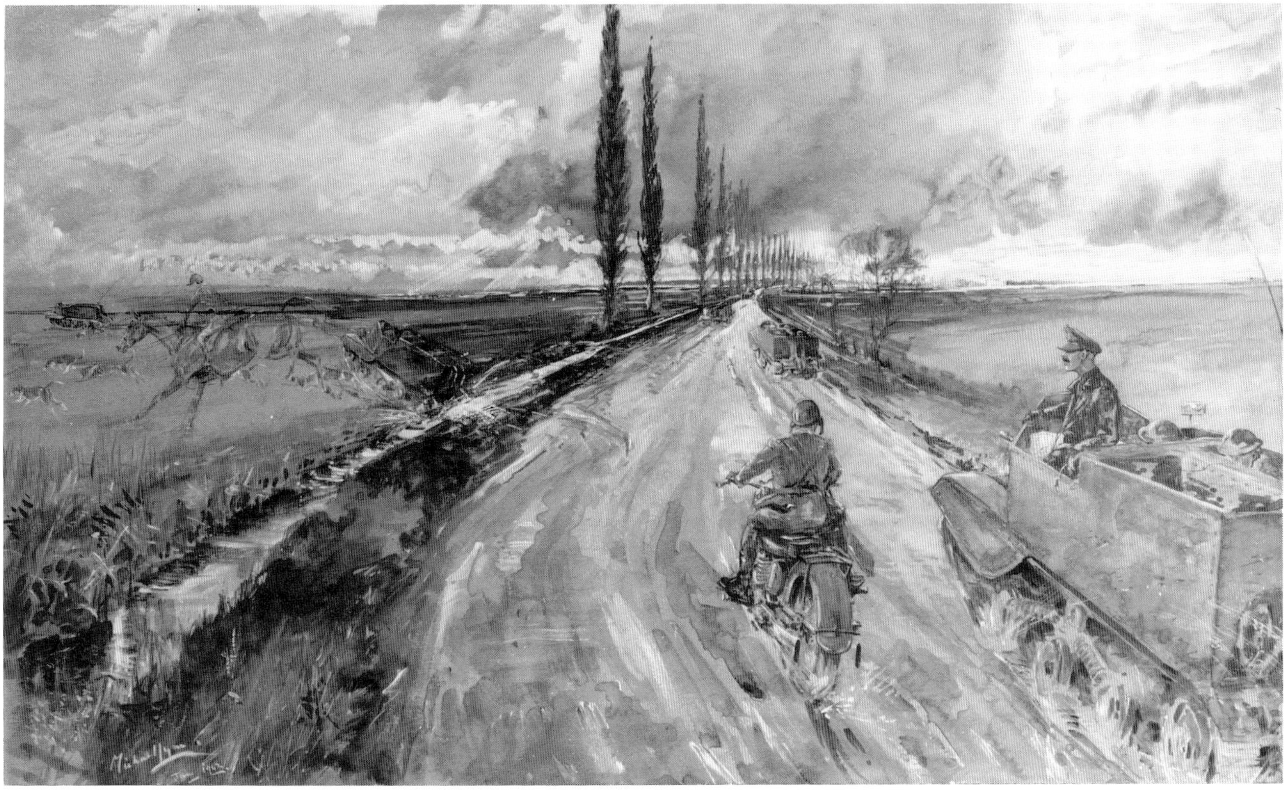

Michael always considered, with characteristic modesty, that his own war record was poor in the extreme, pointing to the exploits of his two brothers, Richard and John. Richard was already in the Territorial Army at the outbreak of war as Assistant Adjutant of the Second Herefords, the regiment his two younger brothers joined on 3 September 1939. He was posted to Burma in 1941, joined the Burma Rifles and was on the Burma – Siam border at the time of the Japanese invasion. He fought throughout the campaign and then during the retreat, lead his troops for fourteen weeks in an heroic and successful attempt to reach India through the Burmese jungle and Japanese lines. He then became ADC to the general officer commanding the 33rd Indian Corps. and was awarded the Indian Frontier Medal.

Whilst ADC, it was Richard's misfortune to become involved in a severe motor accident. He was being driven by an Indian driver who crashed and abandoned the car. Richard was thrown out and left for dead. When found, he was taken to hospital with a broken pelvis and other injuries.

John Lyne transferred from the Herefordshire Regiment to the Royal Fusiliers in 1940 and was promoted captain and appointed adjutant of one of their battalions. In late 1941 he was transferred to the HQ, South Wales District, and subsequently to HQ Western Command. In July 1942 he volunteered for the Army Air Corps and was promoted major in the Glider Pilot Regiment. After qualifying as a glider pilot, he commanded an operational squadron. On D-Day he was leading his squadron over Normandy when the tow rope of his glider was shot off over German lines, the glider crashing into an orchard. The crew were unhurt, but John had broken his foot. He won the MC for getting his crew and himself back to the allied lines through many hazardous situations.

At the end of the war, John, now a full colonel, stayed in the army and was sent to Palestine for two years to help fight the Israeli terrorists. He was in the St David's Hotel (British Army HQ) in Jerusalem, when it was blown up by the Israelis, but he survived and was again decorated.

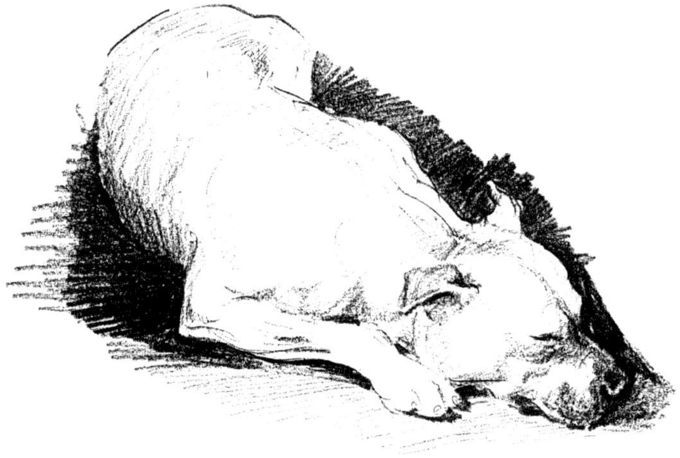

FOUR

THREE NEW HOMES 1945–1955

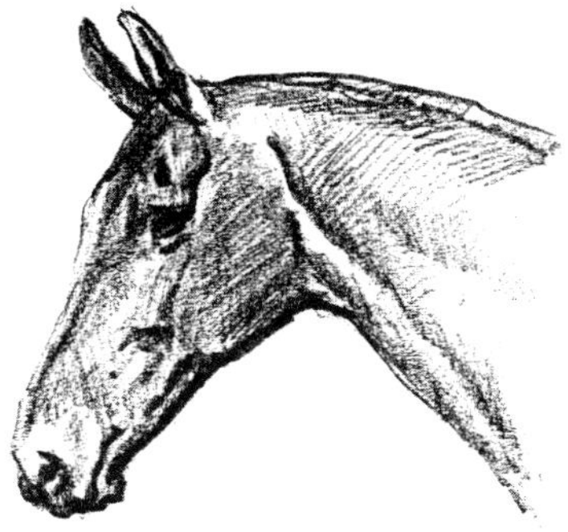

John and Michael Lyne bolstered their morale whilst privates in 1939, waiting to go to their OCTU courses, by dreaming of the tremendous celebrations when the war was over. When the end came, John was in Palestine and Michael in Italy, it was all rather an anti-climax. They both read of the joy and jubilation at home and their long promised celebrations never took place.

One by one the hunting personalities returned from the Army to civilian life. Ronnie Wallace, now a captain, to hunt the Ludlow and subsequently the Heythrop, Lt Col Heber-Percy to become a Joint Master of the Cottesmore and 'Bay' de Courcy-Parry (Dalesman) to be Master of the West Cumberland.

Michael returned to England and rejoined his family in November 1945, determined to re-start as a sporting artist, after a six year break. Although he had achieved recognition in the pre war era, Michael was to find it much more difficult to re-establish himself: it would be uphill all the way, for the golden boy of the late 1930s, over the next five years. Sporting paintings were to be a luxury in the austerity ridden post-war world and commissions, which provided Michael's 'bread and butter' were thin on the ground and often went unpaid. His creative energy was prodigious and this, coupled with the need to communicate visually produced a formidable combination, particularly when motivated by the need to provide for a wife and family.

As a temporary first family home, Michael rented a cottage in Chalford, overlooking the Golden Valley which leads down to nearby Stroud on the western edge of the Cotswolds. The house was not very memorable, but it enjoyed a good southern light and was just down the road from Tom Mallinson, Michael's Joint Master of the United Cotswold Beagles on whose farm the hounds were kennelled during the war years. The Mallinsons were typical of the friends the Lynes made – keen country folk and full of kindness (chocolate biscuits for young Edward, now age four, at a time of very strict post-war rationing). One of Edward Lyne's recollections of that time vividly illustrates the state of chronic food shortage, even in the country.

A large aeroplane flew over the valley very low, shortly followed by an enormous bang, and then a column of smoke driving up from lower down the valley. Michael, never short of courage, ran from the house and disappeared down a steep bank in the direction of the smoke, leaving Jessie and young Edward standing at the bottom of the garden, worrying and waiting. After what seemed ages, Michael's rather smoky face appeared as he strode up the bank. Later in the safety of his home he recounted that the plane had hit a small monastery, partly demolishing the old building and setting it on fire. On arrival, Michael found a monk in a great state of agitation, trying to gain access to that part of the building which, though not destroyed, was blazing lustily. Michael thinking that there must be another monk trapped in there, heedless to the danger, battled his way into what had obviously been the kitchen. He quickly scanned the room but saw no signs of any bodies, alive or otherwise. Returning he informed the still very distressed monk that there was nobody trapped in the kitchen, where upon the monk replied, 'Did you find the sausages?' Apparently, the butcher had earlier that morning delivered one pound of sausages, and these were uppermost in his mind, even though the monastery lay in ruins around him.

Nineteen forty-four had been the last year that the United Cotswold Beagles were a registered pack. Tom Mallinson had struggled to maintain the major part of the pack on his farm near Stroud, using floor sweepings from a biscuit factory and whatever else he could find to feed them, and three or four couple of unentered hounds were on loan to the army at Catterick. Michael returned at the end of 1945 to resume his Joint Mastership and the pack managed to continue hunting until the end of the 1945–1946 season. Unfortunately a combination of feed shortage plus the fact, that not surprisingly, Jessie found whipping-in incompatible with bringing up a lively toddler, led to the break up of the pack. It is ironic that having survived the whole of the war, it was the impact of the grey, sullen, utility and shortage ridden post-war era that brought about the pack's demise.

The story of the pack was however to have a happy ending. Having started from modest beginnings to become one of the best packs in the country, it was fitting that it should be presented to the Royal Agricultural College, Cirencester (who recently celebrated their centenary), to help re-establish their own pack. Daphne Moore relates that the little, badger-pied dog, United Cotswold Safeguard, bred during the war at Catterick, was to become the patriarch of the revived RAC pack and a winner on the flags. A few couple were also sent to the newly formed Marlborough College pack.

In 1946 Michael was asked to undertake a commission which gave him great pleasure. The Ledbury Hunt Farmers' Ball was being held at the Guild Hall, Gloucester, for the first time in eight years, and it was decided to give the long serving ball secretary a gift of two of Michael's Ledbury watercolours. Not only was this badly needed work, but it provided a welcome return to what Michael, after his father's retirement to Ledbury, regarded as his home hunt, and more important still, the hunt which started him on his career over a decade earlier.

The Grand National which had not been run between 1941 and 1945, resumed in 1946, and on 29 March 1947 Michael travelled to Aintree with Tom Mallinson to see the second post-war running of the race. It was incidentally, the first time that the race had been

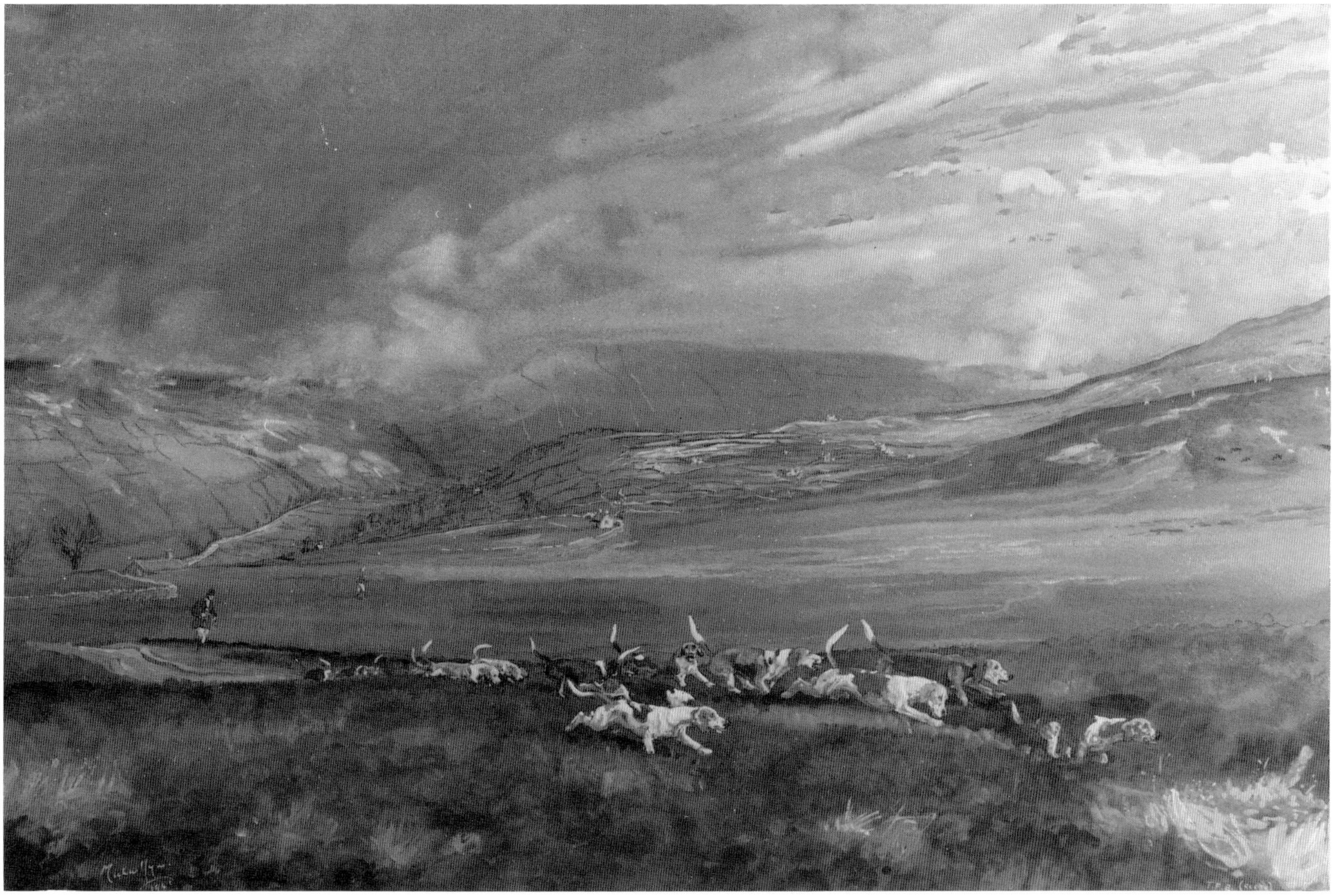

John Parry MFH *hunting hounds in Swaledale above Low Row*, 1944. The hounds are mostly Trinity Foot; the pale coloured hound running second is United Cotswold Safeguard, bred at Catterick and given by Michael to the RAC Cirencester after the war. Major Parry reckoned he was apt to run mute, but he hunted very well. Behind Safeguard is another UC hound, Bandsman, and behind him is his brother Blazer.

run on a Saturday. Such was the climate at the time, that the Prime Minister could suggest that a Saturday running would be in the interest of British industry. In the event the whole of the meeting was run on a rain-soaked course in appalling conditions, following the heavy February snows and floods, and visibility was poor. The field contained such legendary horses as Mr J.V. Rank's Prince Regent, and Lord Bicester's Silver Fame. Michael's interest was centred on the 100–1 chance Toyette, owned and ridden by an old army friend, Major Reggie Waugh-Harris and the subject of a commission for a large watercolour. In addition, the damp rain-soaked race was to produce a further four watercolours which were included in the Ackermann's exhibition at the end of the year, and was also to introduce Michael to a venue which would inspire some of his very best work. One would

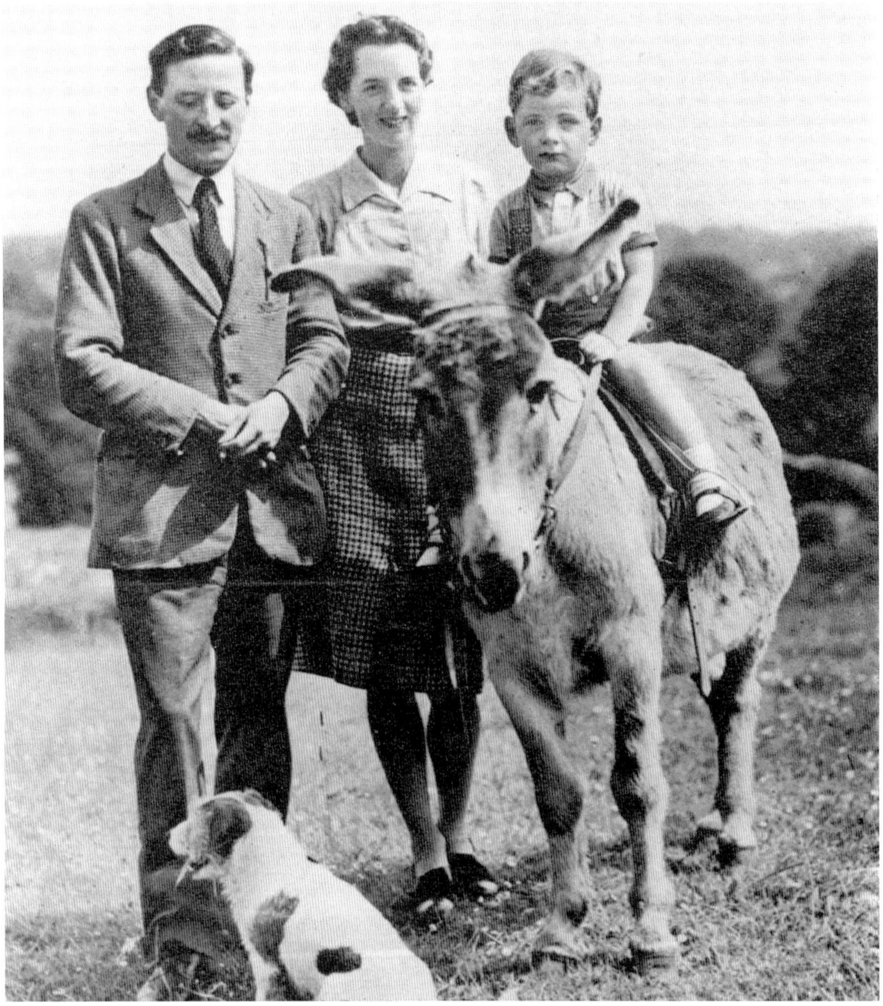

The Lyne family at Througham Slad, 1947, with Jenny the donkey. Edward Lyne was born at Lockerbie in 1942.

like to speculate that he took the advice of the *Horse and Hound* reviewer, 'We hope that Mr Lyne will not forget that pictures of Aintree never get stale.'

Michael, true countryman that he was, found little of interest in the far removed world of the Thoroughbred, but from his earliest days, he had always followed steeple-chasing, whether between the flags at local point-to-points in the Welsh Marches, or under rules at Ludlow and Cheltenham. Aintree however, was to introduce him to a new and very different world.

Since the establishment of the Whitbread Gold Cup in 1961 and the subsequent introduction of commercial sponsorship, it is now very difficult to conceive that the Grand National was the only opportunity for the owner of a high class chaser to make any real money. It was also for the public a spectacle par excellence, and even now with many modifications to the fences, none who have visited Aintree can fail to be aware of its character and atmosphere. Michael was enchanted, although his superb series of Aintree paintings were yet some fourteen years ahead.

The family moved from the cottage at Chalford in 1946 to a grand, old, but rather spooky house, named Througham Slad. This was the country seat of the Cadbury family of chocolate fame, and owners of vast cocoa plantations in Ghana, now Edward Lyne's home. The family lived in the servants' quarters and as the Cadburys would never allow electricity to be installed, it was heated by an open fire.

This old house holds so many memories for Edward Lyne that he says he could easily write a book about just that short period of his life. His father's book *From Litter to Later On* was written, or at least conceived at this time, when the family's much loved terrier Lorna, who came from the gypsies in the Doone Valley, Somerset, whelped the most hectic and lovely family of beagle cross puppies by Pipewell Justice. Michael, worrying how to feed a family with the restraints of post-war rationing, went out one day, about this time and purchased Rosemary, who became their Jersey house cow. Rosemary had belonged to two spinsters, the misses Eddy and Wilby, both of whom had raced Fraser Nash cars with great daring at Brooklands, and whose cars Edward Lyne unsuccessfully went in search of during one of his leaves from Africa. The cars were housed in a Nissen hut, still in racing trim, and sold comparatively recently for in excess of £250,000 upon the death of the last of the two old ladies. Rosemary had had the misfortune to sit upon

Part of Lorna's whelp, Througham Slad, 1947. This watercolour is unused artwork for *From Litter to Later On*, published in 1973.

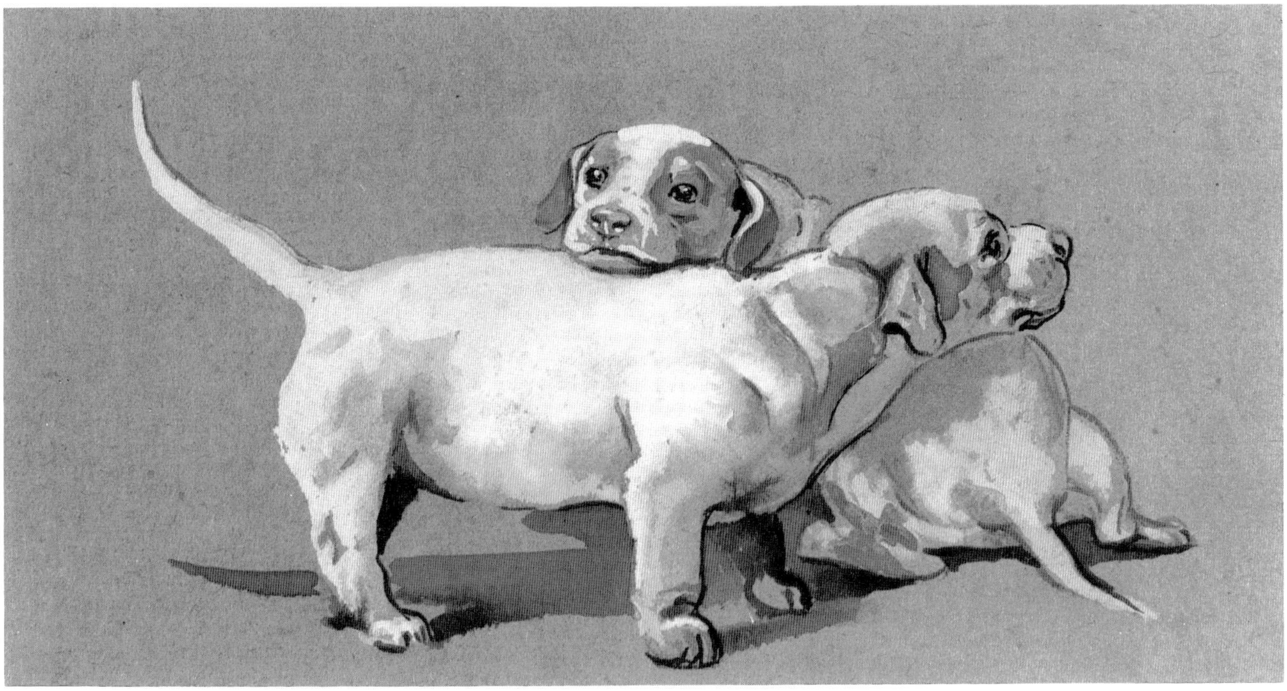

'Most cows distrust dogs, but Rosemary, our Jersey, seemed to sense that Lucy really had no evil intentions and submitted meekly to having her nose licked.' *From Litter to Later On.*

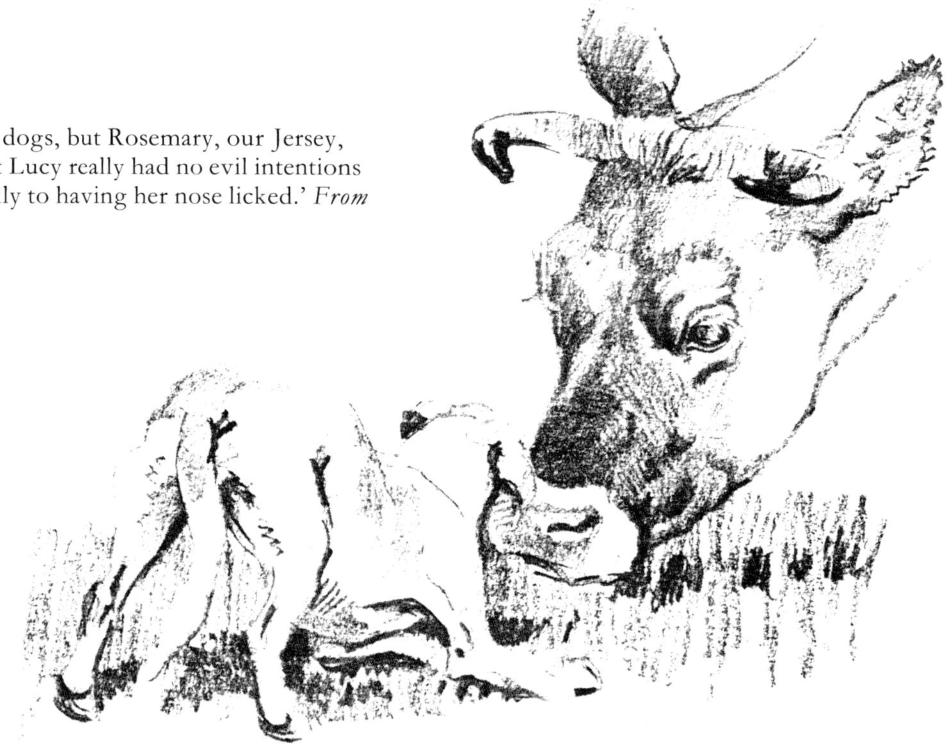

a broken bottle, neatly excising one teat, which is how Michael managed to find her at a now reduced asking price.

Rosemary lived in a meadow to the south of the house; this she shared with an old donkey with a broken ear, Jenny, retired from a Stroud bakery, who through the kindness of the Cadbury's, later became a part of the Lyne family. Michael used to bet his foxhunting friends five shillings (25p) that they could not stay on Jenny's back for more than five minutes. No matter how accomplished the horseman who took on the bet, they were always floored, to Michael's delight, when totally unexpectedly, Jenny would drop one shoulder.

The winter of 1947 was exceptionally hard and the Lynes were snowed in for a total of eight weeks, as they lived at the end of a narrow winding and descending road of some three miles. Michael set himself and his family the task of digging themselves out. It was beyond the bounds of probability for two and a quarter shovels to dig away three miles of snow drifts. Each morning they would awake to find that all their hard work had been negated by the wind causing existing drifts to reform and cover the hard won ground.

A decision was then made that the few scattered families living within approximately fifteen square miles, would pool their human resources to try to make life bearable. The die was cast and it fell to Michael to don snow shoes and deliver the bread to the thinly scattered population. With a sack of bread on his back, he covered many miles of difficult and hilly going. Arriving at one old lady's house, he knocked on the door, an upstairs window opened, and a wizened old face looked out, the mouth opening as if to say, 'What do you think you are doing here?'. Michael looked up and said to the lady, 'I've brought your bread'. Back came the rather toothless response, 'I hope you've brought my usual brown'. Michael, completely taken aback said, 'I've only got white' where upon he got the wigging of his life.

Michael always considered that the years at Througham Slad were the happiest of his life, the ideal ambience for a hard up family and an artist seeking to re-establish himself with uninterrupted work. He had the pleasure of seeing his work well received after the wartime interregnum, the family re-united and the birth of a second child, Diana.

Sir Alfred Munnings and Cecil Aldin both considered that an enforced absence from painting during World War I had improved their art. Michael disagreed, he felt that his

Epsom Races, 1948. Watercolour, 11.5 × 15.25 in (29 × 39 cm).

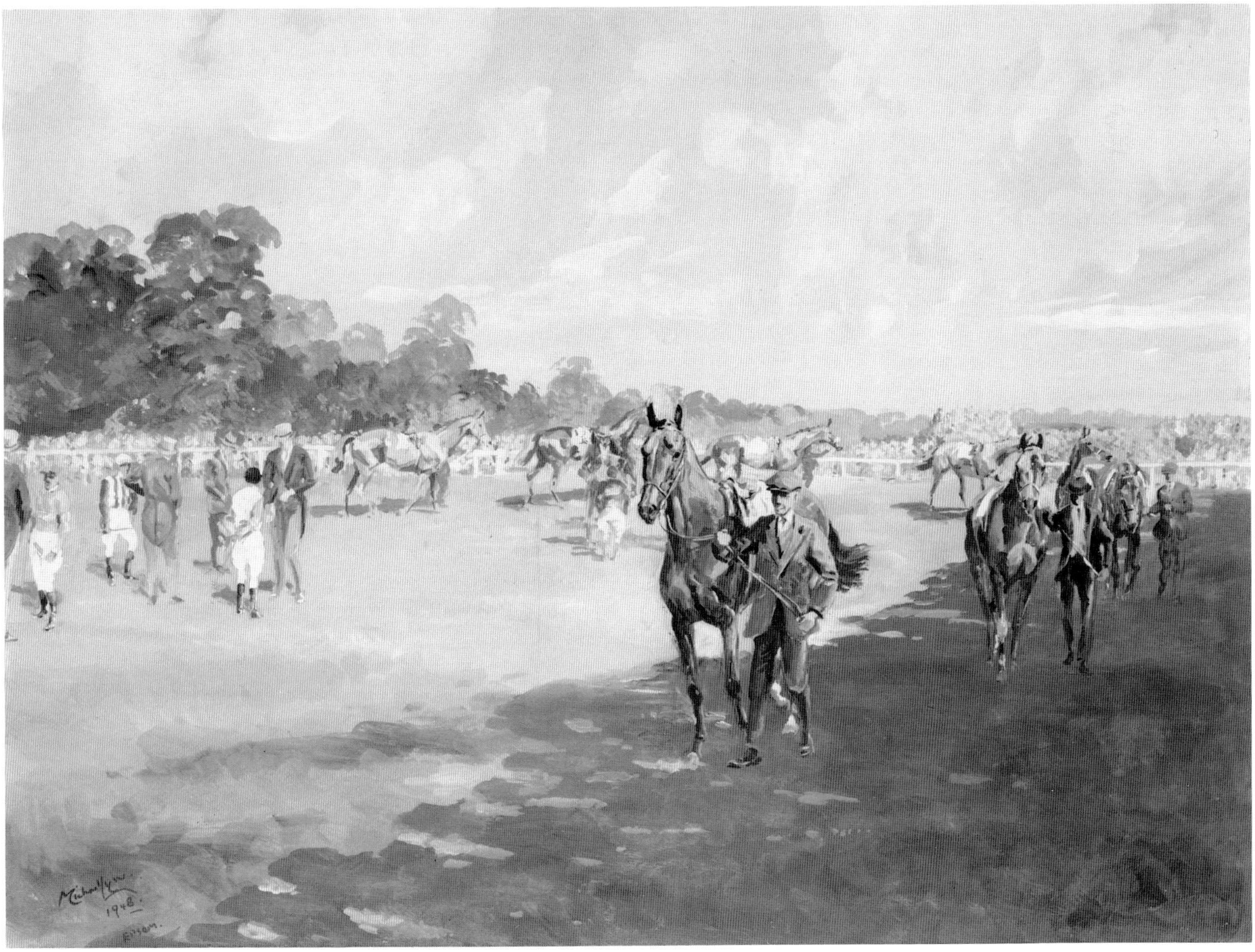

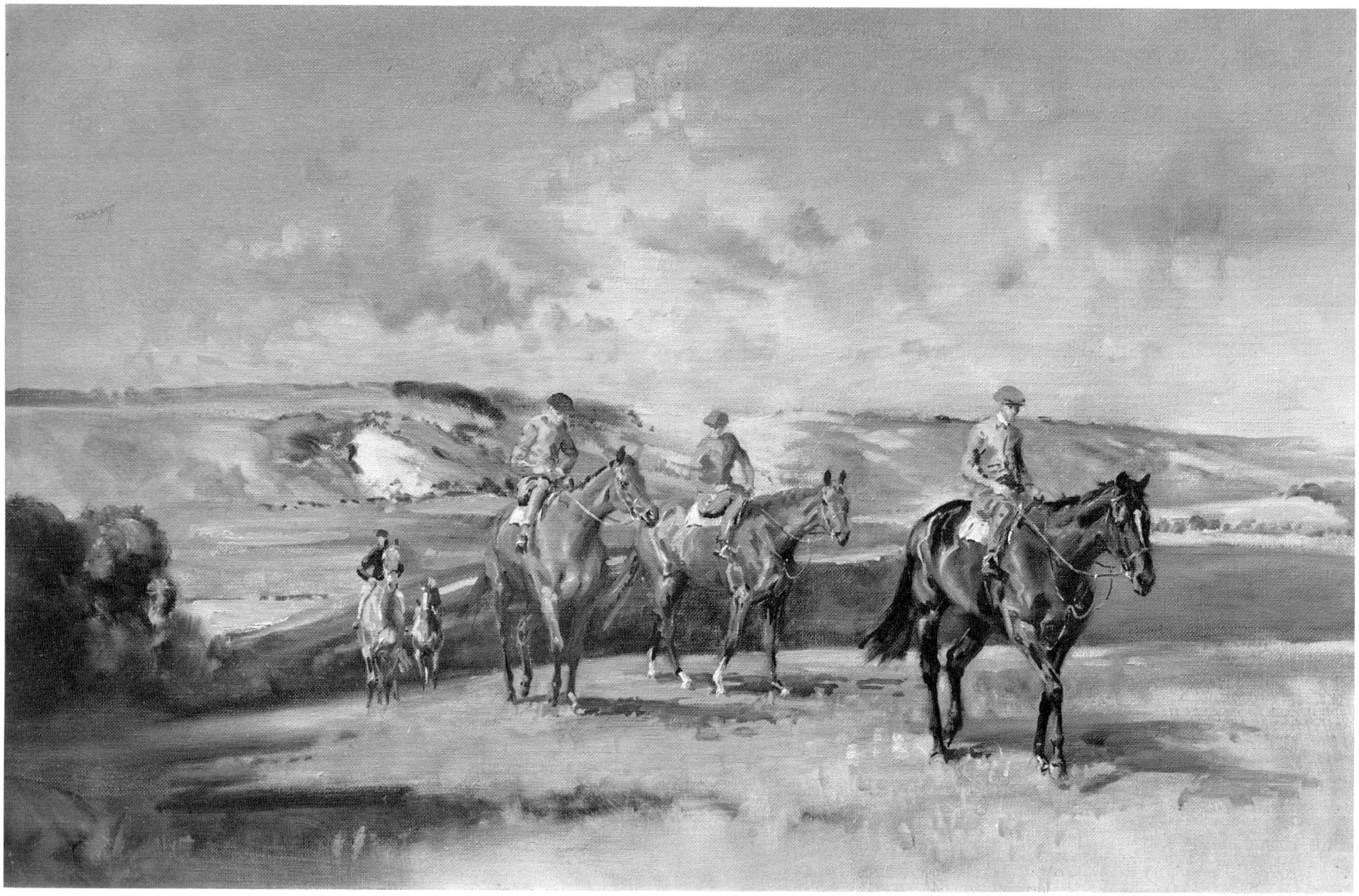

Upper Lambourn. Oil on canvas, 20 × 30 in (51 × 76 cm)

six years of army service was lost painting time, which should be made up as quickly as possible. It was this decision that for the next thirty years was to commit him to a routine of unremitting hard work and prolific output (working throughout daylight hours for the whole of each hunting season) which ultimately was to destroy his health.

In November 1946, exactly a year after shedding his Sam Browne and leaving the army, Michael had his first one-man post-war exhibition at Ackermann's new gallery in Old Bond Street. Ackermann too were readjusting to the post-war world of shortage and drabness under the direction of Miss Mole. They were re-establishing themselves after being bombed out of their old New Bond Street gallery in 1941. In the circumstances, given the shortage of glass and picture moulding, it is surprising the exhibition was held at all, let alone showing sixty-one works by one man.

It was seven years since a sporting art exhibition had been held in a London gallery, and the reviewers loved it. *The Field* commented that 'The exhibition will come as a treat to all lovers of horse and hound. Lyne is in the front rank of our younger artists, and his watercolours reveal a fine eye for country, great understanding of his subjects, spirited action and excellent composition. This show is one that should not be missed.' That excellent judge of painting, Denys Sutton, writing in *Country Life* was no less enthusiastic. *Horse and Hound* stated 'that the always promising Mr Lyne was now reaching maturity and certain to fill the place, so long held by Mr Lionel Edwards'. After commenting on many of the paintings, *Horse and Hound* concluded by stating 'good sporting artists are few and far between these days, and most of the best of them are getting on in years'.

A further one-man exhibition was held by Ackermann at the end of 1947 entitled 'Hunting Season 1946–47' and reviewers were again enthusiastic, dwelling on Michael's spirited action and knowledge of his subject, together with his 'noticeable progress since last year'. By comparison with the 1938 and 1946 exhibitions, the 1947 one displayed an extension in the artist's repertoire, with the inclusion of Grand National material, animal studies and narrative paintings. It was obvious, though perhaps not to Michael at the time, that he would be noticed, promoted and taken up by the hunting establishment. This happened, though it took another three years and came from a very unlikely quarter.

During the presidency of Harry S. Truman, Lewis Douglas was United States Ambassador to the Court of St James' from 1947 to 1950. He had with him a special assistant, Paul Warburg, who visiting Ackermann, purchased a Michael Lyne watercolour from the 1947 exhibition, as a present for his foxhunting brother, Frederick. But the painting grew

Post and Rail Fence, Middleburg, Va., 1951. Included in the 1989 Exhibition catalogue.

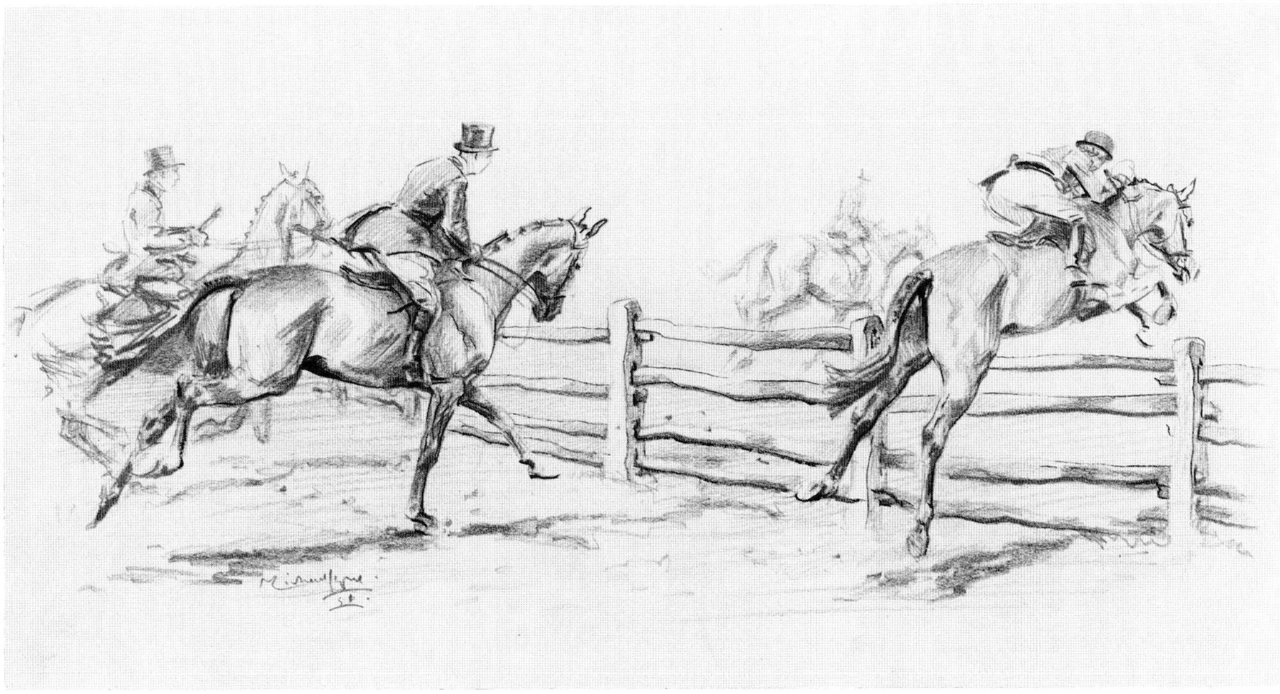

on him and he decided to keep it for his own pleasure and hung it in his official office. Paul Warburg's brother Frederick and sister-in-law Wilma visited London shortly afterwards and were also much taken with the Lyne painting. A visit to Old Bond Street proved abortive, Ackermann had no Lyne watercolours on offer, both exhibitions having been total sell-outs. With typical American vigour, Frederick Warburg, on learning that the artist lived near Stroud, contacted an English banker friend, Richard Fleming, brother of the author and journalist Ian Fleming, whom he knew lived in the Cotswolds. Shortly afterwards, Fleming and the Warburgs made their way to the Lyne home at Througham Slad. In fact they left the Lyne's empty handed other than with a copy of *Horses, Hounds and Country* and a liking both for the artist and his work. Such was Frederick Warburg's enthusiasm for Michael's work, that he quickly persuaded the masters of several of the leading East Coast of America foxhound packs to commission paintings.

In October 1949, Michael packed his old army valise (new luggage was still almost unobtainable) and said goodbye to his family, and boarded the Dutch ship *New Amsterdam* for New York. The crossing was rough and ahead lay almost three months work, for he was due to return home in time for Christmas. Michael feared the worst, even though he had a workload almost equal to a whole winter's work in England. In the event he was confounded, America proved to be a watershed in both his life and work. He was always grateful for this and visited the country regularly during the autumn months, until 1984.

Although an archetypal Englishman, shy and retiring by nature, Michael found in his new American friends much that was appealing, and revelled in the company of his urbane, hedonistic, affluent hosts. Whilst they were his patrons they also became his friends and in them he found something that he never experienced elsewhere and certainly far removed from the ambience of an English country parsonage.

During his first visit, Michael was able to visit eleven out of the hundred or so recognized packs, though through the very nature of his visit, he did not see any of the many unregistered private packs. He was kept busy and returned to England with a large portfolio of drawings which were later to become two dozen or so finished works covering packs from the Myopia Hunt of Hamilton, Massachusetts in the north to the Middleburg Hunt of Virginia in the south. The die had been cast, from that time onwards the United States was to be a real and integral part of Michael's life.

Whatever the impact of the United States on Michael Lyne and his reciprocal feelings for it, home always beckoned. However much he enjoyed his American visits, he was always excited by the prospect of returning home. Sadness at parting from American friends was much more than compensated for by the knowledge that his family, a fine country house, dogs, water fowl and livestock awaited his return. The home to which Michael now returned was not Througham Slad which the Warburgs had visited, but Dunfield House near Fairford, on the southern edge of the Cotswolds, which Michael had purchased,

Off in the Brook, Kilkenny Country. Signed, watercolour, 11.75 × 14 in (30 × 36 cm).

PLATE 7

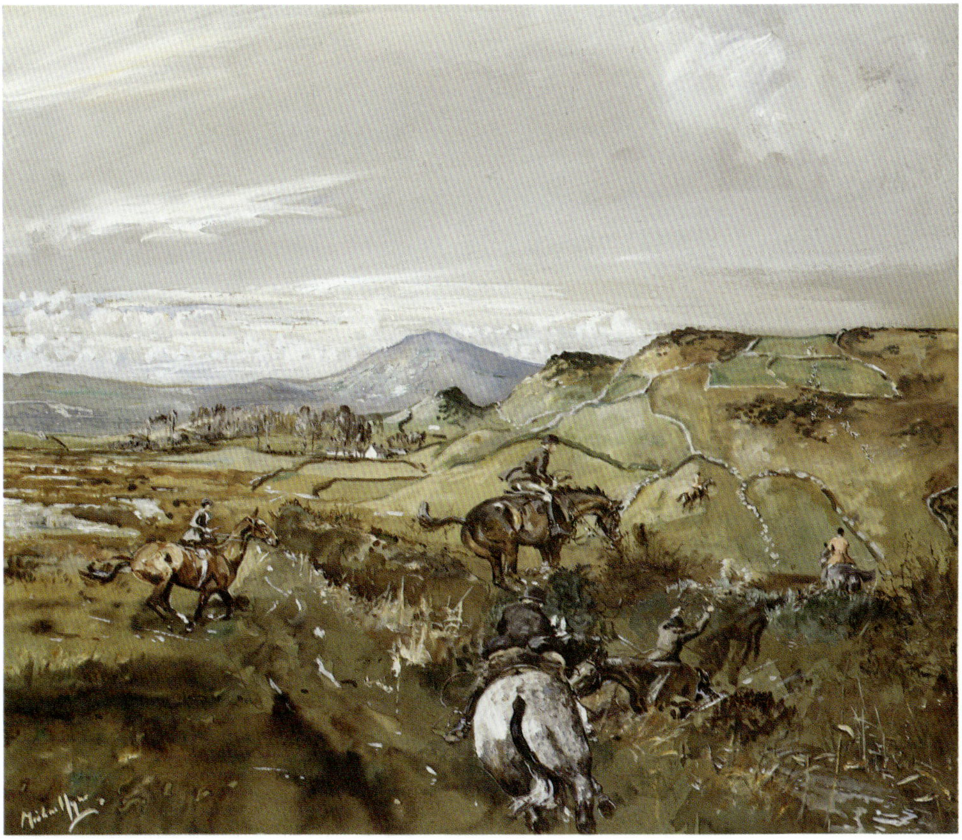

(*below*) *Landscape with Brood Mares, Rokeby, Virginia* 1952. Signed and dated, watercolour, 16.5 × 23.5 in (42 × 60 cm).

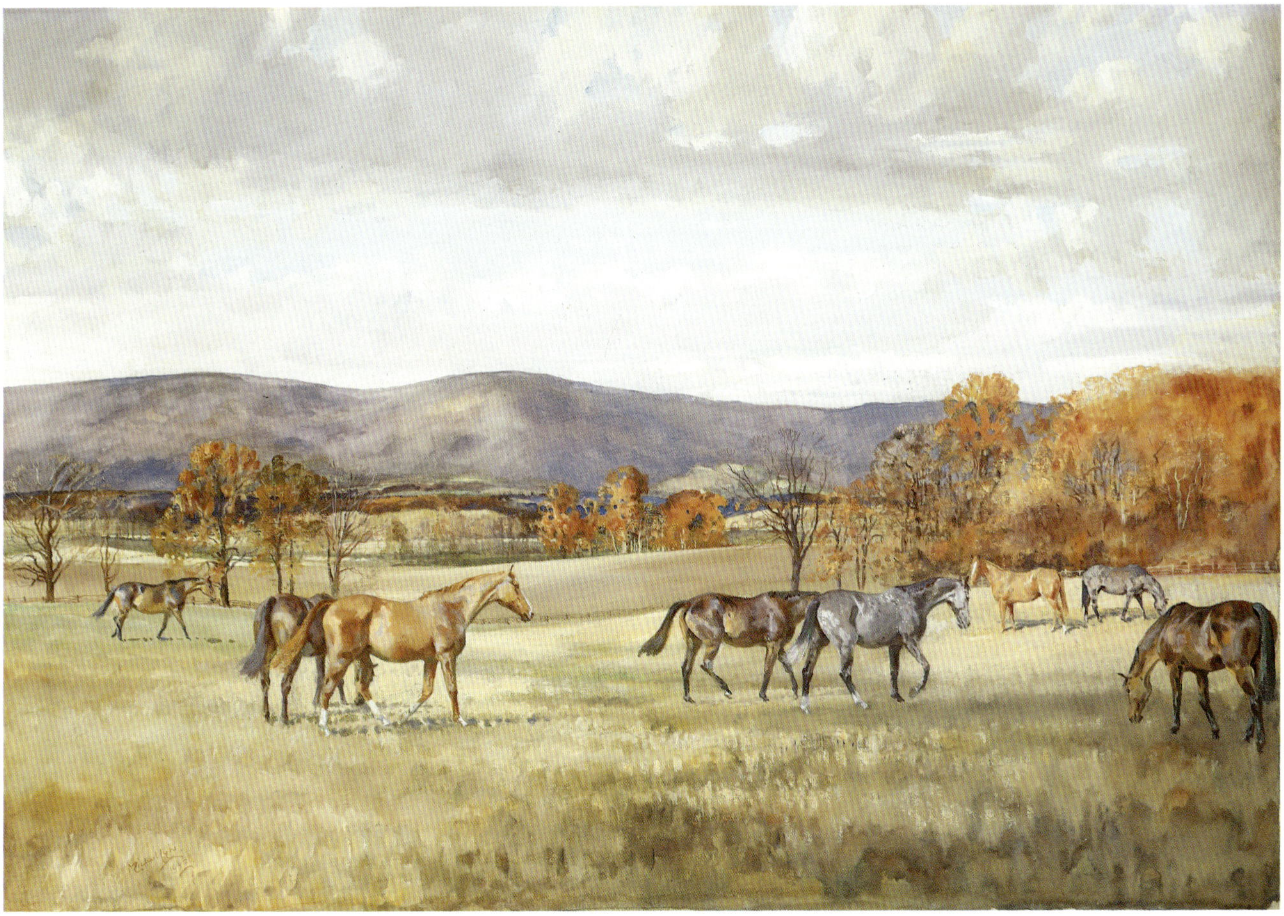

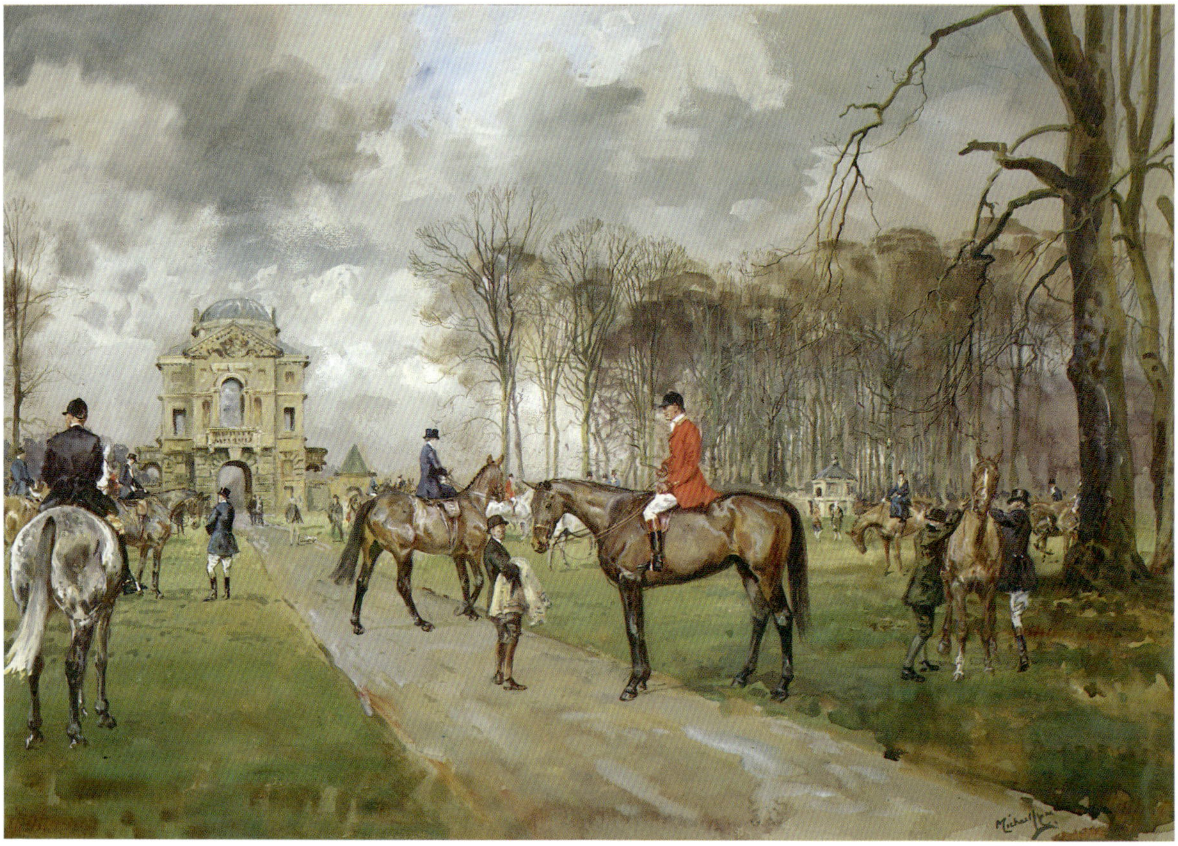

The Duke of Beaufort's Hounds – The Meet at Worcester Lodge – Paul Mellon on Gunsmith, February 1960. Signed, watercolour, 16.25 × 23 in (41 × 58 cm). *(below) The Duke of Beaufort's Hounds – Gone Away from Tog Hill – Paul Mellon on Enough Rope*, March 1960. Signed, watercolour, 16.25 × 23 in (41 × 58 cm).

PLATE 8

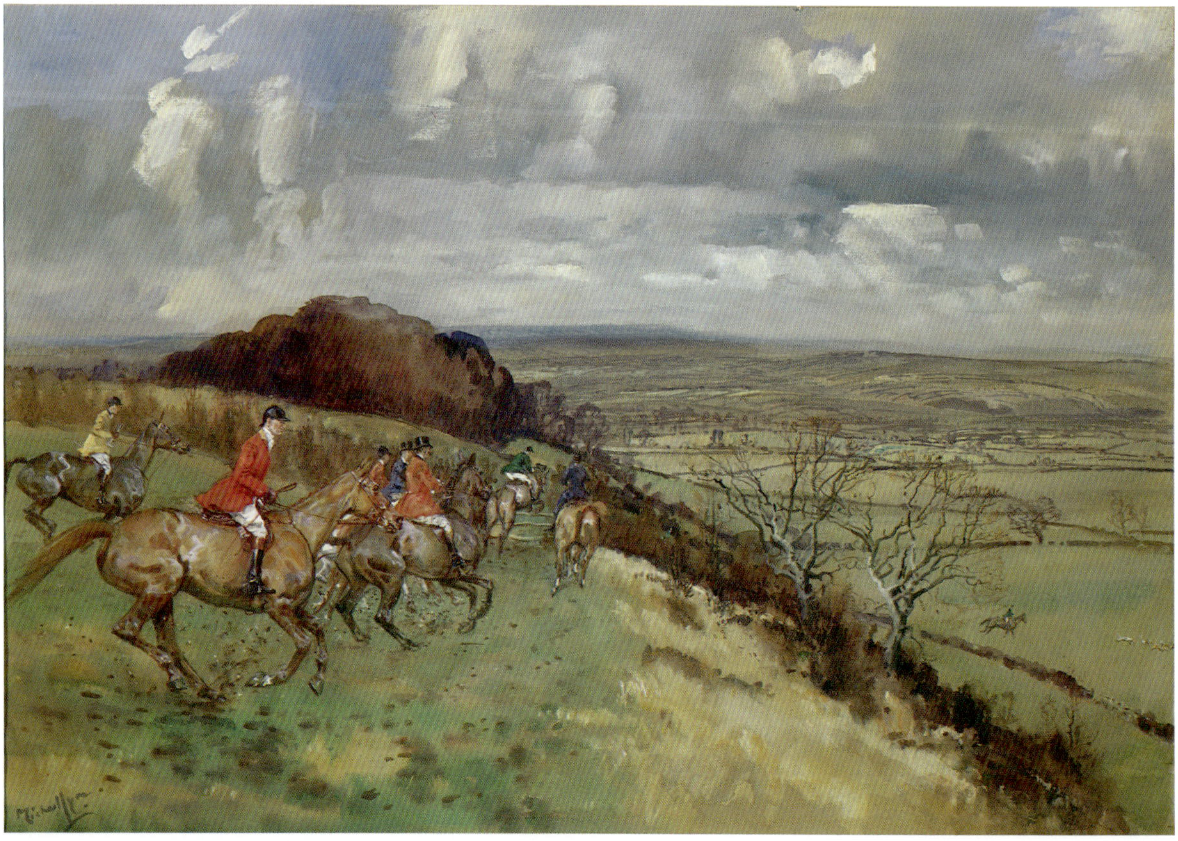

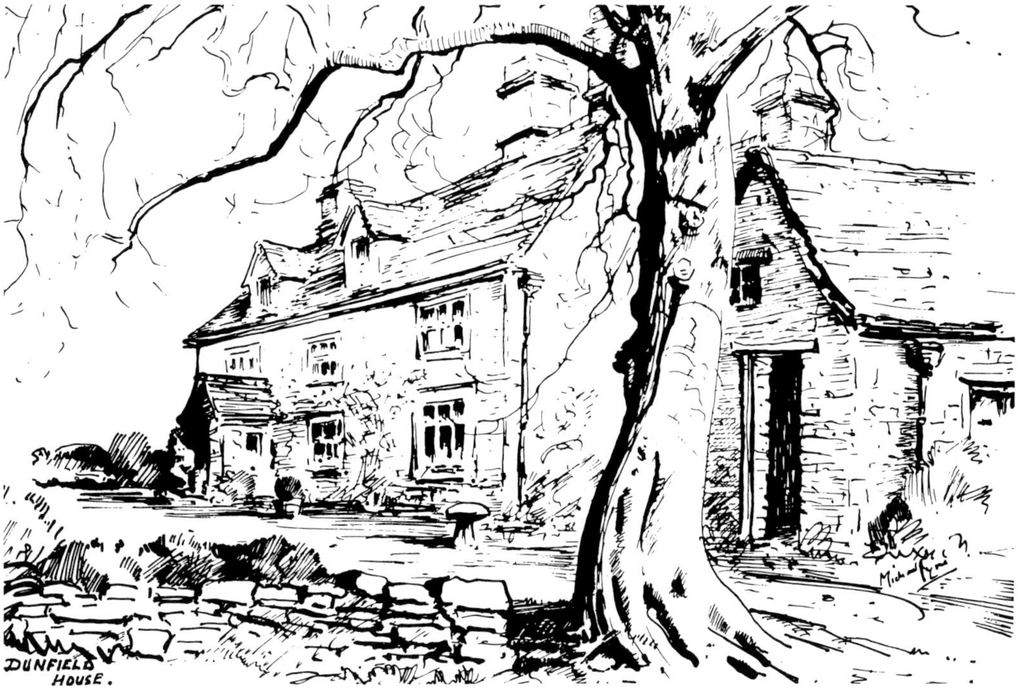

Dunfield House: the Lyne family home from 1948.

with the aid of a thousand pound wartime legacy from one of his godfathers, during the winter of 1948–1949. He had wished to own a permanent home in an area accessible to the Hunting Shires and eventually found Dunfield House, which lay in a very small and quiet hamlet, with an open stream running the length of its narrow road, and easy driving distance for Michael's pre war Morris Ten to reach the main hunting countries.

Dunfield is a typical old Cotswold farmhouse, set amongst apple orchards, comprising a large stable yard, many outbuildings, and a freshwater-fed pond of some half an acre. It was the pond above all else which attracted Michael to the property, and it is fitting that his ashes now rest on its bank. All this sounds idyllic, but the whole property, having stood empty for four years was in need of much attention.

Edward Lyne's recollections of that period conclude that to his sister Diana, it must have been magical to lie in her pram outside the front door surrounded by the tallest weeds imaginable, all of which had some indefinable attraction to almost all the British butterflies. To Edward, aged seven, each new day was to be one of adventure, as he hacked his way through briars, thistles and giant docks, gradually getting his bearings and learning the lay of their land. One day Edward recalls thrusting his way through some particularly inhospitable undergrowth, ducking under a curiously horizontal growing yew tree, only to spy a little Cotswold stone miniature house. Edward ran back to tell his parents that

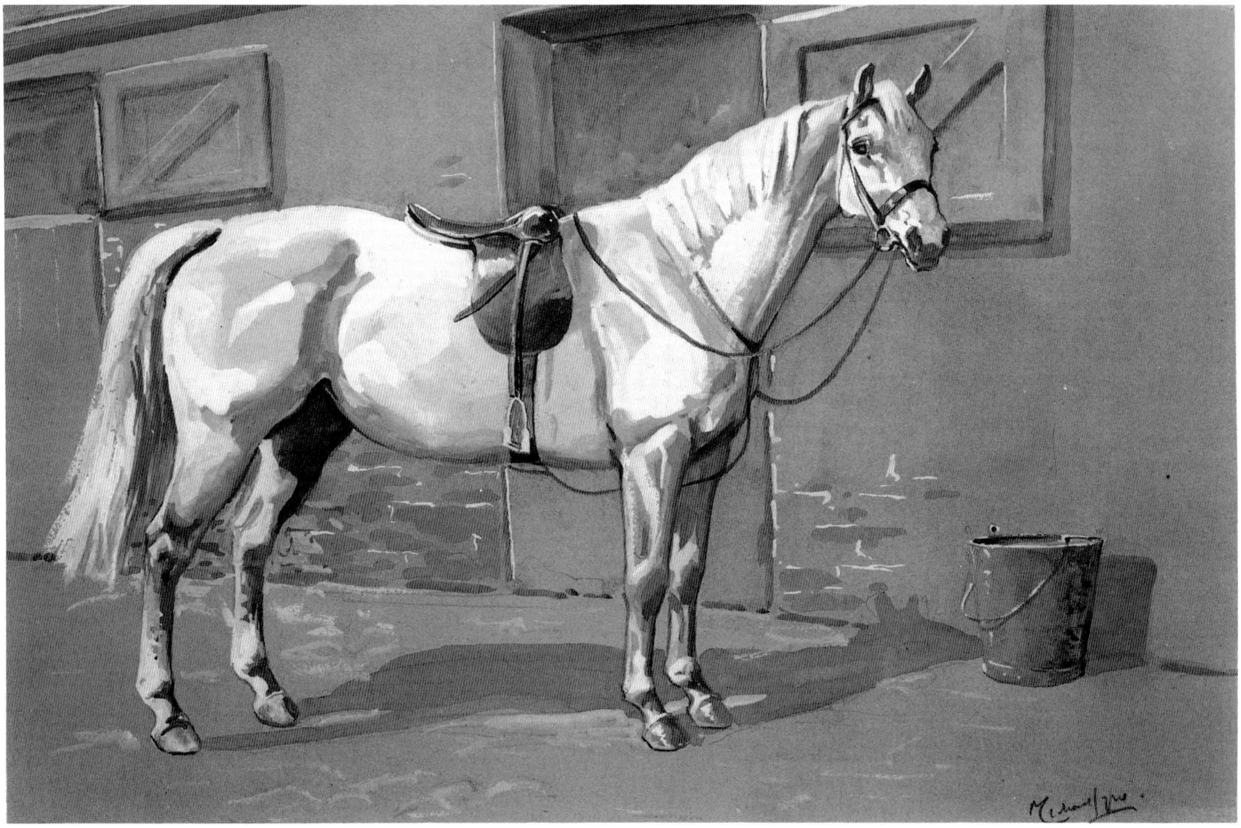

Grey Pony outside Stable, 1947. This watercolour illustration was for Henry Wynmalen's book *Riding for Children*, published as a Puffin Picture Book in 1949. The caption in the book reads: 'Here is "Silver" ready to be mounted.'

he had found the house he wanted to live in. His father went with him to inspect, and when he opened the creaky door and peered inside, he roared with laughter. Edward had found an architectural oddity, in Cotswold parlance a 'dunnock' or outside lavatory, but with a difference. It was a very sociable two seater!

The lawn was one of Michael's priorities. It could be seen from old photographs taken in the 1920s, when Squire Faulkener had lived at Dunfield, that there had been a big lawn on which a maypole was erected each May Day. The Lynes pondered how they might regain the lawn. First Michael took a few hanks of grass out with some hefty shoves of an old push mower, a gift from Tom Mallinson, but soon realized that it would take a lifetime to achieve the desired result, the lawn area being some fifteen hundred square yards.

Michael next tried a flock of geese. They did not make much impact either, but were nevertheless happy companions and each night were locked in an old loose box, safely away from the local fox. At that time Edward was sleeping under canvas in a bivouac which his father had made for him out of an old tarpaulin with an iron gate frame covered with chicken wire for his bed.

Partial success with the lawn was achieved when Jessie Lyne attended a house sale at nearby Hannington. She arrived back with the inevitable pair of somewhat lumpy armchairs, probably to replace former chairs purchased from a secondhand emporium, owned by Mr Hayes in Fairford, who had as a sub-tenant, a bookmaker (illicit in those pre-betting shop days). The most famous of Mr Hayes' chairs, delivered as always by the man himself on a horse-drawn cart, went by the name of 'Hippo'. However, it was not chairs that were the pride of Jessie's collection, but a complete set of gardening implements including a pony (donkey in their case) mower of massive proportions.

The mower was oiled and set. Jenny the donkey harnessed up and attached with the traces, Michael happily holding on the handles of this Iron Age masterpiece. Suitable commands were given but neither Jenny nor the mower moved an inch. Realizing that one had to command from the front, Michael transposed himself to Jenny's head and again urged her on with singular lack of success. It was thus that, until Dunfield acquired its first motor mower, Michael and Jenny, both by now in harness, pulled this great machine from one end of the lawn to the other. Michael always ending this Herculean weekly task in a far greater lather than Jenny.

By now the family had two cows, Rosemary and her young heifer calf Sylvia, as well as Jenny to feed during the winter months, so there was a need to obtain and save fodder. Michael, as always, quickly thought up the answer. Dunfield was surrounded by miles of country roads with wide grass verges which the local council mowed once the summer grass had grown to a fair height. Passers-by soon grew accustomed to the Lyne family armed with hayrakes and pitchforks gradually working their way down the sides of the local roads, turning the grass and making hay for later collection.

They must have been long hot summers in those days, since it never took long to have the hay in fit condition to cart away either in the family's new Austin A40 Countryman or on an attractive little costermonger's cart pulled by Jenny. Sadly, neighbours and passers-by were soon to be denied the spectacle of the Lynes at work on the verges of Gloucestershire and Wiltshire, Michael having decided that he must put his two acres to work and set about mowing, single-handed, one of his orchards with a scythe. This was a marathon task, particularly when remembering that he had cows to milk twice a day, dogs, bantams, geese and ducks to feed and a livelihood to make as an artist. Once cut, this two acres of grass had to be turned by hand until dry and was then placed upon tripods made from willow branches cut from trees growing along the nearby stream.

Michael employed, the following year, the services of Mr Strange, an old man living in the next village who came along with his two horses and a horse mower. During the hunting season, Mr Strange could be seen hunting with the VWH hounds, riding one of those two horses, a half legged grey with a wall eye!

The year 1950 was bittersweet for the Lyne family. Michael's brother John, to whom he had a strong affinity, died of polio, having left the army and recommenced his practice as an estate agent. Michael had written at some length about his visit to the United States in *Country Life* and illustrated the article with a delightful drawing of Elias Chadwell, the Millbrook Hunt, New York State and now a second visit was planned for the autumn. This would again be by sea, but shorter, only four weeks, and this time Michael would be accompanied by his wife Jessie. Also, unlike his first visit, Michael now had a full wardrobe.

On his first visit Michael had some difficulty in getting together a suitable wardrobe for socialising and hunting, as rationing still affected clothing and food alike. Friends came to his rescue and one gentleman in particular who went locally by the name of 'Hungry Ned' gave some kid leather breeches and a fine black silk top hat. There was one feature of Michael that defied gentlemen's outfitters, and that was the size of his head: it was very small. Hungry Ned's head did not appear any larger than Michael's, but there was no mistaking that this top hat was going to need some modification if he was going to be able to see where he was going. Michael carefully inserted lavatory paper beneath the headband until the top hat was a snug fit. The family were called to inspect and assure him that the hat looked right. He put his head between his knees and the hat, having defied gravity, the family were convinced that no mishap would befall him in the hunting field.

The first meet of the American visit occurred on a crisp day. Michael, who had been provided by his host with a fine Thoroughbred, honed to a high degree of fitness was introduced to the Master of Hounds, and in the best tradition of formal hunting etiquette, each doffed their hats. Embarrassingly for Michael, from out of the headband of his shiny silk topper floated slowly to earth what could only be lavatory paper!

A significant feature of this second visit was to be the first United States Exhibition of Michael's work. It was held during early November at Scott and Fowles Gallery, Fifth Avenue, New York, and consisted of sixteen full sized watercolours of East Coast packs, including Frederick Warburg's Middleburg Hunt. The catalogue contained an interesting and perceptive comment about Michael's paintings:

'The countryside in Michael Lyne's watercolours with its flaming colours and the dishevelled clouds in the sky above it, waits expectantly, as if it were there for no other purpose but to provide the scene for fox hunting – as if it could realize itself only by having people in pink coats follow hounds across its tawny fields.'

United States' influence was to make a further significant contribution to Michael's artistic development by convincing him that he should paint in oil colours in addition to watercolours.

Following his second visit and a period of dissatisfaction with the very low quality of post-war watercolour materials, Michael started to paint in oils and found that the wider,

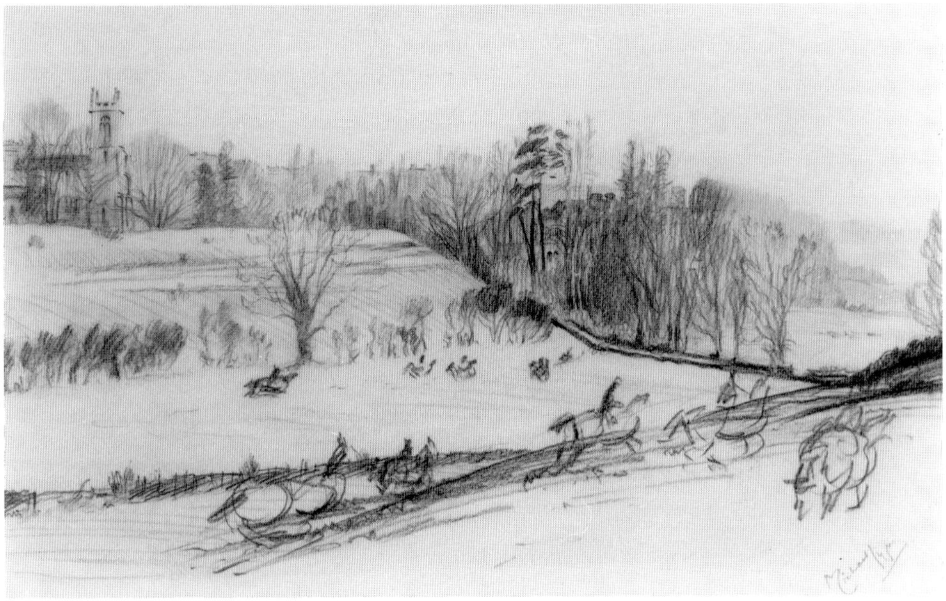

The Heythrop at Lower Slaughter, 1953. Watercolour, 17 × 23 in (43 × 58 cm). The working drawing (*above*) was made on the spot and gives a good indication of how Michael Lyne made adjustments to his paintings in the years after World War II. He was anxious that his work should be both correct topographically and acceptable artistically. The relationship between the two conflicting requirements were reconciled.

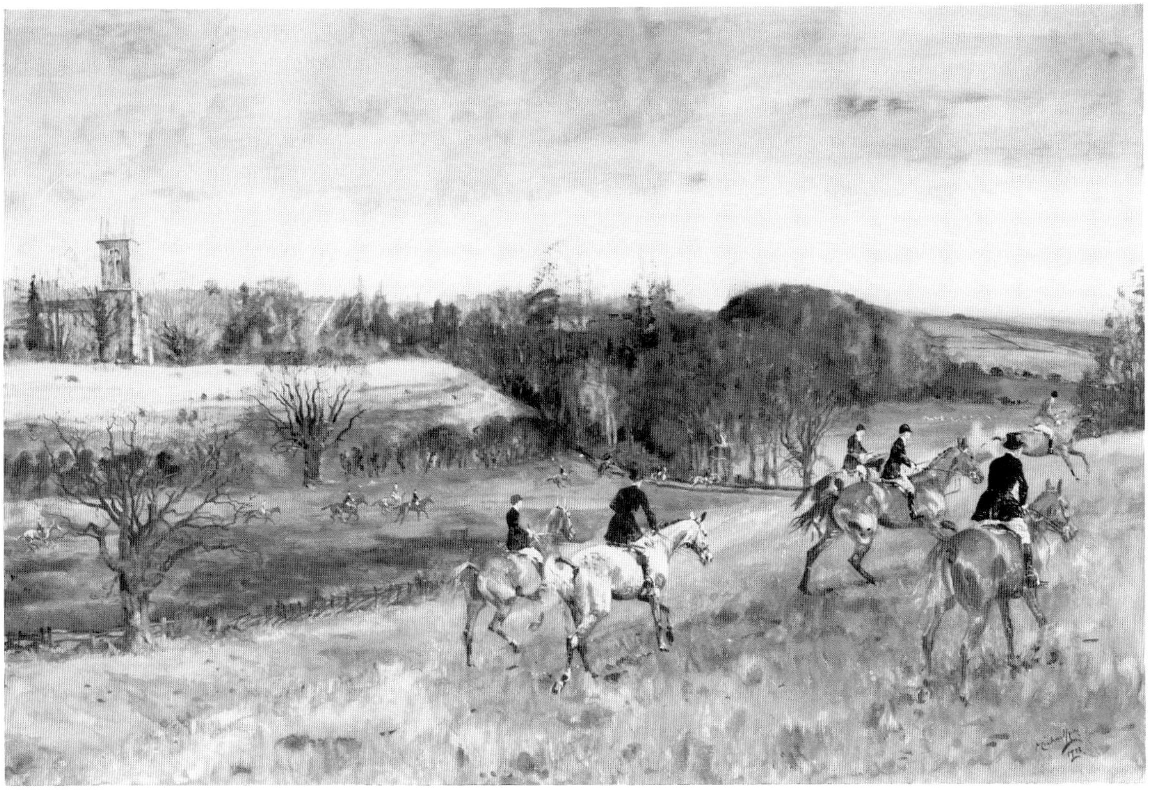

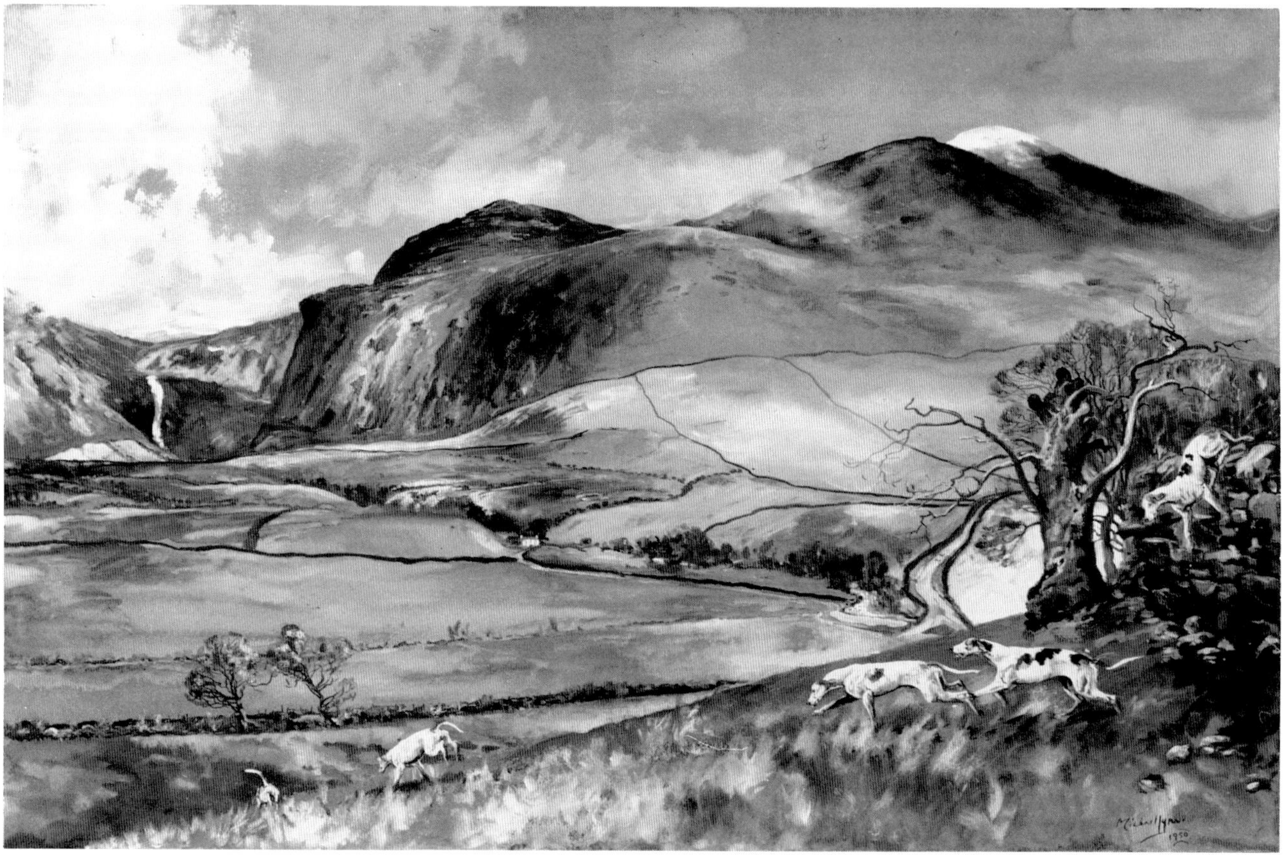

The Blencathra Foxhounds, Fell Hunting near Dead Crag, Cumberland, *c*1950. Watercolour approximately 12 × 20 in (30 × 51 cm). Included in the Retrospective Exhibition at the Tryon Gallery in 1989.

more vibrant colour tones related much more accurately to his own mental images of the subject matter than the muted tones of the traditional watercolour paints which he had used exclusively until 1950. Another dimension had been added to his art and he discovered in full the gift of natural stylish colouring which he inherited from his Jewish great grand-mother, although it must have always been present in his work, for one critic complained at the 1946 Ackermann Exhibition that the colouring of some of the painting did not accord with that of the English countryside in winter.

In 1951 came the third and final post-war one-man show at Ackermann. Thirty-five watercolours were on display, including three studies of American packs, the Middleburg Hunt, Piedmont Foxhounds and the Millbrook Hunt, in addition to such new material as paintings of Ascot, the Lake District, the Pond at Dunfield and Coursing. Michael's art was maturing and developing and his search for subject matter going far beyond the confines of the hunting field. This was to be a blueprint of the Michael Lyne in his mature years and the precursor of the one man shows of the 1960s and 1970s.

In addition to preparing paintings for the Ackermann exhibitions, Michael started to write and illustrate articles regularly for *The Field* and *Country Life* on rural and sporting subjects, and was soon engaged in book illustration. The first post-war book which he illustrated was Glenda Spooner's *Royal Crusader*, an autobiography of a horse, published in 1948. The following year saw the publication by Puffin Picture Books, the children's wing of Sir Alan Lane's Penguin Books, of *Riding for Children*. Michael provided the illustrations and the Dutchman, Henry Wynmalen, the text. The book was well received and was to be followed in 1954 by a minor classic, *The Horse in Action*. Again Wynmalen provided the text and Michael the illustrations. This time it was not charming pictures of children with ponies, but every action of a horse depicted in a detailed sequence of drawings, an assignment which taxed Michael's skill, observation and patience to the very limits, and an achievement of which he was very proud. The work itself was inspired by Maler Ludwig Koch's illustrated equestrian classic *Die Reitkunst Im Bilde* published in Austria some thirty years earlier.

From 1948 hardly a year passed without a book illustrated by Michael being published, and a clutch of articles from pen and brush being included in one or other of the illustrated

The Millbrook, near Wethersfield, New York State. Oil on canvas, 24 × 36 in (61 × 92 cm). The late Senator Frederick Bontecou (on the grey), for many years Master of the Millbrook, was a close friend of the Lynes.

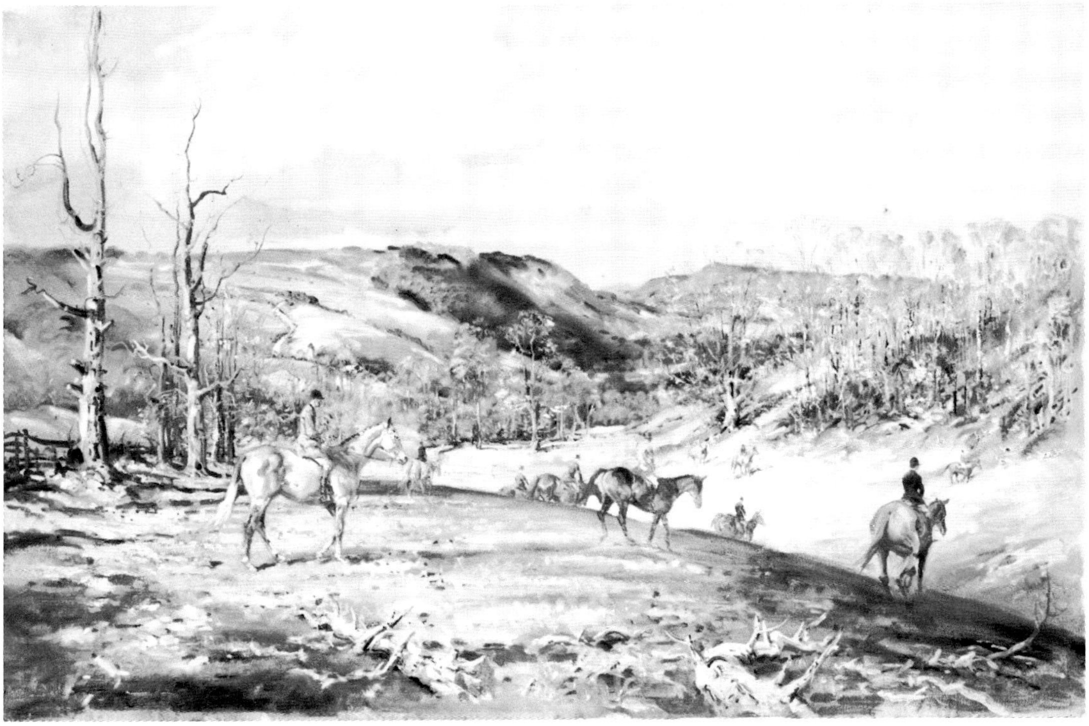

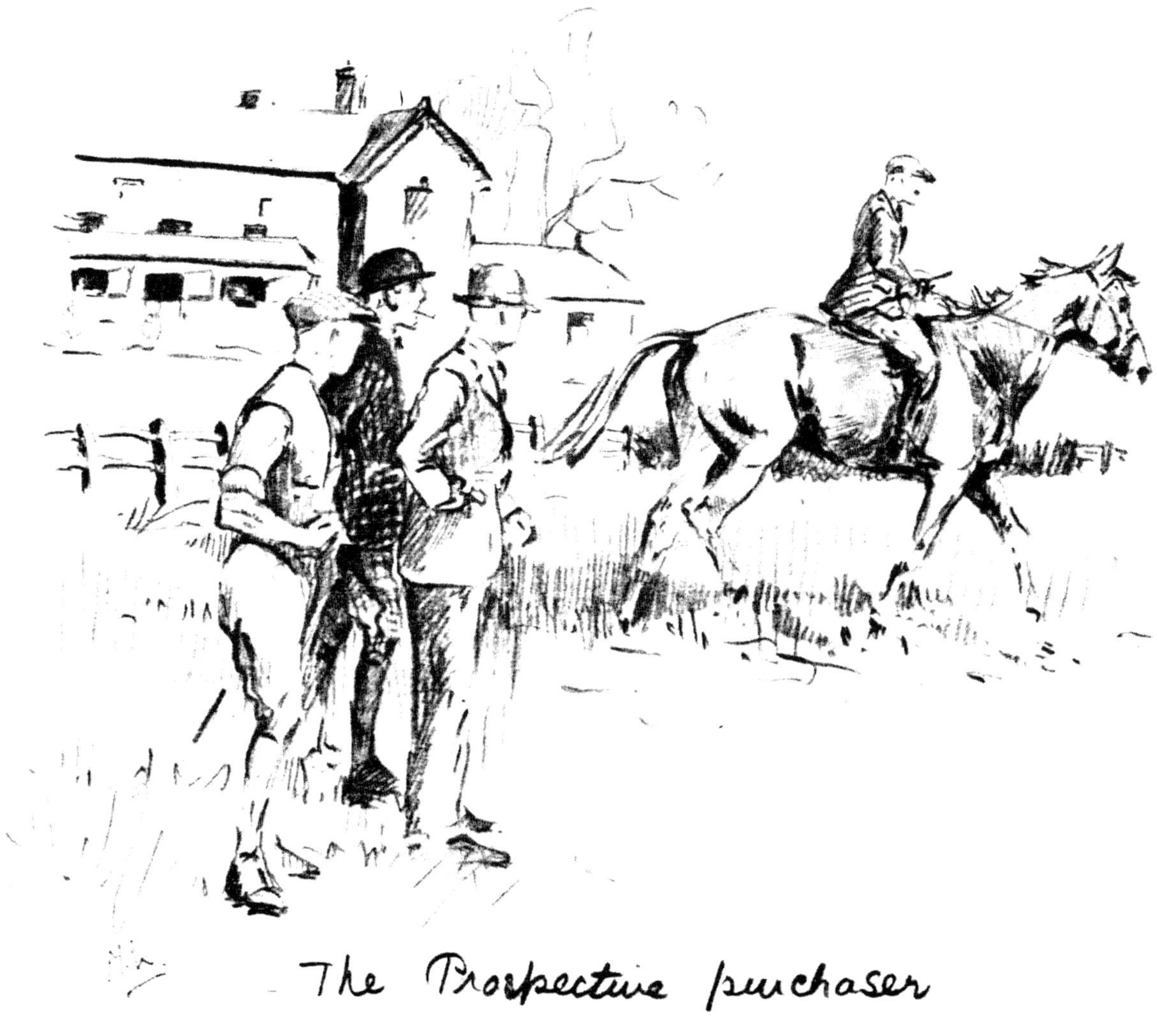

From *Skilled Horsemanship*, 1937. 'The first book I ever illustrated.'

country magazines, though the second half of the 1960s was less prolific, due to the very high level of demand for Michael's oil paintings.

As the 1950s progressed, other visits to America were undertaken, Michael and Jessie Lyne becoming more adventurous and travelling by air, from London via Shannon and Gander to New York. They established the custom of staying with the Frederick Bontecou's of the Millbrook Hunt, New York State, to recover from the journey and adapt to American way of life. This was a most welcome innovation, for Michael was never a good traveller, and later in life hated leaving home, even for a day. As a younger man, he always lacked the confidence to make a journey enjoyable, feeling that he was on the wrong aeroplane or train, and he was never able to cope with the minor irritants of travel. Michael accepted this fact with his customary good humour, and would recall wryly, a story against himself. He tried to use a public telephone in New York, and was in trouble with the instrument and the foreign currency, the call not being toll free. He became aware of a highly attractive woman in the adjoining booth, obviously aware of his difficulties, and giving him encouraging smiles. She soon joined Michael and helped him obtain his number when he was able to make his excuses for not attending the party to which he had been invited. This should have been his opportunity to become an unfaithful husband, but Michael saw that he parted amicably from the attractive lady, recalling that her parting comment was rather amusing: 'Say, you must be a Duke of something.' 'Not so,' said Michael, 'but why?' 'Gee, it's the way you talk.' She was awfully pretty was Michael's final comment on the episode.

It was also a source of much pleasure to Michael and Jessie that Richard and Charm Fleming of Northleach, who had brought the Warburgs to Througham Slad and helped to initiate the American connection, become family friends, and lent the Lyne children, Edward and Diana, ponies to ride each summer. About this time, the two house cows disappeared, having been milked by an old man from the village for a number of years. After very careful vetting, a new home was found for them near Newbury. Michael felt the time had come for him to have a horse on which to hunt, thus enabling him to gather material and new ideas for his paintings. This resulted in the arrival of Rodney, a 15.1 grey hunter, who can be seen in so many of Michael's pictures. They remained partners for life, hunting regularly with the VWH.

During August 1955 Michael's father died and was buried in the graveyard of his old church at Upton Bishop.

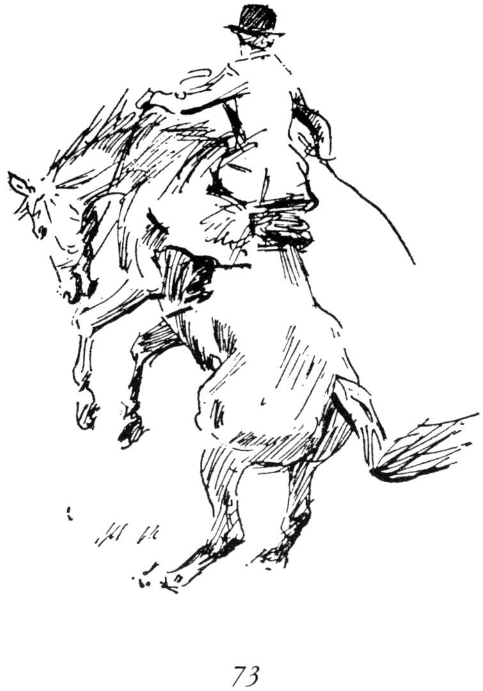

FIVE

TOP OF THE LADDER 1955–1974

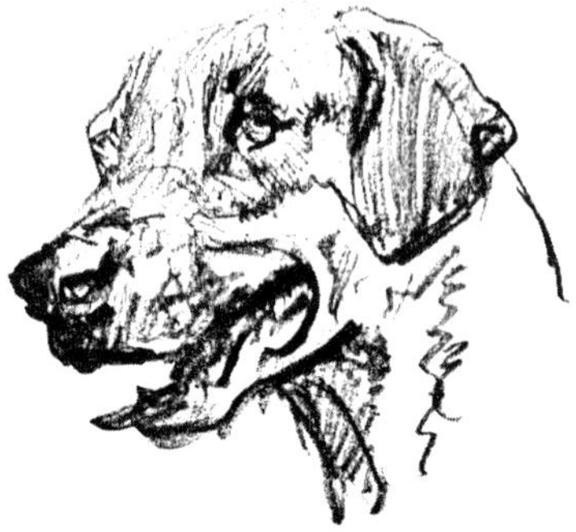

During the mid-1950s life at Dunfield fell into the set pattern common to many English country houses of the time. The war years receded into memory, though Captain C.E.M Lyne led the local British Legion parade each Remembrance Sunday. The Lyne's two children were growing up, Edward entering his public school, Radley. Michael had hoped that he would eventually become Master of the Radley College Beagles, unfortunately these hopes were unfulfilled.

Whilst the two house cows had gone, the donkey remained to keep company Rodney, who was the centre of attention. The bantams, a particular favourite of Michael's, flourished and now numbered seventy-two, having been first kept in 1950, for the benefit of the children, with a handsome cockerel, Jackson and a thirteen-year-old spangled hen. In time, the bantams were to be replaced by the Dunfield Waterfowl collection, as the Salukis enjoyed eating the bantams! The large pond, once part of a medieval castle moat and covering half an acre, was fed by a spring which was one of the many sources of the River Thames. Since the Lyne's arrival at Dunfield in the late 1940s, Michael, assisted by Edward, had systematically cleaned the pond of weed. It was this feature that had first attracted Michael to the property and as work progressed, he became more and more attached to it. Fortuitously in 1949, during his first American visit, Michael visited the Dillon Ripley waterfowl collection, and was so impressed with what he saw, he decided to have some of his own on the Dunfield pond. Michael confided this idea to one of his new American friends, Russell Arundel MFH, of Warrenton, Virginia, over dinner one evening. Returning to England, he received a telephone call from Washington advising that a pair of wood duck (Carolina's) were on their way to London. At London Airport Michael saw their packing case, but was told by an officer of the Ministry of Agriculture & Fisheries, that unless he had an import licence, he could not import them, and they must either be destroyed or returned to the United States. Michael was not easily put off and contacted Sir Peter Scott at Slimbridge, who promptly imported the pair on his own Wildfowl Trust licence for Michael.

The changing population of the pond has been tended and harboured for almost forty years and is a source of never ending delight. At its peak, the collection contained twenty-five different species, all of which are celebrated by lovingly crafted wooden miniatures

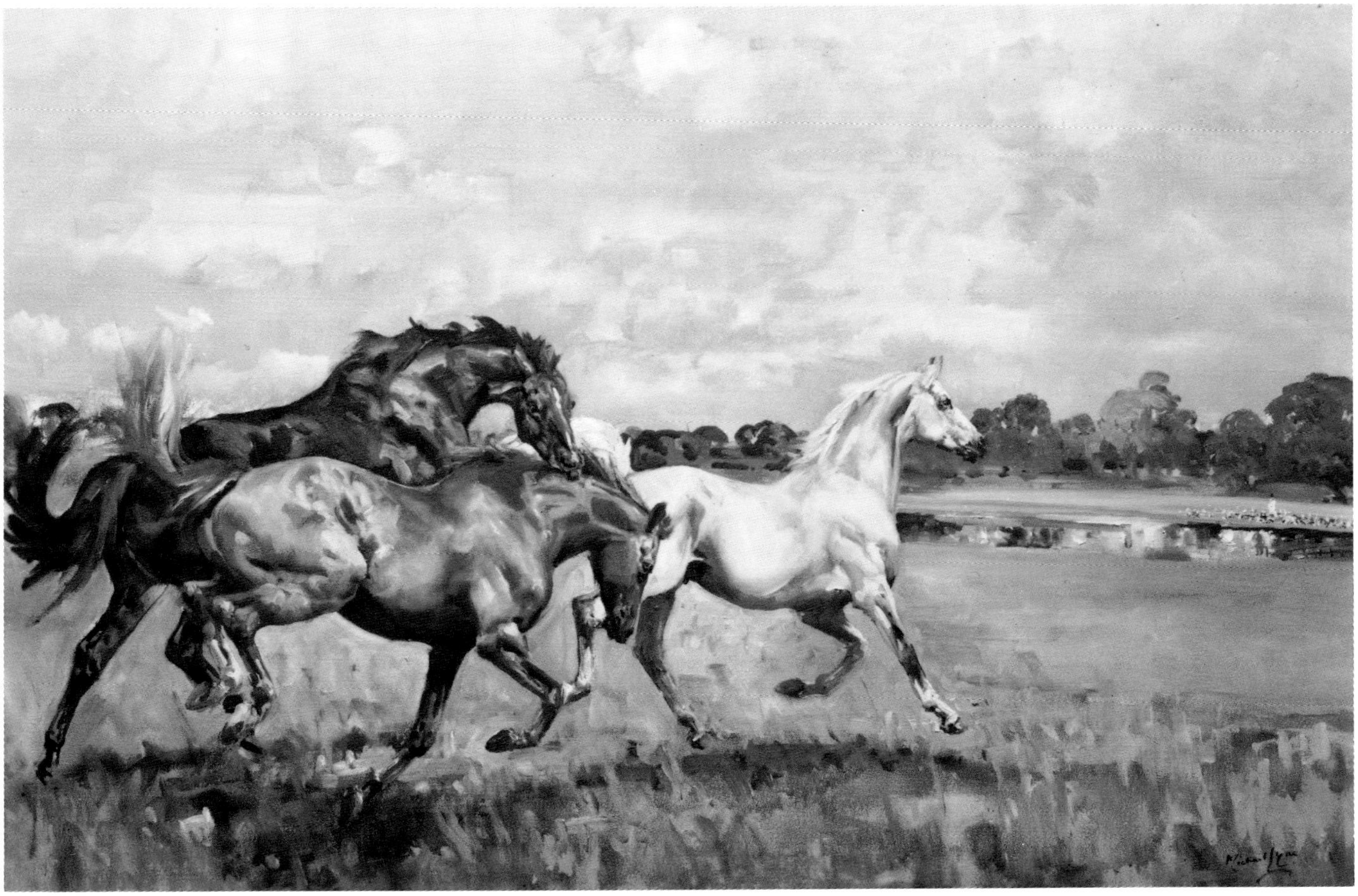

Out to Grass. Oil on canvas, 24 × 36 in (61 × 92 cm). Michael Lyne had a great fondness for a well-made grey and always included at least one painting of a grey in each London exhibition. This picture was included in the 1979 Frost & Reed Exhibition.

on the drawing room mantel shelf. Today, Jessie Lyne still tends the rump of the collection.

Michael, like Winston Churchill, found great relaxation and enjoyment in stone-walling and the use of concrete; it was a therapy, a relief from the pressures of painting and providing an income for his family. As the 1950s progressed, so did the reclamation and restoration of Dunfield and its grounds with an ever-increasing number of walls, pathways and fountains. Each year saw an improvement and the garden was planned to remind the Lynes of their favourite haunts, ferns along the pond approach from Exmoor and rowans to recall stalking in Scotland.

Michael continued to hunt regularly with the VWH, but also enjoyed hunting wherever he went during the season. So extensive were his travels in England, Ireland, Scotland and the United States that he ultimately hunted with over forty packs of hounds and had happy memories of each.

The Suez crisis in 1956 saw a major disruption in life at Dunfield. It was unfortunate for Michael that he had hired a West End Gallery for a one man show, having severed his connections with Ackermann some years previously. This took place at the height of the crisis. Needless to say, the exhibition was not a success.

One of the more lasting effects of the crisis for country people and those dependent on transport and mobility for a living was the introduction of petrol rationing. Horse transport had disappeared almost totally at the end of the war. The car was no longer a luxury to countrymen such as Michael, who had isolated homes and were forced to travel extensively on business. The 1956–1957 season proved to be a difficult one for reaching hunting countries, and Michael was forced to make extensive use of railways. Fortunately the railway system, though elderly and inefficient, had not yet suffered the Beeching axe,

The Attack, 1960. Oil on canvas, 28 × 36 in (71 × 92 cm). From a reconstruction of an event at Dunfield after Michael had found the head, and some remains, of his peahen.

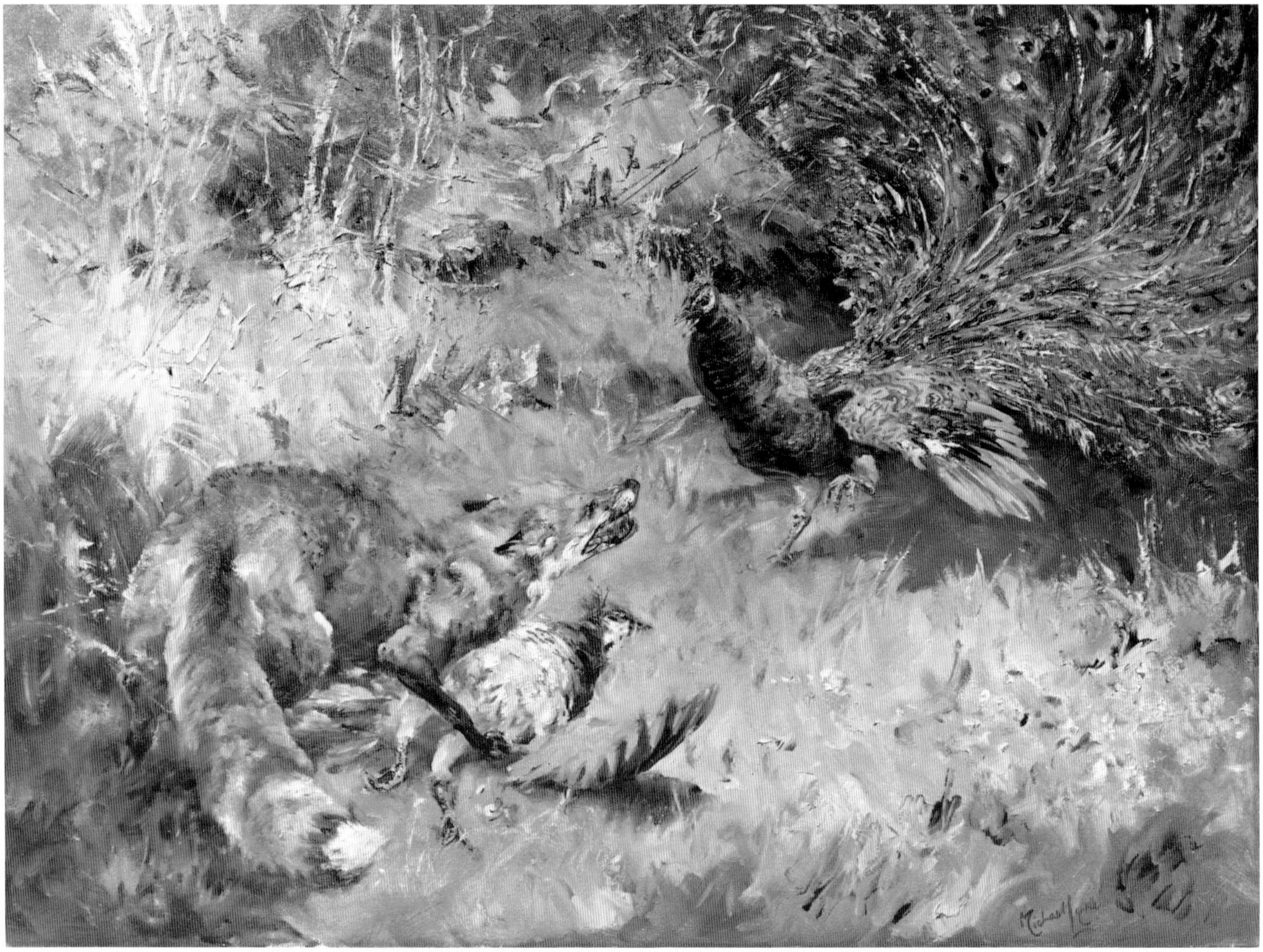

and still gave access to the more remote hunts. Home life suffered too from the shortage. Edward Lyne, then fourteen and home from Radley for the summer holidays, recalls that luckily his uncle Richard, who worked for Esso as an estate manager, had earlier purchased a little forerunner to the motor scooter that we know today. It was a Corgi, having collapsible handlebars and a telescopic seat, and was designed to be dropped from aircraft for military use. It also had a frugal thirst and was an ideal machine for such times as Suez. At least it made Michael mobile. The rest of the family had to rely on pedal power.

Michael, a parson's son, and Jessie also being of a religious disposition, attended Kempsford church every Sunday. The church lay some two miles from Dunfield, fortunately along fairly level going. For the duration of the petrol rationing, Kempsford parishioners saw the Lyne family going to morning service each Sunday, spread out along the top road, Michael complete with bowler hat, as he was a churchwarden, riding the Corgi, Jessie on the old army Bitch Bike, Edward and Diana pedalling for all they were worth in the rear.

Edward also recalls at this time a family meeting with Michael's close friend Dalesman, 'Bay' de Courcy Parry. Both men, in addition to their fondness of hounds and hunting, had well developed senses of humour and mischief would be perpetrated when they were together, as was the case when they all met up on Exmoor. Dalesman and Michael left Jessie to look after Edward and his sister, and set off into the distance. They seemed to be away for a great deal of time. When finally they reappeared, they both had grins stretching from one side of their faces to the other. They told the children with great delight that they had been in search of sausages or Spermophile as they called them, and had come across a multitude of tracks. When the children enquired what exactly Spermophile were, Dalesman and Michael went into vivid descriptions of how they were little furry animals with cloven hooves, which when skinned and fried made the most delicious eating, and were the sausage the children knew and loved to eat. Edward, spurred on more by genuine curiosity than the gluttony of his sister, insisted that they be taken to see the tracks, and if at all possible, help to catch them. Sure enough, at the foot of a big, old beech tree in the rather bare earth, the children saw their first sausage tracks. Each track was similar in shape to that of a cow's hoof, but very much smaller, being somewhat less than half-an-inch in length.

The group followed the tracks for what seemed miles, it was obvious that the pack of Spermophile numbered in excess of twenty and were travelling at quite a lick and had covered a lot of ground since leaving the old beech tree. The two children forgot just where or why they lost the tracks, but by then they were tired and hungry and ready to forget Spermophile in favour of the picnic which their mother had been making.

Both children managed to get to sleep that night, no doubt dreaming of those little sausage animals, and hoping that on their next meeting with Dalesman, who was Edward's godfather, they would have a more successful hunt.

Michael and Dalesman were delighted at having so much fun at the children's expense. They had made the tracks with the ends of their pocket knives, and were also chuckling to themselves about the inventive name they had thought of for these little animals. What caught Michael, as well as the rest of the Lyne family, by surprise, was the arrival by post, some weeks later, of a rather smelly and none too well wrapped parcel. Despite Jessie's protestations, Michael insisted on opening the stinking parcel on the kitchen table. All watched as the string was cut and the rather stained brown paper was peeled back to expose a pelt, not exactly cured, and a page out of an old book. There on this page was an illustration of a small furry animal, not unlike that described by Dalesman and Michael. Beneath the plate was the word Spermophile.

About this time, Michael was in the habit of mounting his daughter Diana on Jenny, the aged donkey, who Michael always said was a contemporary of his, and taking her with him on his morning ride on Rodney, the grey hunter, around the village. Jenny was reliable, but still retained her habit of dropping a shoulder and hooking off her rider. Poor Diana suffered regularly, sometimes in the village and sometimes in the Dunfield yard.

Michael and Jessie continued to make frequent visits to the United States during the autumn, but also occasionally in the spring. As the years progressed and flying developed, the journey became easier and less exhausting. The established itinerary was followed, calling at hunting friends along the East Coast and making short stays with each. The Lynes always flew from London to New York and were well aware of the welcome that they would receive from the Bontecou family of Millbrook, New York State. Frederick H. Bontecou was a Master of the Millbrook Hunt and one of the first generation of Michael's American patrons. Michael rated him as one of the best sportsmen he had ever seen, particularly in view of his participation in the King George V Cup-winning United States team at the 1924 International Horse Show when he rode his own horse, Bally MacShane.

Moving south, a favourite stopping place was at Lutherville, Maryland, at the home of J. Fife Symington, which was first visited in 1952. With typical humour, Michael was fond of recalling how he and Jessie were more or less hijacked by Fife Symington whilst staying at a hotel working on a surprise commission in Baltimore, and suffering from the strain of keeping the picture and arrangement secret; Fife installed them in the Symington home. He is an extraordinary man, in many ways the complete antithesis of Michael, coming from an old established industrial family, spending a very full life working as a principal executive for Pan Am Airways, with such exotic sabbaticals as being American Ambassador to Trinidad and Tobago. Between 1939 and 1969 he had two periods as joint Master of the Greenspring Valley Hounds and owned the great horse Palau, a big fine Thoroughbred.

In Virginia an obvious stopping place was with Frederick and Wilma Warburg (the couple who first invited Michael to the United States) at Middleburg, where Frederick Warburg was Master of the Middleburg Hunt and a very keen collector of Michael's work.

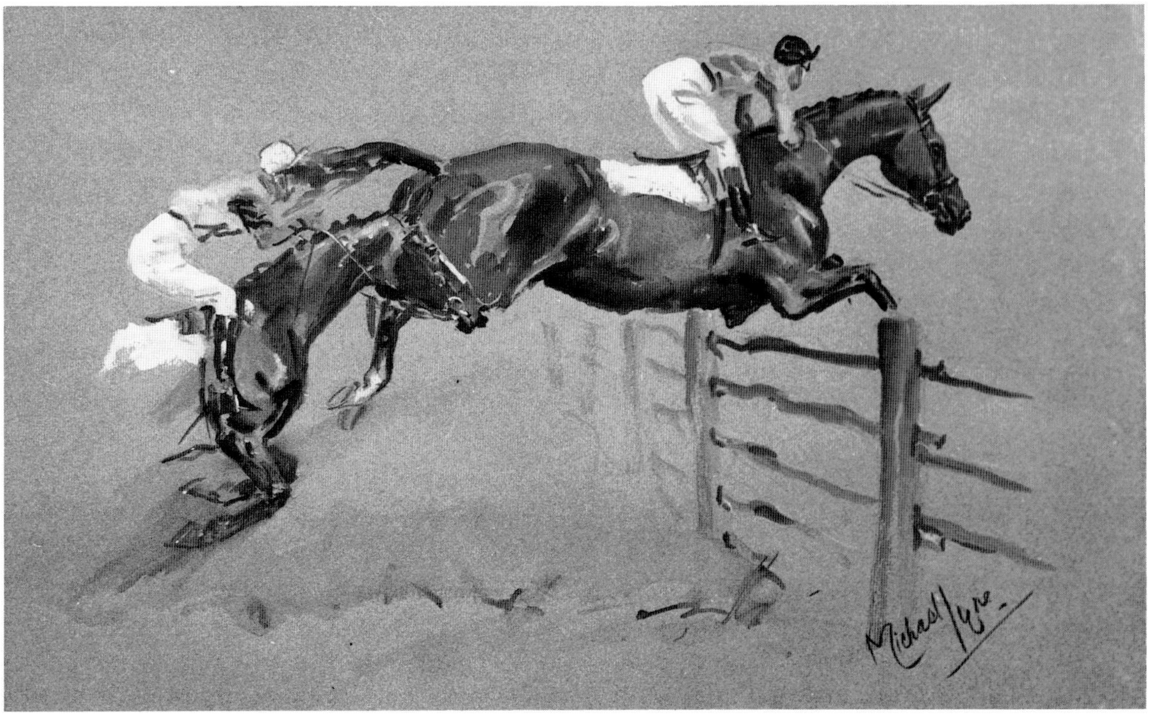

Timber Racing, The Plains, Warrenton, Va. Watercolour study, 8 × 10 in (20 × 26 cm).

One rarity in the Warburg collection is an eight inch high car mascot of a fox in full hunting kit, carved from wood and hand painted. At the same time as Michael made this car mascot, he produced a series of cut-out and hand-painted fox masks as house presents for his friends and hosts. Edward, home from school for the holidays, made the flat cut-out shapes with his fret saw, and they were subsequently finished and painted by his father.

As a keen hound man, the Middleburg kennels were of absorbing interest to Michael, with their old established pure American blood lines. At nearby Warrenton, the Lynes stayed with Russell and Marjorie Arundell. The late Russell Arundell, in addition to being Master of the Warrenton Hunt, had a very distinguished political and business career and lived in a mansion on top of a mountain. The mansion had the unique distinction of having had a palatial room added to house a large commissioned painting by Michael.

Michael always enjoyed the experience of staying at Wildcat Mountain, for as a keen naturalist he was fascinated by the wild life of the estate, including bear, wolf, wild turkey and large wild cats. The eerie sound effects of wind and rain caused him to comment 'a wild night on the mountain is as good as a dramatic radio play'.

Returning to New York, the Lynes would journey back through Maryland, Pennsylvania and New Jersey. It was in New Jersey with the Essex Foxhounds, hunted by Buster Chadwell, that Michael had what he considered the best day's hunting of his life. He was aboard a very glamorous and fast liver chestnut mare which was so narrow he felt that his knees

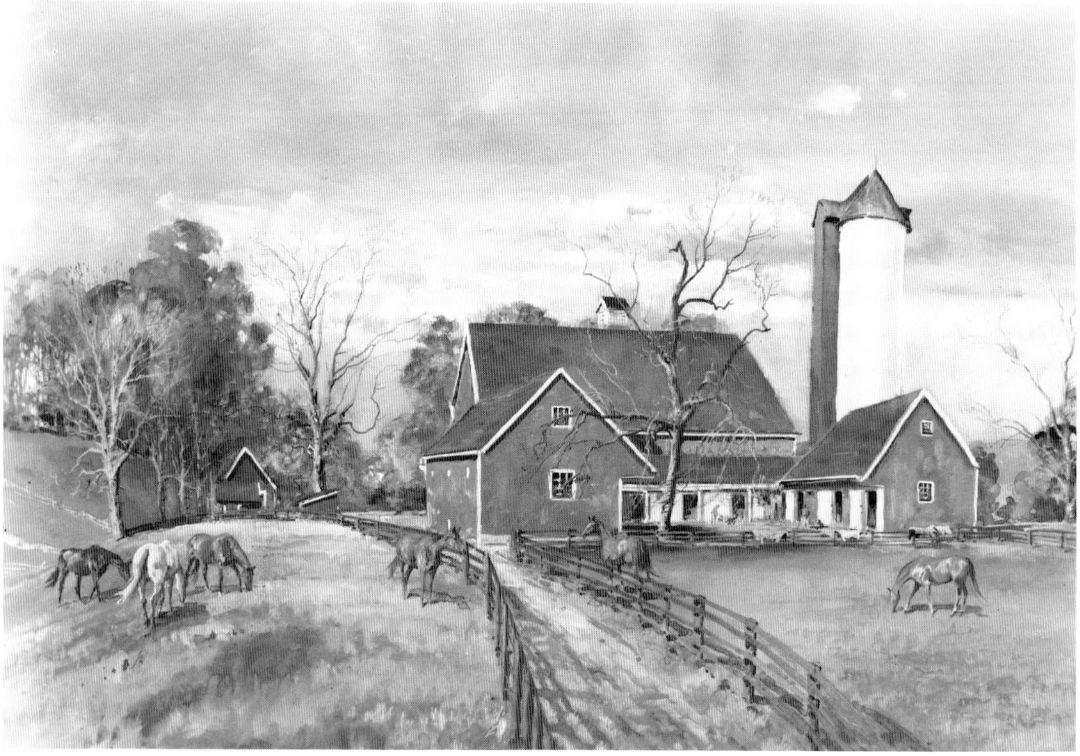

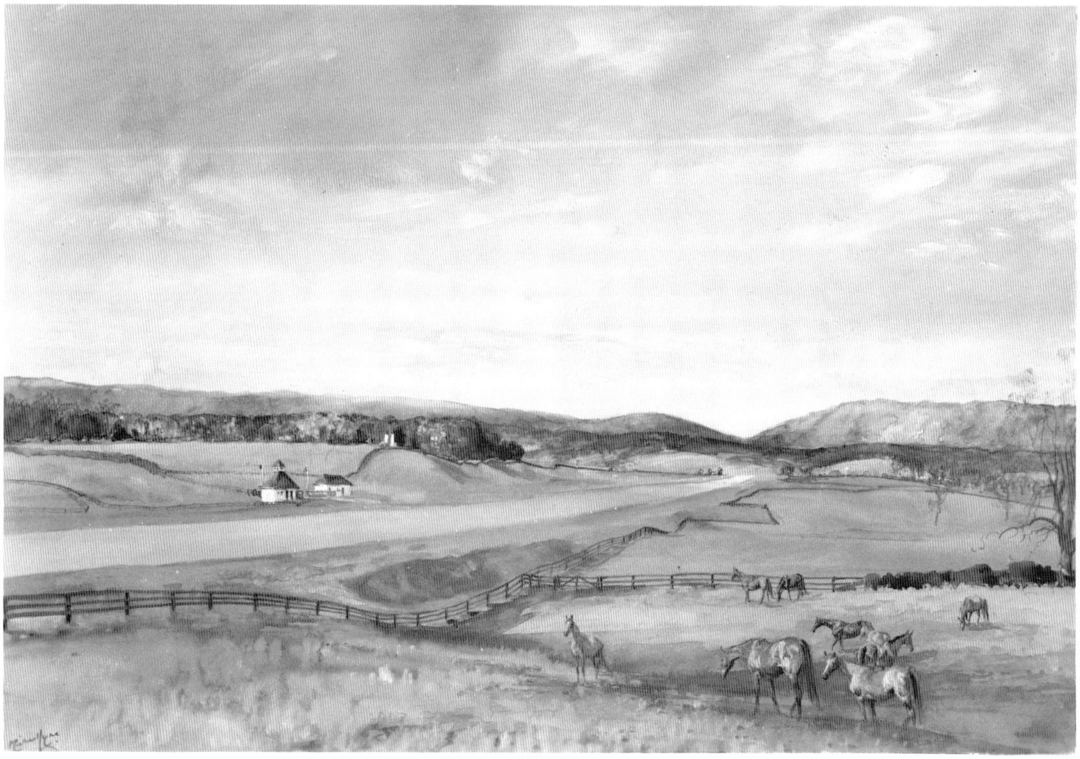

(*above*) *The Hunter Barn, Oak Spring, Rokeby Farms Estate* and (*right*) *The Airstrip at Rokeby Farms*. From a set of four watercolours from 1961, commissioned by and the property of Paul Mellon. Each picture approximately 17 × 24 in (43 × 61 cm).

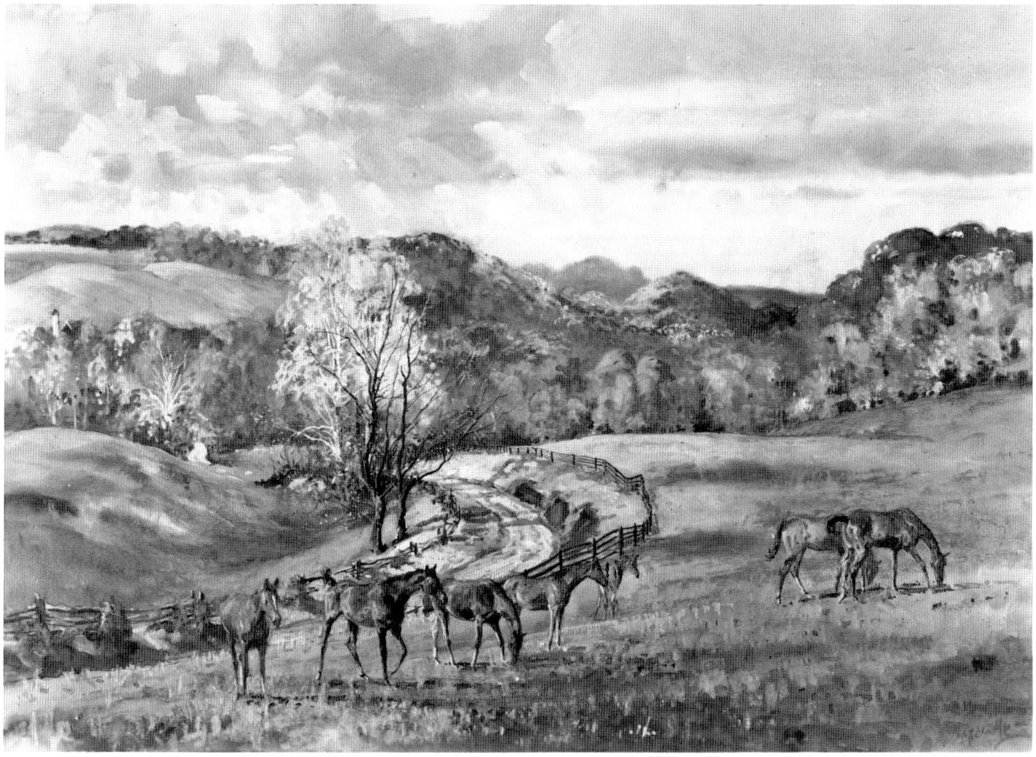

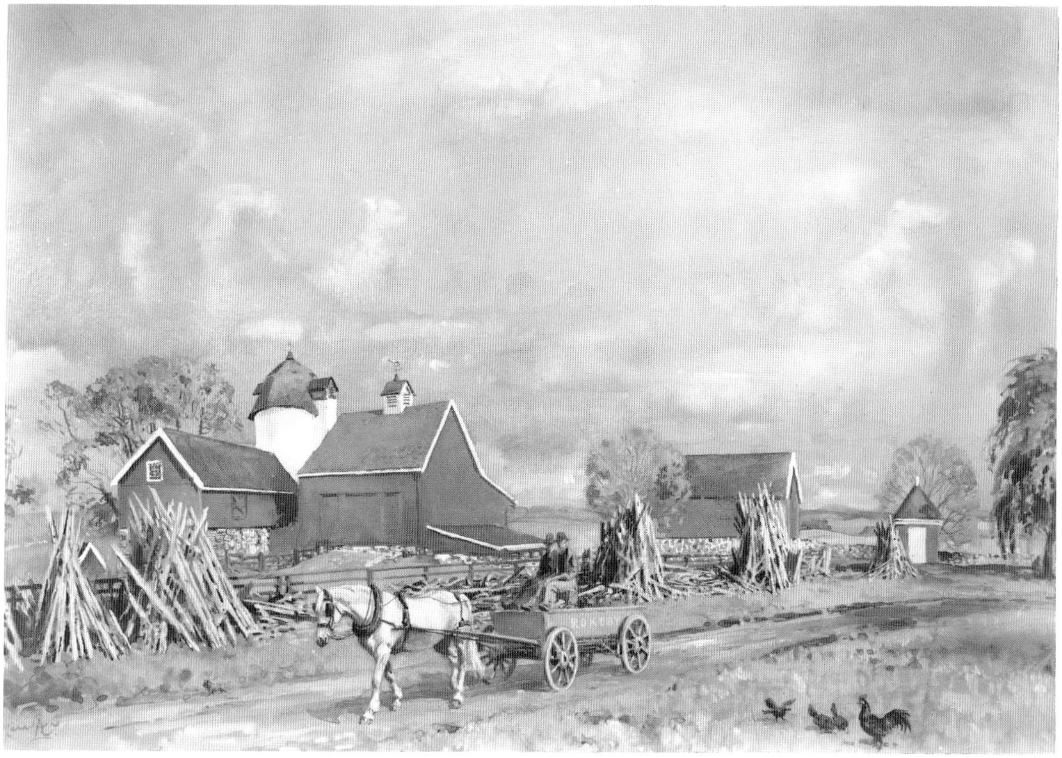

(*above*) *Yearlings at Oak Springs, Rokeby Farms Estate* and (*right*) *Rokeby Farm with manure cart in foreground*. From a set of four watercolours from 1961, commissioned by and the property of Paul Mellon. Each picture approximately 17 × 24 in (43 × 61 cm). *Rokeby Farm* was published as a limited edition print by Frost & Reed.

would touch if he squeezed too much, and as a second horse, he had a magnificent large bright bay Thoroughbred.

Finally the world of foxhunting would be left for that of carriage driving on the New York estate of the Chauncey Stillman who died in 1987 and had both a large collection of road vehicles and a fine team of hackneys. In addition Mr Stillman was a collector of old and modern master paintings and had one of the main reception rooms of his mansion decorated with frescos by the leading Italian artist, Pietro Annigoni. One of the collection's major paintings was Pontormo's three-quarter length portrait of *Duke Cosimo I de Medici* sold by Christie's New York, in the summer of 1988 for twenty million pounds.

Of all Michael's American work, the paintings which gave him the most pleasure were the ten which were commissioned by Paul Mellon, both in England and the United States. Michael had the highest regard for Mr Mellon, both as a patron of the arts and a lover of horses and hunting, and gladly accepted the challenge to produce work of the highest quality. He also enjoyed enormously life on the Mellon Estate at Upperville, particularly the early morning hacks with his host before Mr Mellon left for his Washington office.

In April 1966 Michael and Jessie left England for America on their shortest visit ever, in the form of a long weekend at the Maryland Hunt Cup, at the invitation of Fife Symington. They flew out on a Thursday afternoon and returned on the Monday afternoon. The journey got off to an inauspicious start with engine trouble delaying departure from Heathrow, and the Lynes arrived at Lutherville at 2.00 am on the Friday morning. Friday was taken up with Michael selecting a vantage point from which he could view the race from a Land Rover. He selected a spot adjoining the 3rd and 13th fences. The race is run over four miles, 856 yards short of the Grand National distance. Fences for each race differ, but both are formidable: the American course has no thick Aintree style fences, open ditches or water jumps, only solid, uncompromising post and rail fences, each up to five feet nine inches in height, dictating that the race is run at a much faster pace than the Grand National, with no possibility of error at any fence. In the event the winner was Jay Trump, a previous winner and winner of the 1965 Grand National, when trained by Fred Winter. Michael insisted that he was alone in the Land Rover to watch the race and it says much for his powers of observation and memory that he was able to retain the image of a spectacular and crashing fall, despite the rigours of social high life in the evening of the race. He returned to the course on Sunday to complete his watercolour sketches, flew home on Monday afternoon, and was working in his studio on Tuesday, making preliminary notes and sketches before laying out on canvas his impressions of the race. The finished picture *A Fall at the 3rd Fence* is one of his masterpieces and remains in the Symington collection (*see Plate 11*). In addition Michael painted a complementary picture, *The Second Circuit at the 13th Fence*. *A Fall at the 3rd Fence* was subsequently featured on the cover of the *Chronicle of the Horse*, the weekly American equestrian magazine, as were many of the pictures shown in London and America by Frost & Reed.

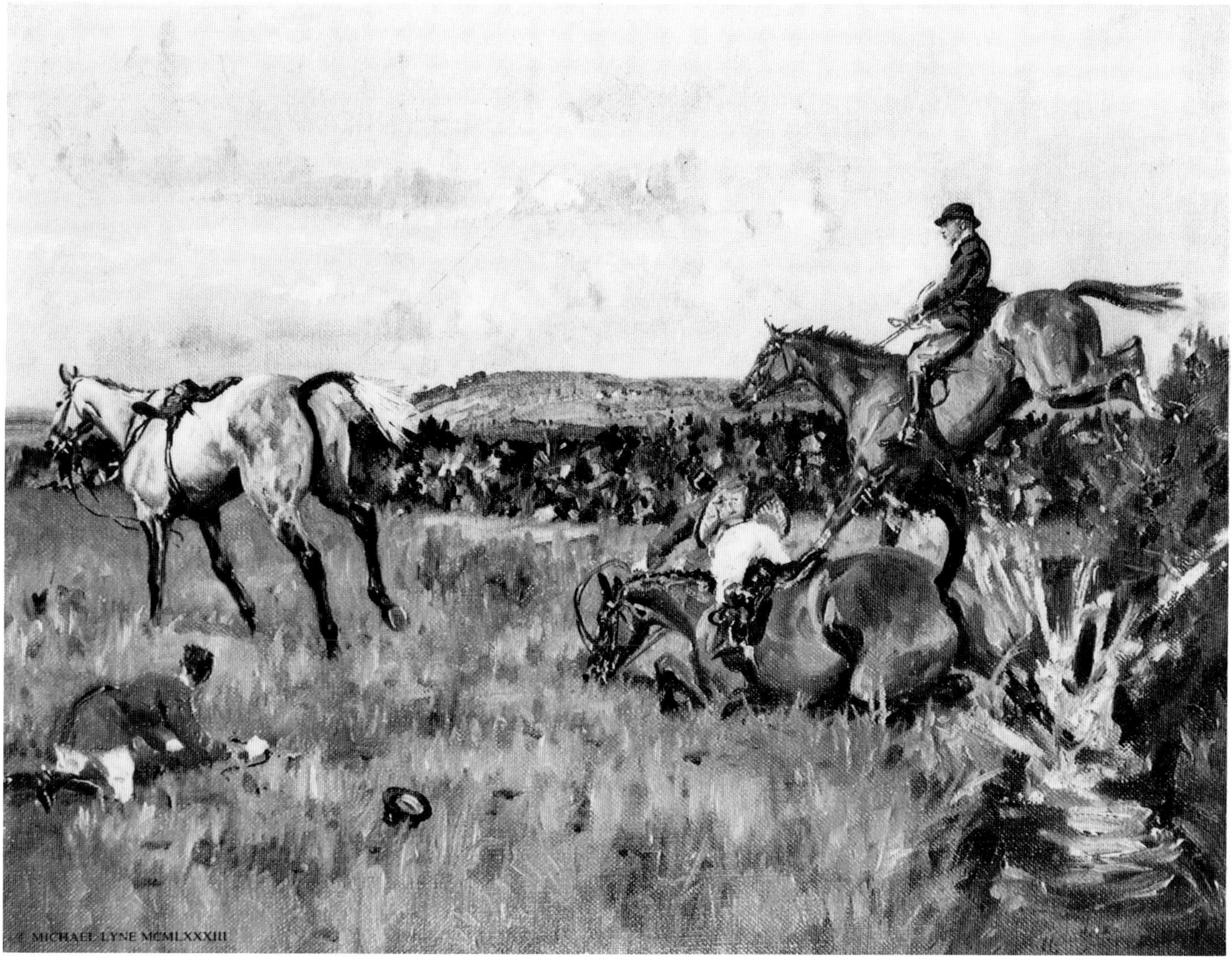

An Irish Bank, *c*1961. Oil on canvas, 16 × 20 in (36 × 51 cm). Published as a limited edition print by the Heale Gallery.

During the early 1970s the Lyne's frequently visited Ireland to see their friends the Blands of Port Laoise, County Laoise. At that time Ernest Bland was secretary of the Royal Dublin Society, one of the world's leading equestrian show societies, and encouraged Michael to judge at the famous Dublin Show held annually in August. One class which Michael particularly enjoyed judging, as a previous owner, was the donkey class, competing for the Swinfen Trophy. Having finished judging one August, Michael rejoined his family in the Royal Box and much to his teenage daughter's amusement, commented that the stallion class, then in the ring, all seemed to have five legs!

Many fine packs were visited and many superb paintings completed. Michael's first Irish

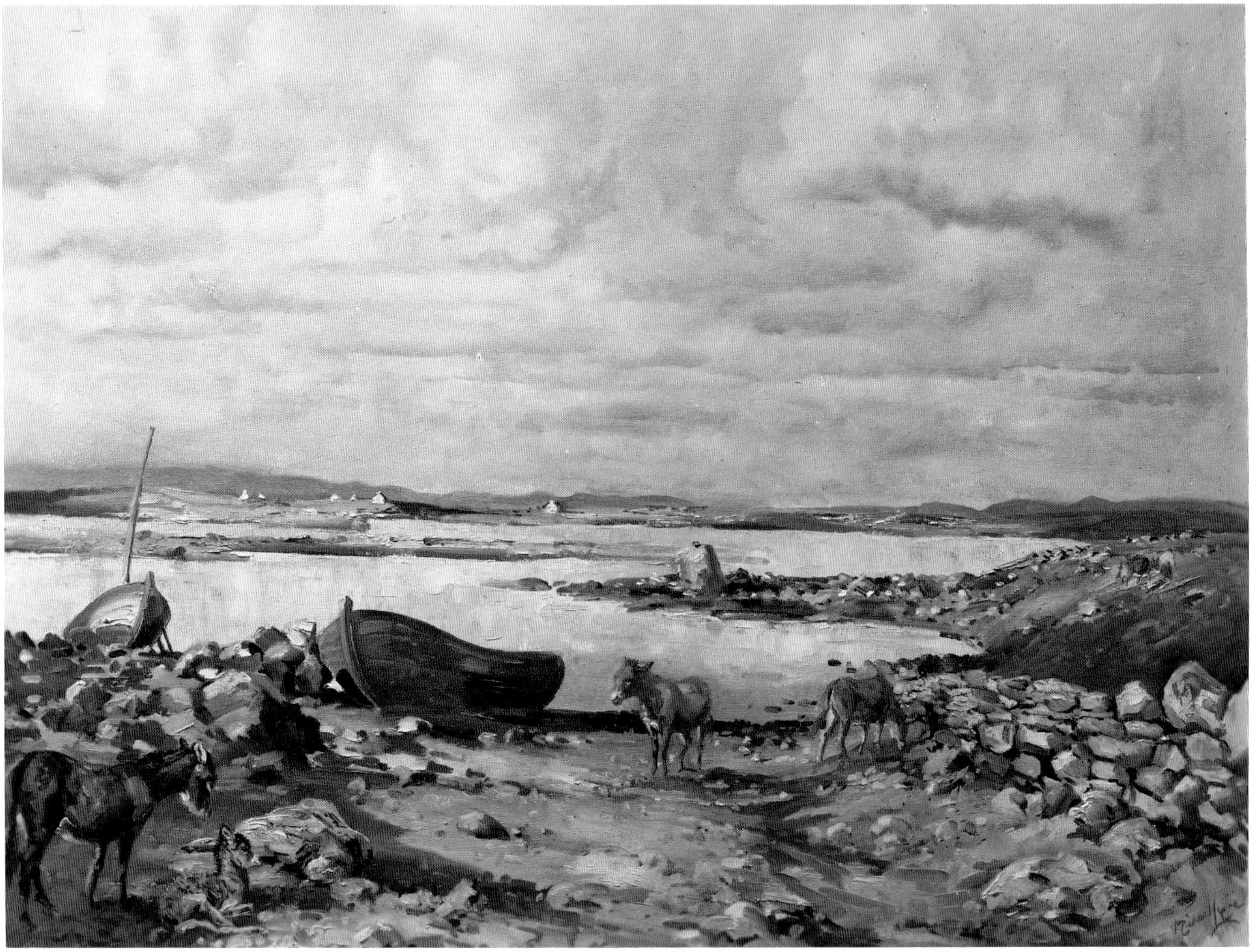

Connemara, *c*1971. Oil on canvas, 28 × 36 in (71 × 92 cm). This was painted during a visit to Dalesman, who was then living at Westport, County Mayo.

visit was in the mid-1930s to gather information and make preliminary studies to illustrate *Rhymes of an Irish Huntsman* by Stanislaus Lynch and apart from during and immediately after the war, he was a regular visitor to Ireland and much enjoyed both the hunting, and the social life which is so inexorably linked to Irish foxhunting. Paintings produced as a result of Irish visits range from the small dramatic *Irish Bank* conveying all the fearless dash of the Irish hunting field to the tranquil *Kildare Hunt Walking Out*. At the feet of the huntsman exercising hounds is a small Jack Russell, Poker, which Michael subsequently purchased out of the Kildare Kennels.

One of the most spectacular paintings of the Irish hunting scene is the aerial view of *The West Waterford at the 'V' Gap* (*Plate 6*) in the Knockmealdown Mountains, County

Tipperary. Near the scene of the painting a notable huntsman, Samuel Grubb, was buried with his horse and over the grave is a large equestrian statue.

Michael enjoyed his days in the Irish hunting field and would agree with the saying 'there's no fox like an Irish fox', and the banks and wide drains were always a great challenge to him. As a young man in the mid-1930s, he had been much taken with a trencher-fed foot harrier pack of black and tan hounds he hunted with (better known as Kerry beagles) of the Kenmare Hunt, Waterville, Co. Kerry. Every member of the field encouraged hounds to draw and in particular their own hound, in the event of a check and hounds failing to recover the line by their own efforts, the nearest man to them assisted, and if his cast failed, someone else took over. Towards the end of the day Michael saw one man call his hound to him and feed her with some very good looking raw beef 'to hearten her', he told Michael.

Dalesman spent part of his retirement in Westport, Co. Mayo, and always looked forward to visits from Michael and Jessie, both to show them the wild Mayo country, the pleasures of local hunting, and to inveigle Michael into judging at the Westport Horse Show.

The Lynes also made several visits to France with Michael's old army friend, John Treffry, Master of the Cury, and his wife. The object of the visits was to hunt deer in Normandy and wild boar in the Ardennes, and Michael favoured two packs in the forest of Compiègne, those of Monsieur Jean Bocquillon and Madame de Rothschild. The visits to the Ardennes were less successful, but the party was able to locate several hunts and follow hounds. Michael recorded the visits and a striking painting of Madame de Rothschild's staghounds, *Forest of Compiègne – The End* (*see Plate 5*) was included in Frost & Reed's 1976 exhibition together with an equally impressive *Buckhounds in the Forest of Compiègne* (*see p.114*).

In England, Exmoor was always a favourite both for hunting with the D & S Staghounds

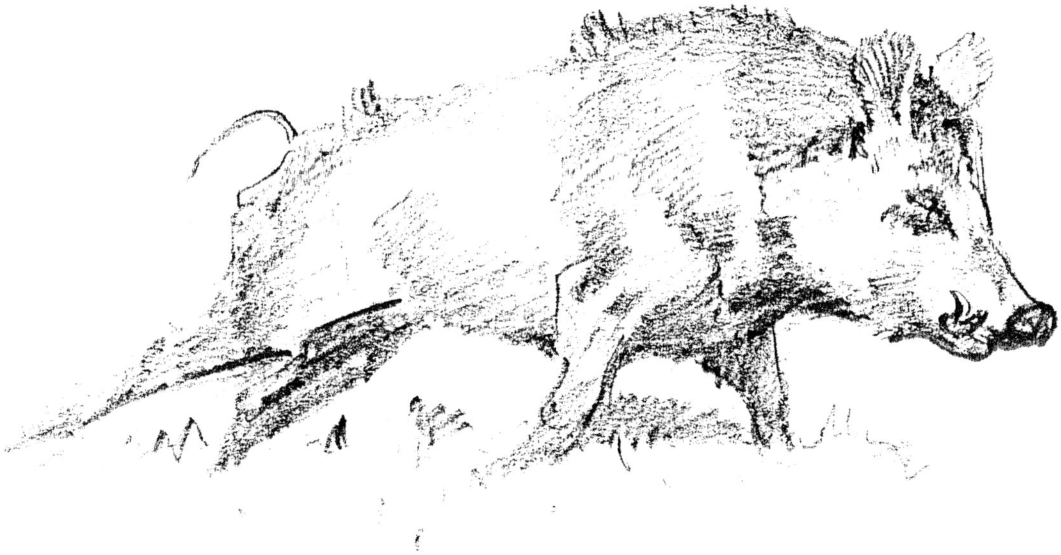

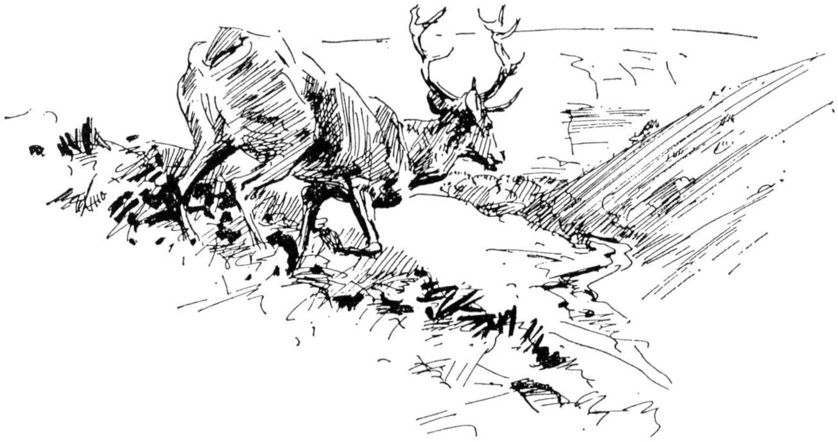

and for painting. Barely a year passed without the family travelling to the moor. Scotland too became a firm favourite, through Michael's friendship with Colonel Harry Nicholl, Master of the Haydon Foxhounds, who had a deer forest at the Black Corries in Argyllshire.

Michael as 'a good hound man' was never a keen shot, but stalking appealed to him greatly, both for the skill involved and its nearness to nature. To him the charm of stalking was the complete involvement of the individual. It was neither shot nor trophy that was best in this sport, but the stalk itself, though having said that, Michael invariably recalled that on his first outing, he achieved a hit, an eleven pointer.

During the 1960s, the two Lyne children were growing fast, Edward had left Radley, passed through the Royal Agricultural College at Cirencester and was about to embark on an apprenticeship as a mechanical engineer. Diana was still at school, but longing to be grown-up.

Michael had not been represented by an agent since parting company with Ackermann in the early 1950s. With hindsight, he always felt that the 1950s were the time of his break-through into full public acceptance after the hard post war years, and it could well have been this knowledge that gave him the necessary confidence to go solo, coupled with a steady stream of commissions in both England (including paintings for the Duke of Beaufort and Lord Knutsford) and the United States. However, he did form a strong alliance with the British based dealers Frost & Reed, through their Bristol director, Mr K.M. Gallop. Michael could always look forward to a representative display of his watercolours in the window of their Clare Street, Bristol gallery during the Badminton Horse Trials period. Other than this annual window display, Michael had no showing of his work in England during the mid and late 1950s, apart from the disastrous West End venture during the Suez crisis, but Frost & Reed produced a series of five limited edition prints.

Sir Alfred Munnings, President of the Royal Academy from 1944 to 1949, together with his fellow Academician Sir William Russell Flint and the marine painter, Montague Dawson, were all represented at that time by Frost & Reed. Understandably the company did not wish to represent another sporting painter whilst Munnings was alive, but with his death in 1959, the way was open for Michael who joined them in the early 1960s. This act, other than the initial United States visit, was the most significant in his professional life.

For almost a score of years, Frost & Reed successfully promoted his name and work on both sides of the Atlantic, held a series of eight one-man major London exhibitions between 1964 and 1979 and published a superb series of limited edition prints, at Michael's request. By any yardstick, it was an outstanding association and only ended with the breakdown of the artist's health in 1979.

It is not my intention to give a massive amount of information relating to the association, but full details of the exhibitions are listed in Appendix II and of the limited edition prints in Appendix III. These alone could account for a lifetime's output by many artists.

By the end of the 1950s, Michael had virtually abandoned watercolour painting, other than for making sketches when on location, in favour of painting in oils. In his own words, he liked nothing better than to get his teeth into a nice juicy oil. This in turn led to his owning, for the first time, a studio. Previously he had used one of the Dunfield bedrooms with good light, but in 1961, a loft over part of the range of outbuildings was converted and commissioned as a studio, with overhead natural light, to enable Michael to continue his custom of working through all the hours of daylight. The income generated by Frost & Reed, from these paintings, enabled Michael both to pay for his children's education and undertake extensive restoration and modernisation of Dunfield's fabric.

Also in the spring of 1961, at Frost & Reed's instigation, Michael returned to Aintree for the first time since 1947, and was so captivated by the Grand National that he watched the race regularly for a decade from the old Canal Turn stand, and created some of the most dramatic, powerful and understanding images of the race that have ever been produced. As a traditional and dedicated field sportsman and countryman, he was never greatly attached to flat racing and the Thoroughbred, but had greatly enjoyed National Hunt racing from his earliest days. Thus the visual stimuli of Aintree obsessed him and his powers and talents were stretched to the limit to produce a series which was to convey the unique atmosphere of the Liverpool course in the most stunning manner possible, doing full justice to both horse and rider. The Grand National has always produced its own peculiar brand of hero, and it is the great fortune of the likes of Jay Trump, Highland Wedding, Rondetto, Foinavon and The Rip, to have been recorded in action, by Michael, for posterity.

With the new studio and the switch to oil painting, came a marked change in the artist's style of painting, moving away from the highly worked and meticulously detailed pictures of the previous years, to a broader, more fluid style of greater simplicity where impression took over from precision, concentrating on the essence of the subject and the passing moment or event, capturing the fugitive effects of light and atmosphere, the constantly changing weather, light and moving shadows. The use of colour became more positive and highly charged with textured surfaces, rough and rasping, making a very individualistic and idiosyncratic statement. The content of Michael's paintings also changed. At that time the sporting art critic and historian Stella A. Walker, was deeply concerned by the somewhat sterile unimaginative approach, traditional presentation and conception of many modern sporting artists, to the extent that she wrote an article on the subject for *Horse and Hound* in January 1967. Michael was most impressed by what Mrs Walker said and corresponded with her on the subject. A delightful letter exists in which Michael says 'you (Mrs Walker) fuel my talent'. In practical terms the artist had a new perspective on his painting and this enabled him to produce such inventive pictures as the savagely realistic *Kennel Fight* (1967), *Stag Hunting – The Lay-on* (1967), and the complete break in tradition with *Aerial View* (1975), though a prototype had been painted in the late 1940s.

In Stanley Wade, the then Chairman and Managing Director of Frost & Reed, the company possessed a superb entrepreneur and promoter with a fine eye for a painting, who did full justice to the new sporting artist on the company's books, promoting him so successfully that for twelve years Michael produced an average of one oil painting each week, often of vast size (40 x 50 in, 102 x 127cm). He virtually abandoned private commissions, other than a small number in America. All paintings from 1958 were listed in a record book kept by Jessie, who acted as her husband's business manager.

The first one-man exhibition of the Frost & Reed series was held at the opening of the 1964–65 foxhunting season, and was effectively Michael's first London show since 1951, attracting wide attention among the art critics. The exhibition was a sell out, as were several of the subsequent shows, and justified Frost & Reed's decision not to sell the whole of the works exhibited to an American dealer prior to the private view. The content of the show can be summed up by Stella A. Walker's statement that all the painting had 'rich thick brushwork, imaginatively used with telling effect and style'. The art magazine *Apollo* noted 'a sensitivity to the transience of light and shadow in open country'.

The second exhibition at the opening of the 1965–1966 season, included a series of seventy preparatory watercolour sketches, both for paintings in the exhibition and in the preceding 1964 exhibition. This innovation delighted both the critics and public for it was considered that few, if any artists, would be prepared to reveal their working methods and allow the public to see the scene as they saw it with on-the-spot sketches or as they remembered it with sketches made shortly afterwards. It also gave an opportunity to see what changes, if any, Michael had made on mature reflection to improve the composition of the final oil painting. An interesting and typical idiosyncrasy of Michael's was always to have a picture of a grey horse in each exhibition.

Diana Lyne has many memories of the private views, not least Frost & Reed's concern that she had a male companion. On one occasion she recalls being introduced to her brother, Edward, on another to a young barrister who, wanting to take her out to dinner, was sent packing by Michael who barked 'she's only fifteen'.

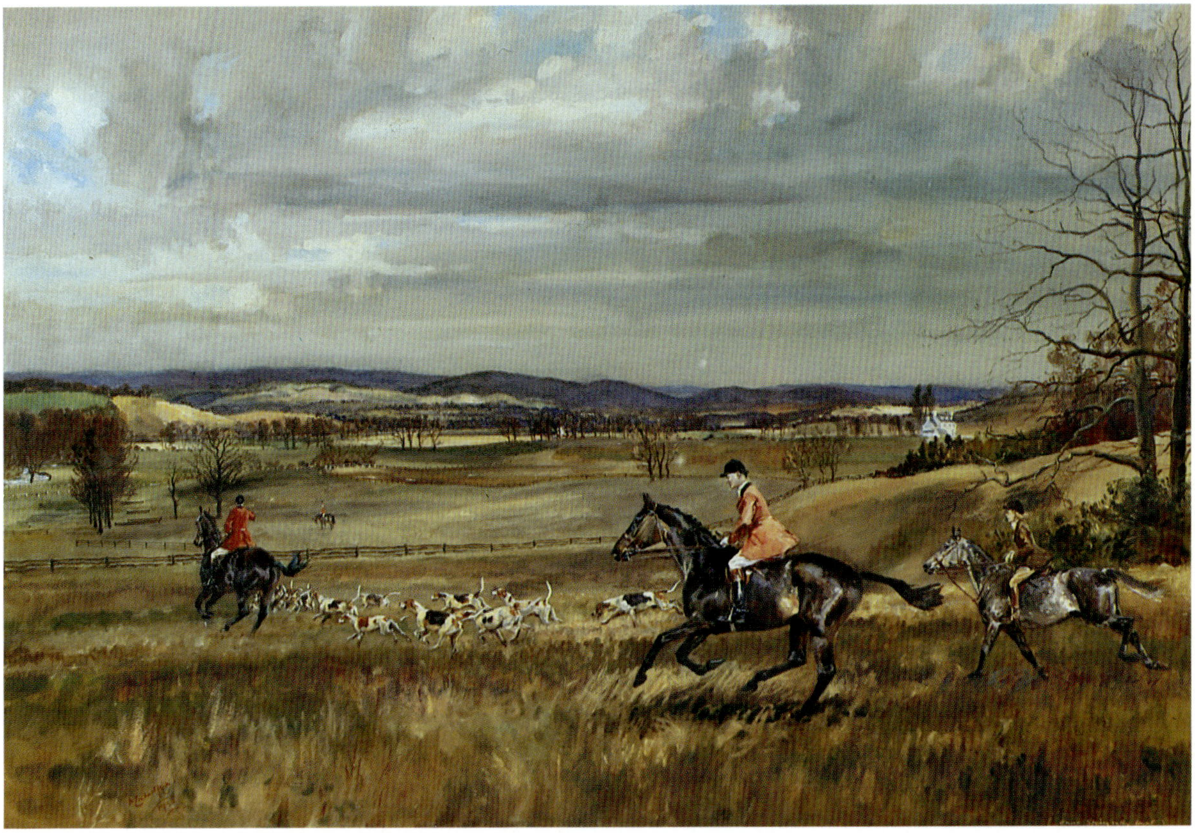

Green Spring Valley Hounds, Maryland. J. Fife Symington MFH *and daughter*, 1952. Signed, watercolour. (*below*) *The Orange County, Virginia, running towards the Blue Ridge Mountains.* Signed, oil on canvas, 24 × 36 in (61 × 92 cm). Only the Hunt staff wear uniform: there is no scarlet in the field other than visitors.

PLATE 9

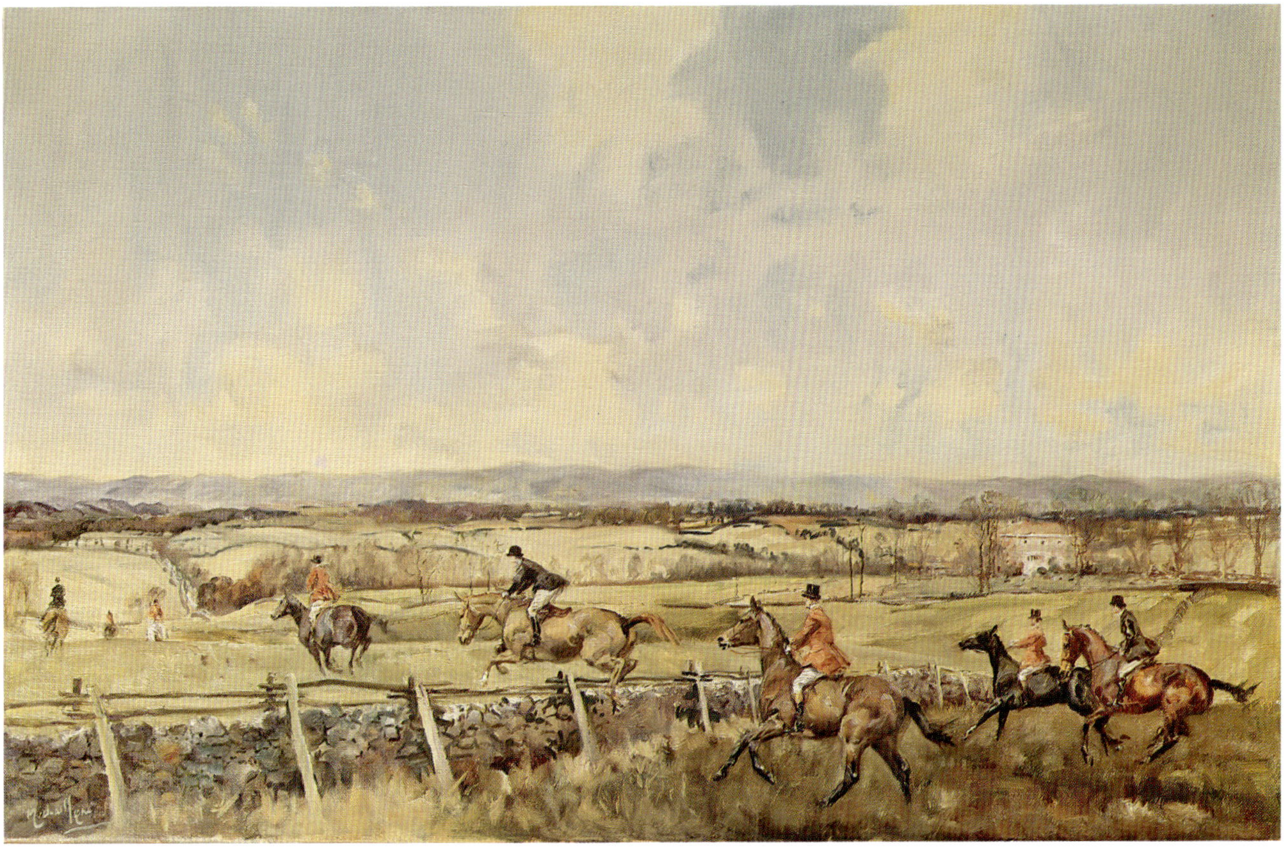

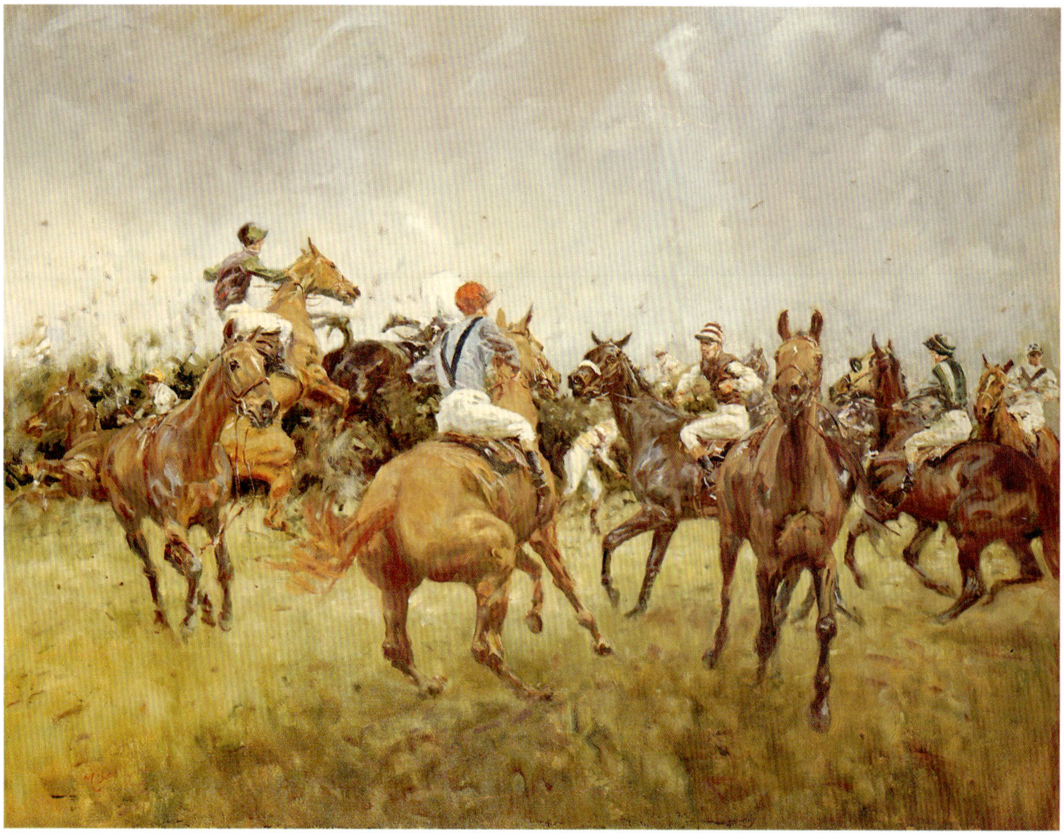

1967 Grand National – The Twenty-Third Fence, 1967. Signed, oil on canvas, 40 × 50 in (102 × 127 cm). Foinavon, the ultimate winner of the race, can be seen in the hood to the right of the picture.

PLATE 10

(*below*) *1965 Grand National – Canal Turn*, 1965. Signed, oil on canvas, 28 × 36 in (71 × 92 cm). On the right, having already jumped safely are Phebu (22) and Kapeno (13). Landing just behind them is Rondetto (4) and Freddie (2), who finished second. Taking the jump is Loving Record (10), Tant Pis (19), and in the centre is Jay Trump (5), the winner. About to jump is Rainbow Battle (27) and finally side by side come L'Empereur (11), Peacetown (11) and The Rip (6) the Queen Mother's horse.

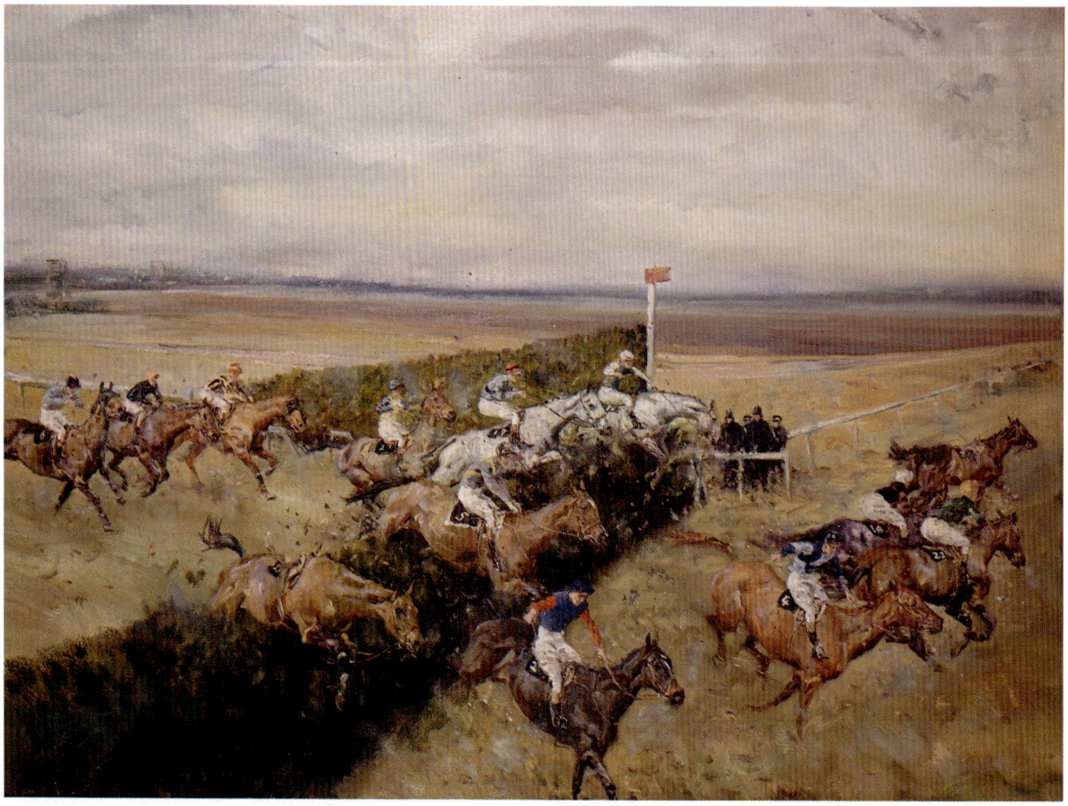

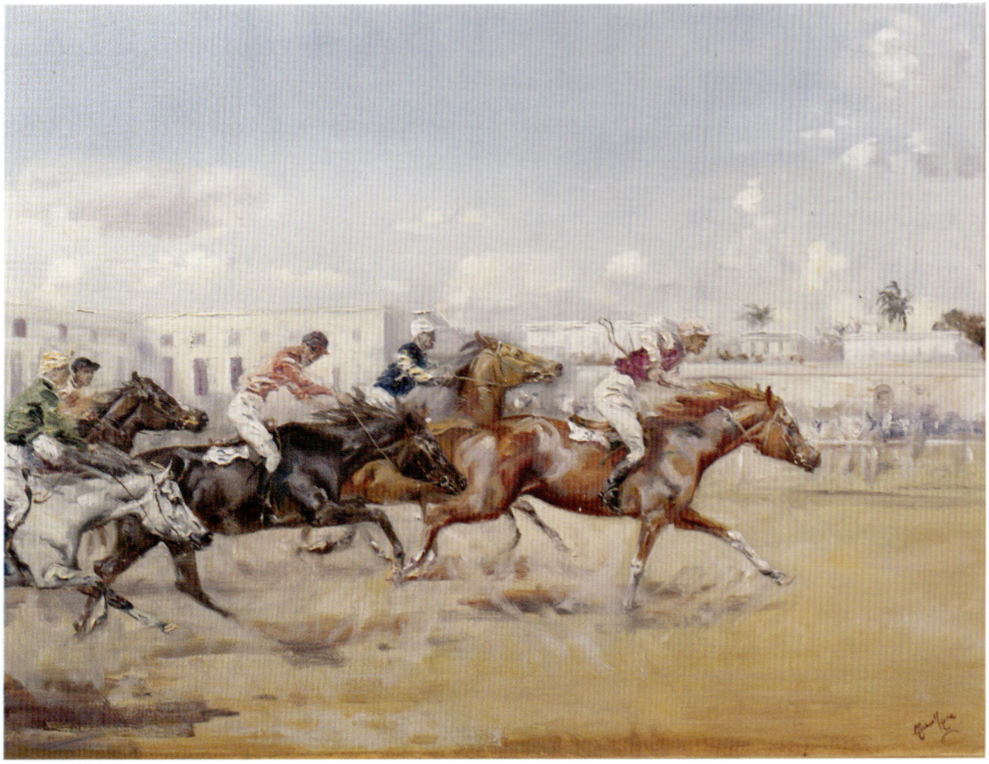

Arabians Racing at Busetta Racecourse, Tripoli, 1968. Signed, oil on canvas, 28 × 36 in (71 × 92 cm). Painted during a holiday with Edward Lyne, who was working in North Africa at that time.

PLATE 11

A Fall at the Third Fence : The Maryland Hunt Cup, 1966, 1966. Signed, oil on canvas. This painting was commissioned by J. Fife Symington and shows (from left to right), Flying Cub (4, B. Griswold), Mountain Dew (1, Janon Fisher Jnr), El Moro (3, Louis Neilson), Boating Party (R. Jones) and Jay Trump (5, Tommy Smith), the winner. Jay Trump had won the Grand National the previous year.

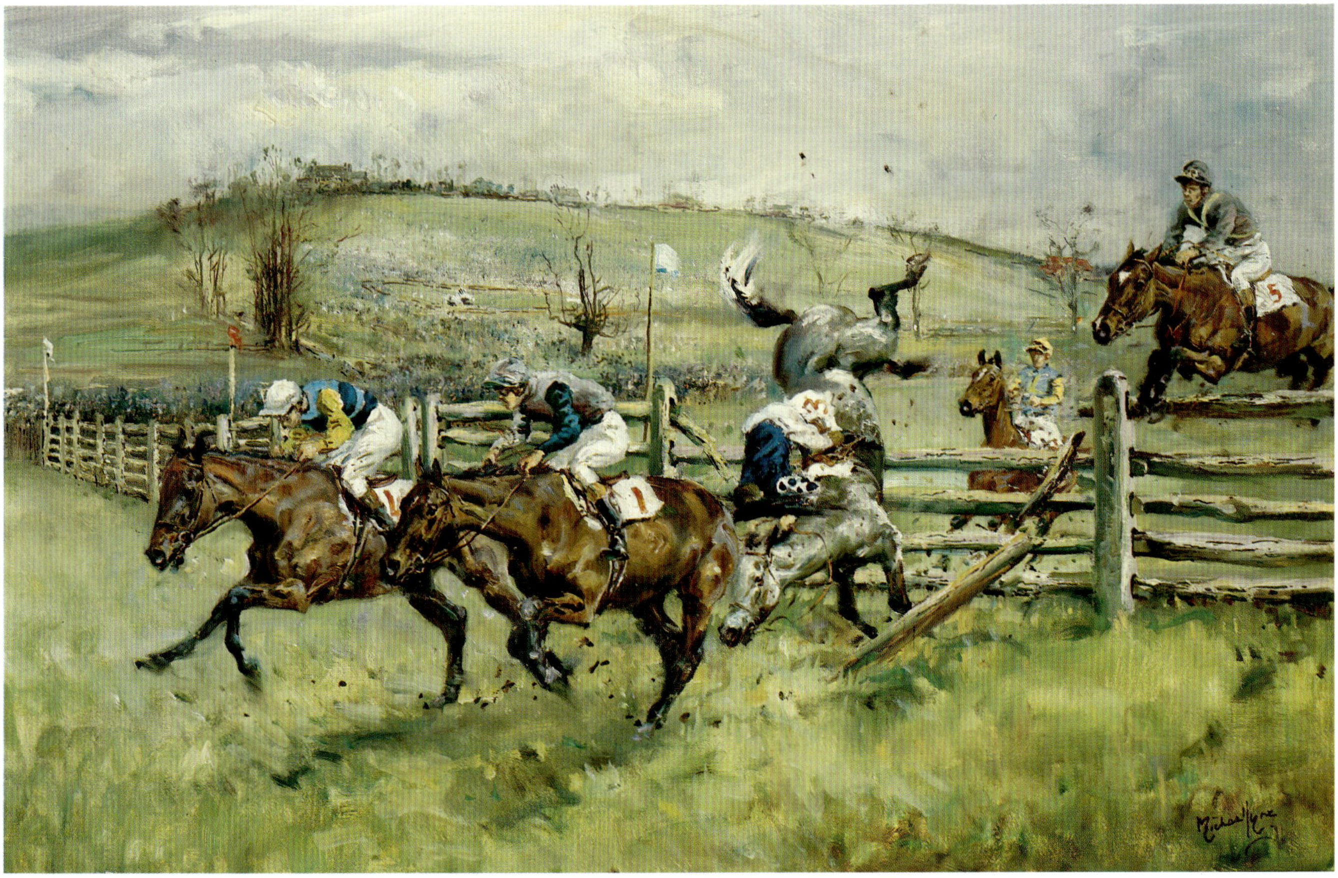

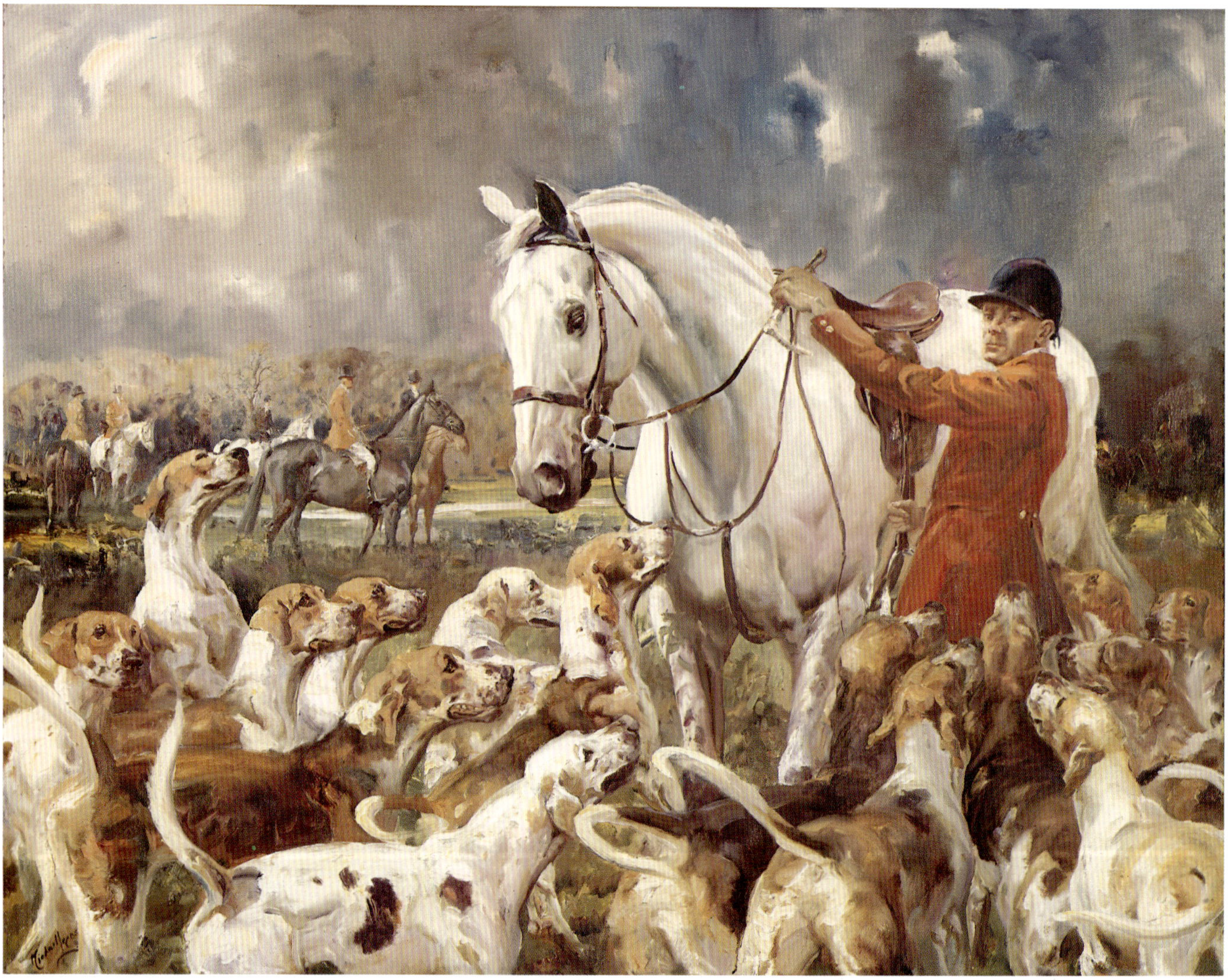

The Huntsman, 1968. Signed, oil on canvas, 28 × 36 in (71 × 92 cm).
Michael Lyne's hunter Rodney was used to model the grey.

PLATE 12

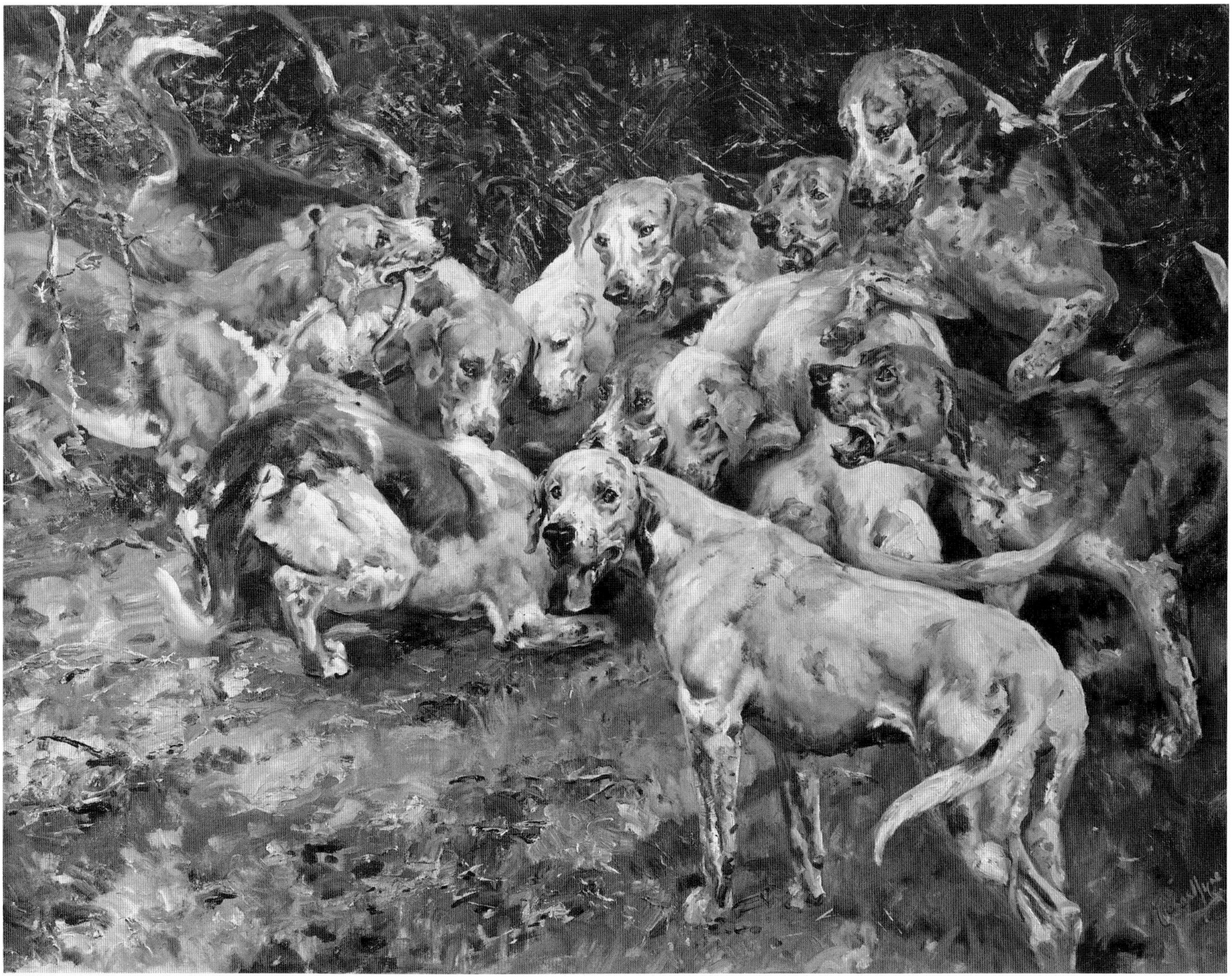

Marking to Ground, 1967. Oil on canvas, 40 × 50 in (101 × 127 cm). This is one of the series of paintings inspired by Stella A. Walker's *Horse & Hound* article in January 1967. It was exhibited at Frost & Reed in 1969.

Further exhibitions in the series were held in 1967 and 1969, and each was deemed to be of absorbing interest, showing the artist's contrasting styles and the varied manipulation of paint and approach to composition.

Commercial pressures on Michael were enormous, both in preparing for the exhibitions and in satisfying the large general demand for his paintings in England and the United States. Many of the best paintings were sold direct to Frost & Reed clients and never exhibited in London. Michael accepted the challenge and did his best to satisfy his ever

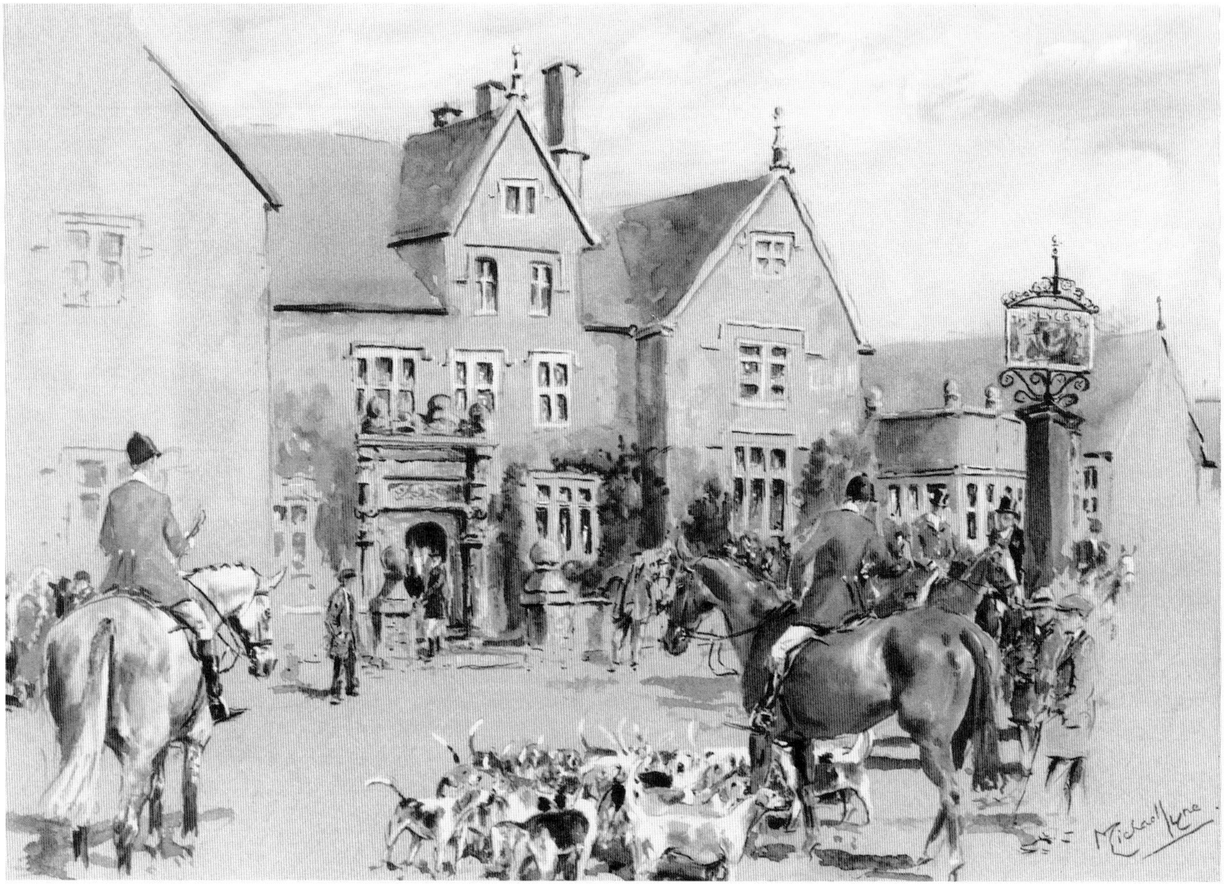

The North Cotswold, A Meet at the Lygon Arms, Broadway. Watercolour, 8 × 10 in (20 × 26 cm).
Exhibited at the Tryon Gallery Retrospective Exhibition, 1989.

increasing public. He attempted throughout to maintain his own high standards of painting, recording, and presentation, though at times this proved very difficult.

In 1971 Michael was invited to send four paintings to the World Hunting Exhibition in Budapest, where they would be displayed in the British Pavilion. The paintings depicted hunting, coursing, stalking and fly-fishing. Despite promises by the Hungarians to return the paintings speedily to London after the close of the exhibition, they remained in Budapest for some considerable time, much to Michael's annoyance, and were subsequently returned with no explanation, but accompanied by a large and impressive certificate bearing Michael's name which now hangs in the downstairs loo at Dunfield.

About this time the Lyne's daughter, after a sheltered and cosseted childhood and convent education, was to leave home for her first job at a Maidenhead hotel. Michael took the opportunity over Sunday lunch to warn her of the dangers of the great outside world and the wolves it contained. Having finished his lecture, he noticed a small mark on his daughter's neck and commented on the fact. Diana blushed and said, 'Well yes, it was one of the wolves that I have just been warned about,' whereupon father and brother Edward both burst out laughing.

Having completed a summer at Maidenhead, Diana was eager to work in Europe and learn a language. Being a traditionalist Michael would have none of this; if his daughter went abroad to work, it would be to the United States 'where we have friends'. Diana acquiesced and went out with her parents on their autumn trip, staying in America to work as a mother's help. She had strict instructions from her father not to return with an American accent, otherwise she would not be allowed back into the house!

Shortly afterwards, Edward left for West Africa, which was subsequently to become his home, and where he is now Managing Director of his own company. Edward married his wife, Annette, in 1971.

During this frantic period Michael never lost sight of one of his first loves, book illustration, and despite all the pressures on him, never refused to undertake work for those who were his friends. From 1958 – 1962 he illustrated Lt Col Cyril Heber Percy's trilogy: *Hym*, a story of a fox, *Us Four* and *While Others Sleep*. The original pen and ink drawings for

Cheltenham: Top of the Hill, *c*1965. Oil on canvas, 24 × 36 in (61 × 92 cm).

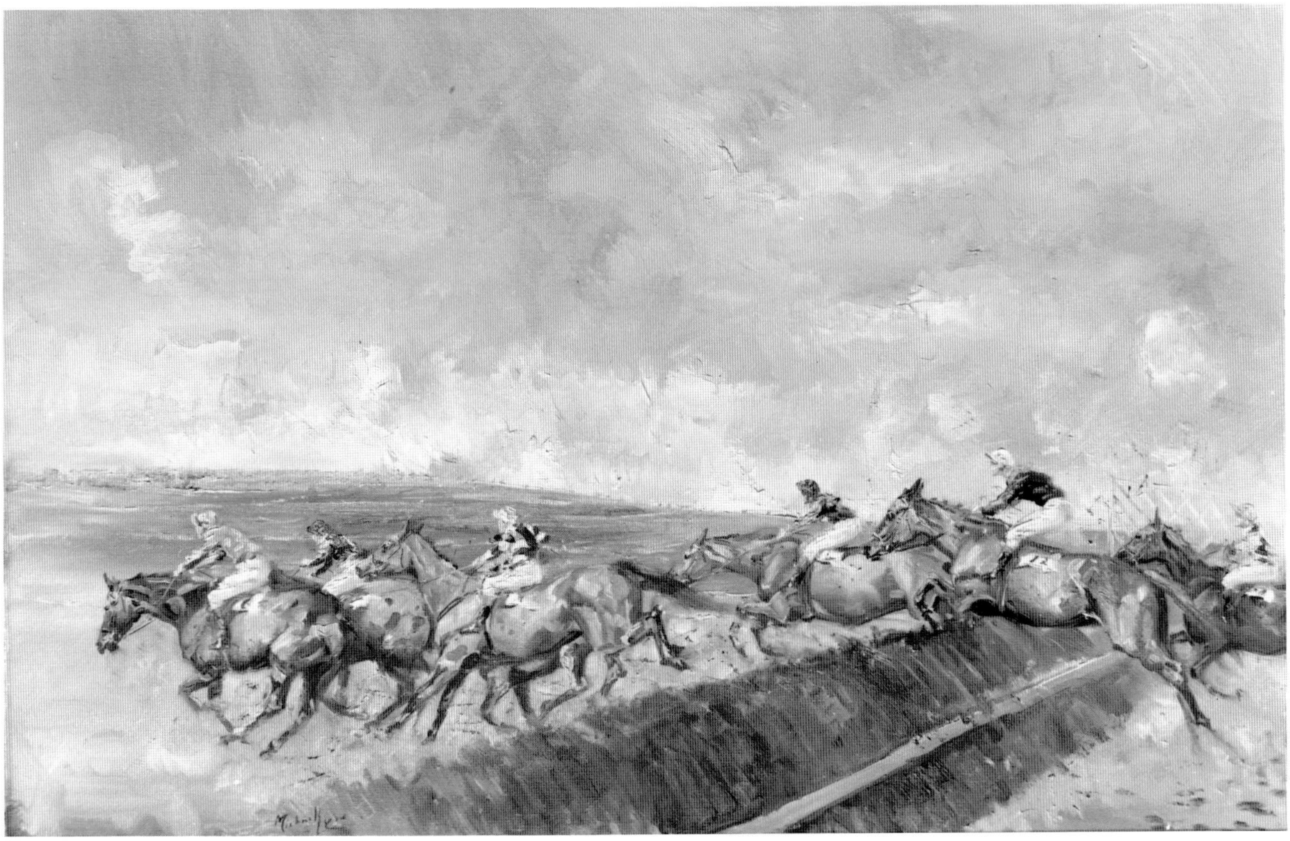

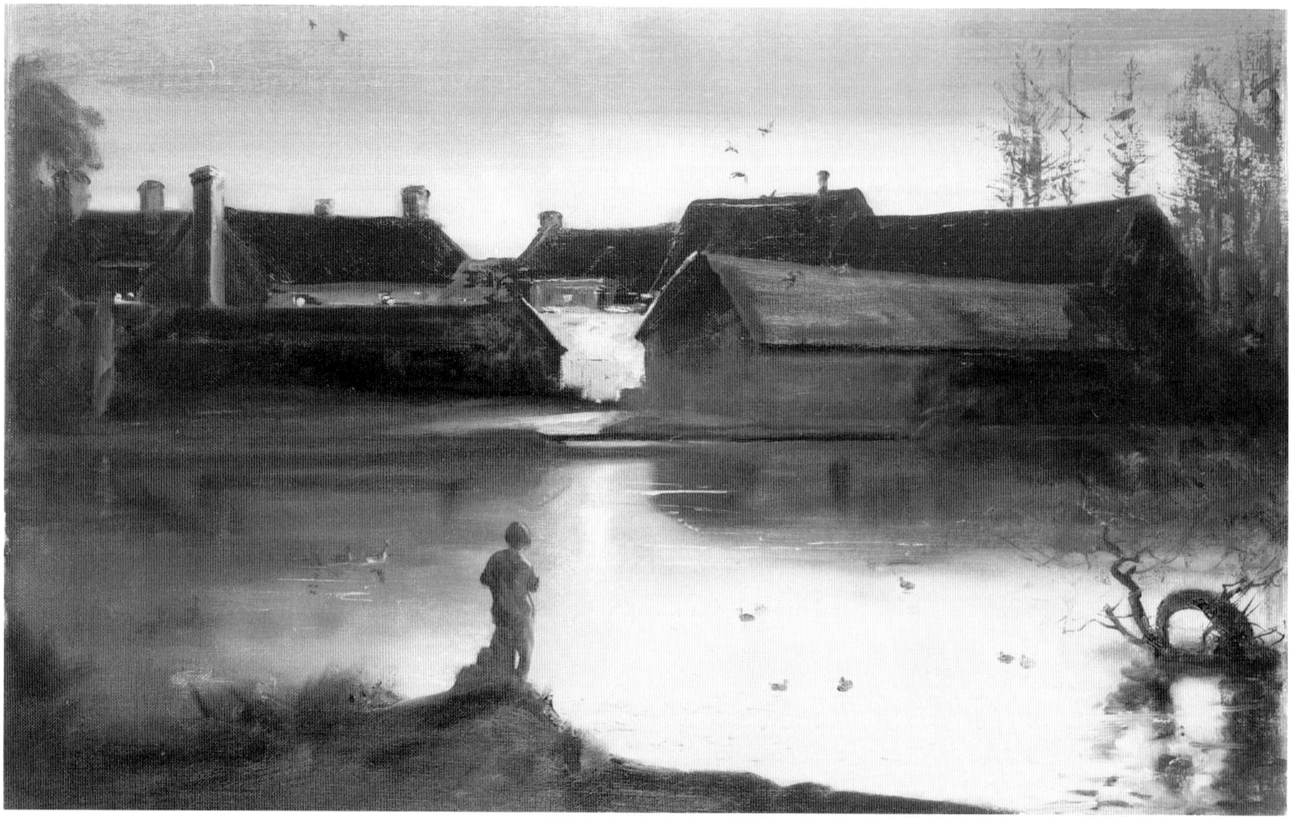

Dunfield by Moonlight, 1971. Oil on canvas, 20 × 30 in (51 × 76 cm). Michael and Jessie were removing a wasp's nest to the paddock. All the house lights were on and this view was that from the far side of the half acre pond adjoining the paddock.

these works now rest in a magnificent Morocco-bound album in the Heber Percy Collection.

In 1965 he illustrated his mentor, Stella A. Walker's, joint publication with Reggie Summerhays, *The Controversial Horse*, in 1963 Bay de Courcy Parry's *Here Lies My Story*, and finally in 1973 Daphne Moore's *In Nimrod's Footsteps*. At the same time, Michael was supervising the production of his own book, *From Litter to Later On* which was originally conceived, written and illustrated some twenty-five years earlier while the family were living at Througham Slad and was finally published by his friend, Richard Grant Rennick.

Unlike some artists, Michael never felt that prints would cheapen his paintings. On the contrary, it was his aim to have a Michael Lyne print in every English public house, and in addition to Frost & Reed, he actively encouraged both the British Field Sports Society, for whom he would gladly spend hours signing broadsheets of his drawings, and subsequently Heale Gallery, to publish further prints.

In the mid-1960s after ten seasons, a crashing fall ended Michael's foxhunting career. Rodney was pensioned off and Michael acquired the foundation stock of the Dunfield

Salukis, descendants of that great coursing Saluki, Knightellington Eshmail. The Arab gazehound was introduced after World War I by returning servicemen from the Middle East and first encountered by Michael at the Rossall Prep School, where the headmaster owned one. In its turn, this led Michael into breeding and what was to become one of his greatest loves, coursing. While the Dunfield Salukis were strictly working dogs, Michael much enjoyed showing them in order to assess his progress as a breeder in good competitive company. One Saluki in particular, Dunfield Djebel was highly successful, thrice qualifying for Crufts, gaining a third prize in 1978, and best of breed in 1979, and becoming Kennel Club Champion in 1980. On the coursing field, Pharaoh Dunfield won the Victor Henderson Memorial Trophy for the best coursing Saluki of the 1969–1970 season, only being beaten once.

Michael and Jessie were members of the Cotswold, Oxford and Saluki Coursing Clubs, and Michael was a steward of the National Coursing Club. He was always a good narrative sporting writer with a quick succinct pen and magic pencil to provide supporting illustrations. As his omnibus volumes *Horses, Hounds and Country* and *A Parson's Son* testify, good gripping stuff, but coursing and Salukis brought out Michael's best endeavours as a writer, two gems being 'All in a Coursing Family' published in *The Field* during March 1975 and 'A Working Saluki Goes to Town', the story of Dunfield Djebel at the 1979 Crufts, appearing in *The Field* Christmas Number 1979 and being written at a time of great personal

Michael and Jessie Lyne at Dunfield in the 1960s with three generations of their salukis.

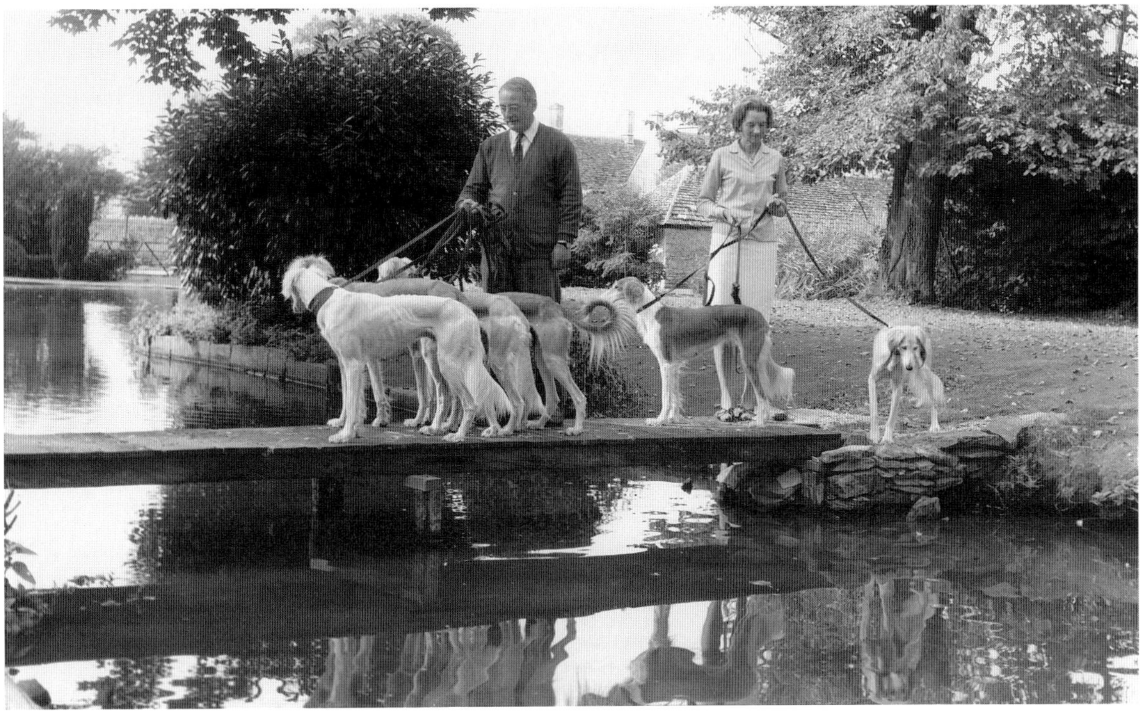

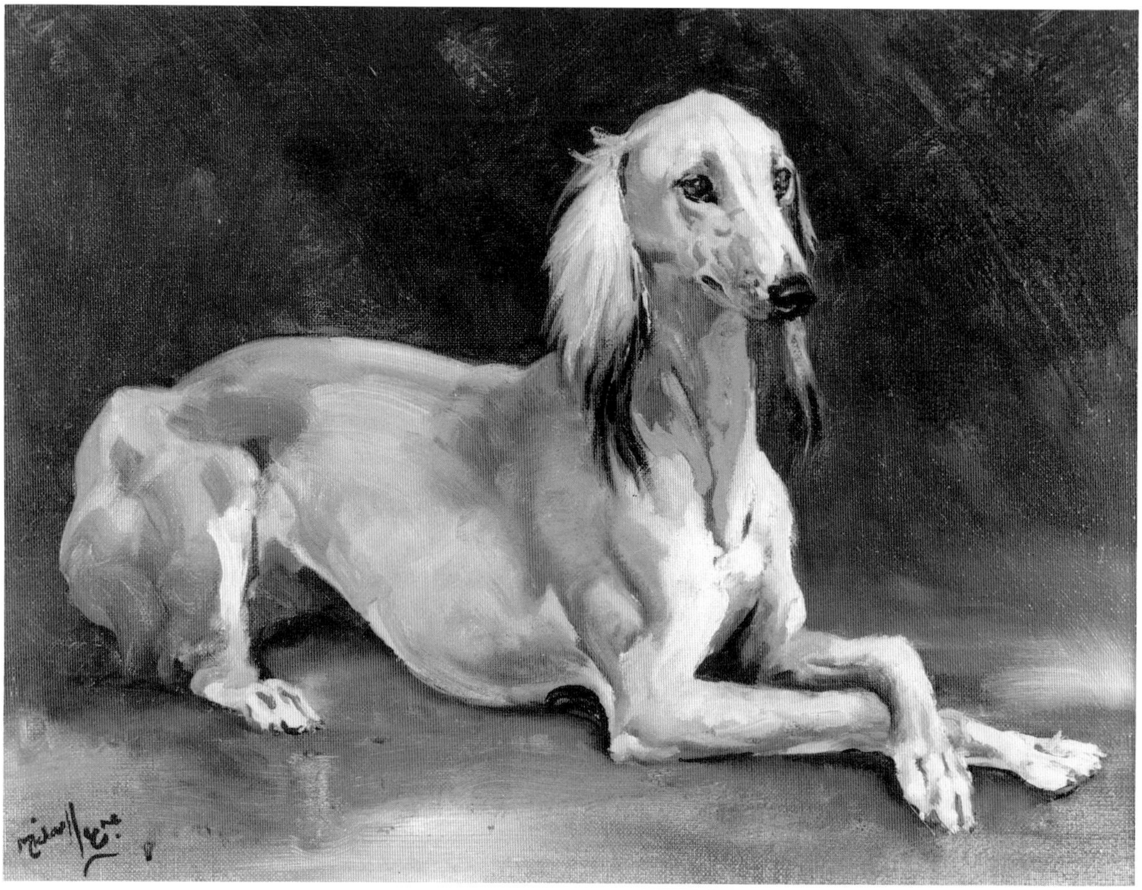

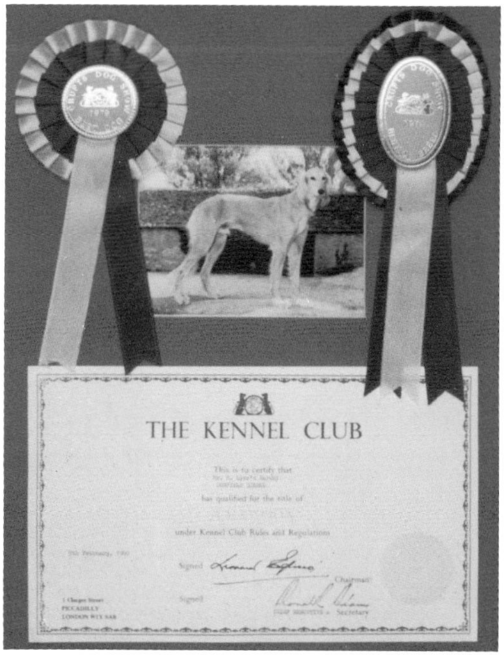

(*above*) *Lotus*, saluki bitch bred by Michael in 1963. Oil on canvas, 20 × 30 in (51 × 78 cm). The Dunfield salukis were descendants of the great coursing saluki Knightellington Eshmail. (*right*) Montage of Michael's saluki Dunfield Djebel: rosettes for Crufts Best Dog 1979 and Best of Breed 1979; Champion Certificate, Crufts 1980.

stress. 'The Truth About Coursing' published in November 1964 for *The Field* and subsequently widely used by the Coursing Supporters Club, is considered by many to be the best modern apologia for the sport.

In addition Michael, as one of the few contemporary artists with an understanding of gazehounds and the technicalities of coursing, produced a whole range of paintings of the sport. While some were static or character studies, they mostly depicted running dogs in action, emphasising power and speed. A set of four large watercolour studies presented to the British Field Sport Society are now exhibited in the Society's travelling main show unit. For the first and only time in his career other than the personal wood carvings for himself and the Warburgs, Michael, in 1974, entered the field of three-dimensional art and produced a set of three small bronzes, consisting of a brace of greyhounds and a hare. Michael found it difficult to work in such a contrasting medium to that which was his norm, but thanks to Frost & Reed, he did not abandon the project. The end result he found pleasing, capturing grace, power and speed, though he always considered that the hare had too much chest.

In his last days, Michael several times contemplated producing a sequel in bronze from his well known painting *The Loose Horse* but alas, the idea never came to fruition. A good indication of Michael's knowledge and dedication to the sport can be gained from an observation by that keen coursing supporter, Peter Hunt, of the British Field Sports Society. He sat, on one occasion, in Michael's car on the Huntingdon Coursing Ground, and viewed a number of courses over a period of thirty minutes. Michael watched each with great concentration and produced a series of pencil sketches, at the same time talking continually about the sport.

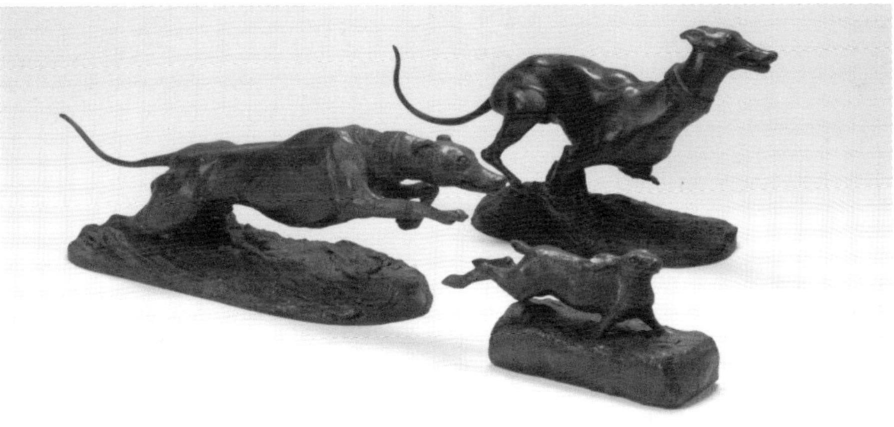

Coursing Group. Bronze, signed edition of 10, executed 1974, greyhounds each approximately 9 × 4 in (23 × 10 cm), hare approximately 4 × 2.5 in (10 × 6 cm). Michael Lyne felt the spirit of his ancestor John Bacon RA urging him to try the challenge of speed in sculpture. This was his only sculpture, as a plan to sculpt *The Loose Horse* did not materialise.

SIX

AUTUMN DAYS 1974–1989

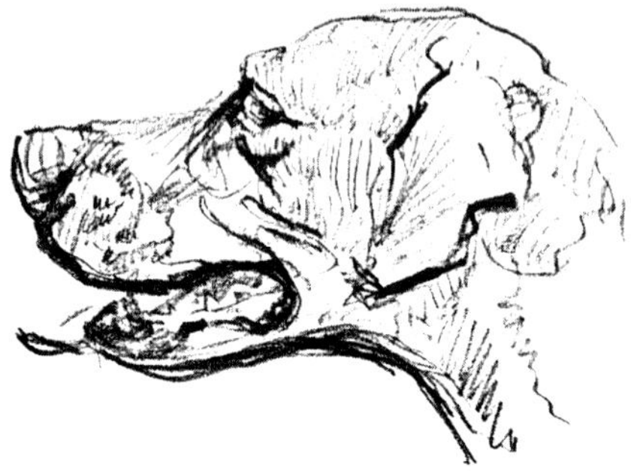

The 1970s saw many changes in the Lyne family. Mrs Joan Lyne, Michael's mother, died in 1974, having seen her youngest son reach the top of his profession as a sporting artist and writer. In the same year Michael's first grandchild Henry, the son of Edward and Annette, was born, an event which gave Michael great pleasure and to some extent ameliorated the feelings of insecurity he was experiencing about his work and health.

The children's old nanny, Mrs Annie Leighton, who had subsequently become Mrs Joan Lyne's companion, joined the household at Dunfield on Mrs Lyne's death and divided her time between Michael's family and that of his sister in Hampshire, until her death some years later.

Diana married Richard Cox in 1978, and Michael much enjoyed arranging the wedding and reception at nearby Bibury Court. The family, now with two sons, live close to Dunfield and are regular visitors.

The early spring of 1974 saw the publication of Michael's book *A Parson's Son*, a limited edition collection of mainly semi-autobiographical writings, many of which had previously appeared in the equestrian and field sports press, supplemented by some new material and a very impressive array of reproductions of the artist's work – one hundred and fifty in all. It was well received by reviewers and the sporting public; though it was not realized at the time, the volume marked a watershed in the artist's life and work.

Michael, by nature, was essentially a very private man and kept his own counsel other than to his devoted wife. It was she who discovered after Michael's death and drew my attention to, the following inscription in the artist's personal copy of *A Parson's Son*:

'1974 (aged 62) I have published two books and illustrated three others, produced a set of bronzes and painted upwards of forty pictures, and had a New York Exhibition. It has also been a successful year showing and coursing Salukis. The year has also seen in my eyes, a remarkable decline in my ability as a painter – being quite ill early in the year may be responsible for this. I am also delighted with the birth of my first grandchild, Henry.'

In all matters, great and small, an honest man, Michael saw what the next five years were to reveal to the sporting art world and his many admirers; that the enormous amount

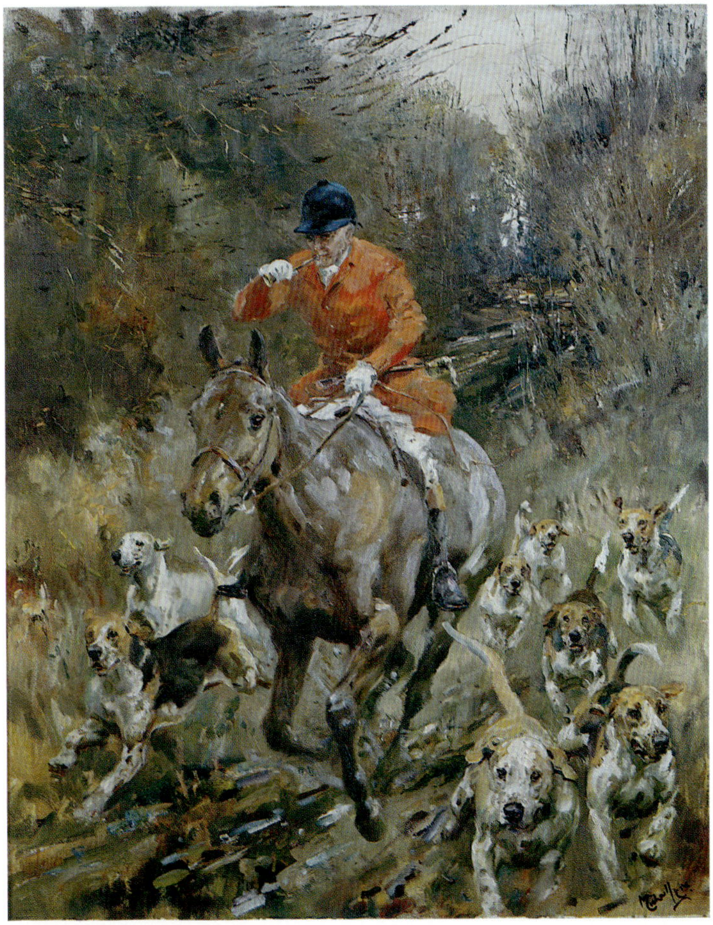

Going to a View Hallo, 1964. Signed, oil on canvas, 36 × 28 in (92 × 71 cm).

PLATE 13

(*below*) *VWH Crossing the River Thames at Kempsford*, 1965. Signed, oil on canvas, 24 × 36 in (61 × 92 cm). Michael Lyne hunted with the VWH for ten seasons and for many years was churchwarden at Kempsford church.

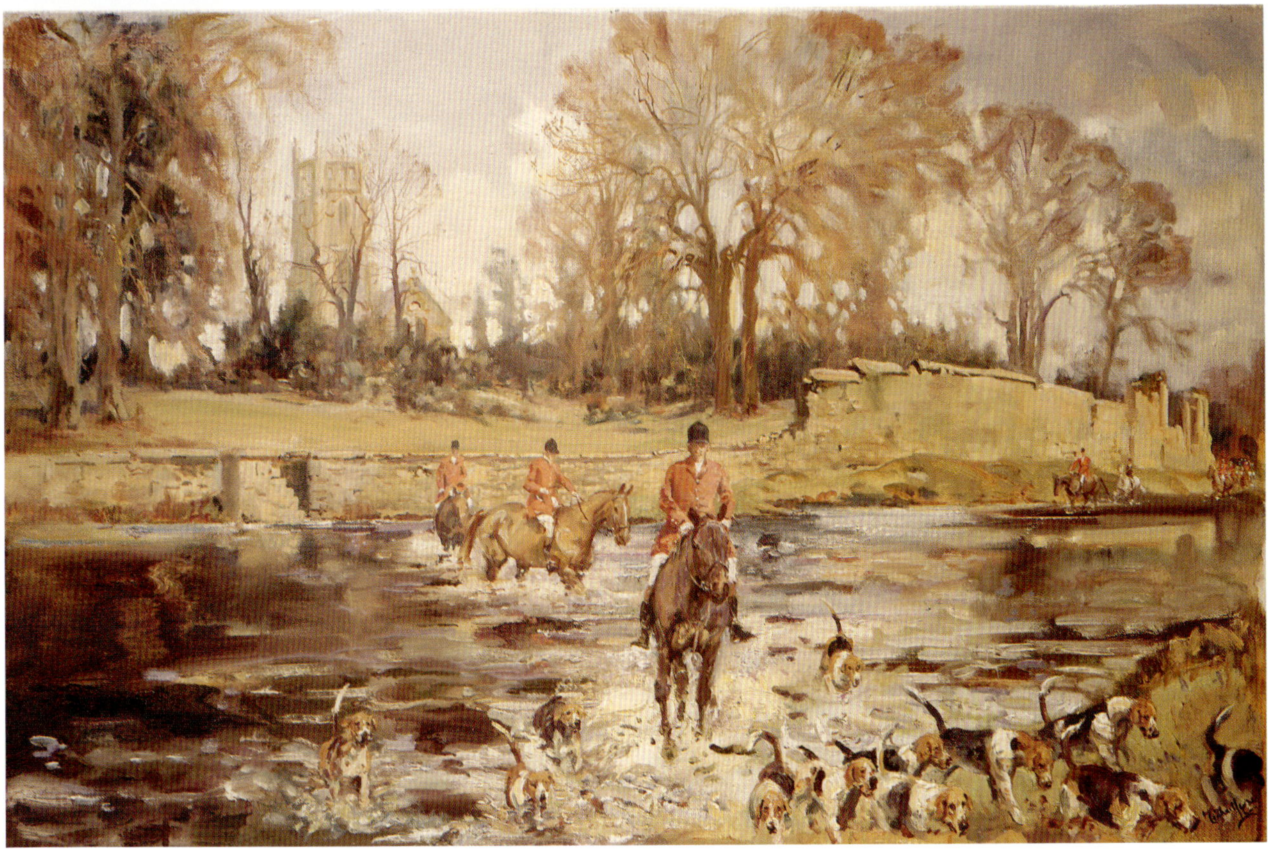

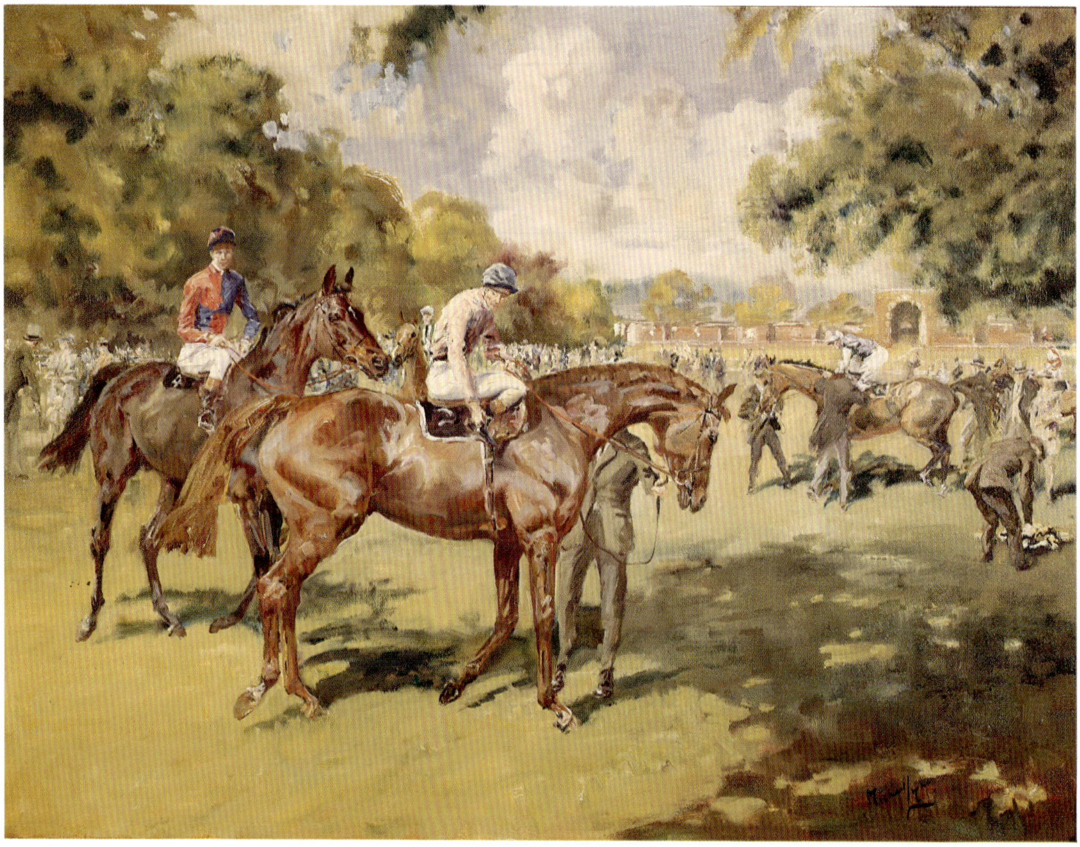

Ascot: The Parade Ring. Signed, oil on canvas, 28 × 36 in (71 × 92 cm).

PLATE 14

(*below*) *Ascot: The Start*, 1964. Signed, oil on canvas, 18 × 24 in (46 × 61 cm).

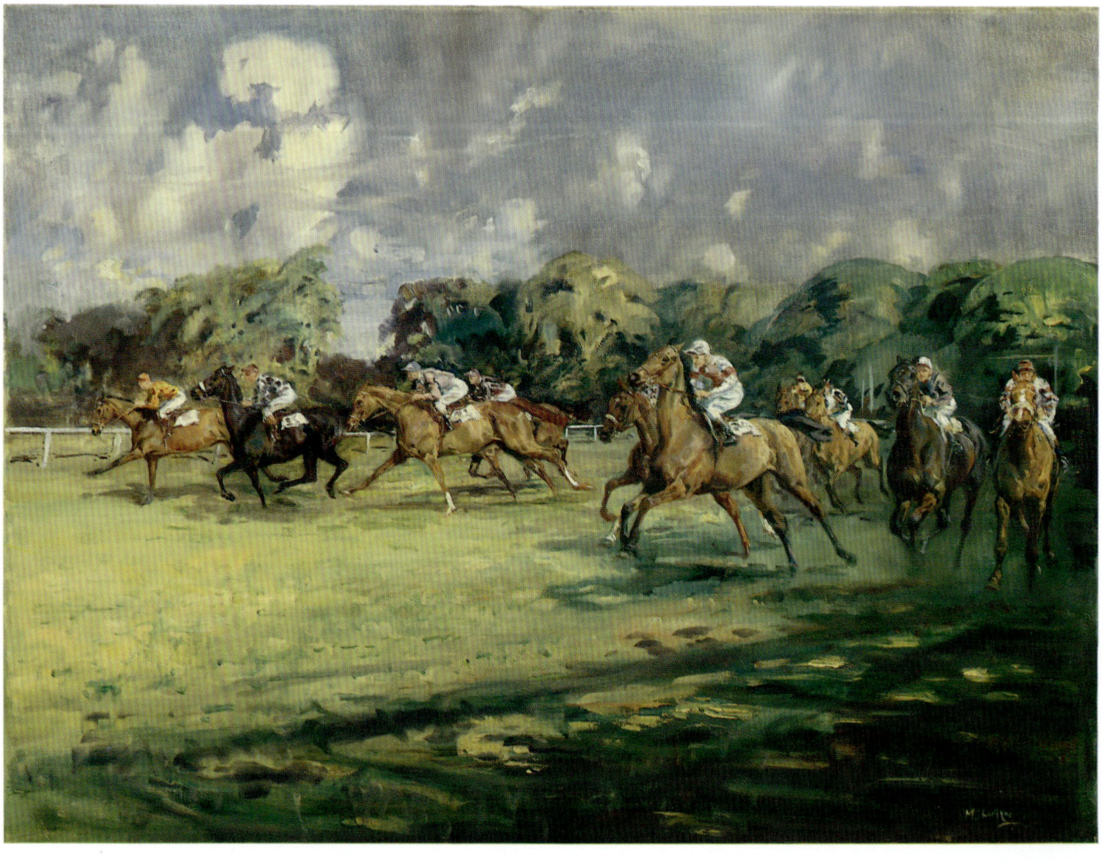

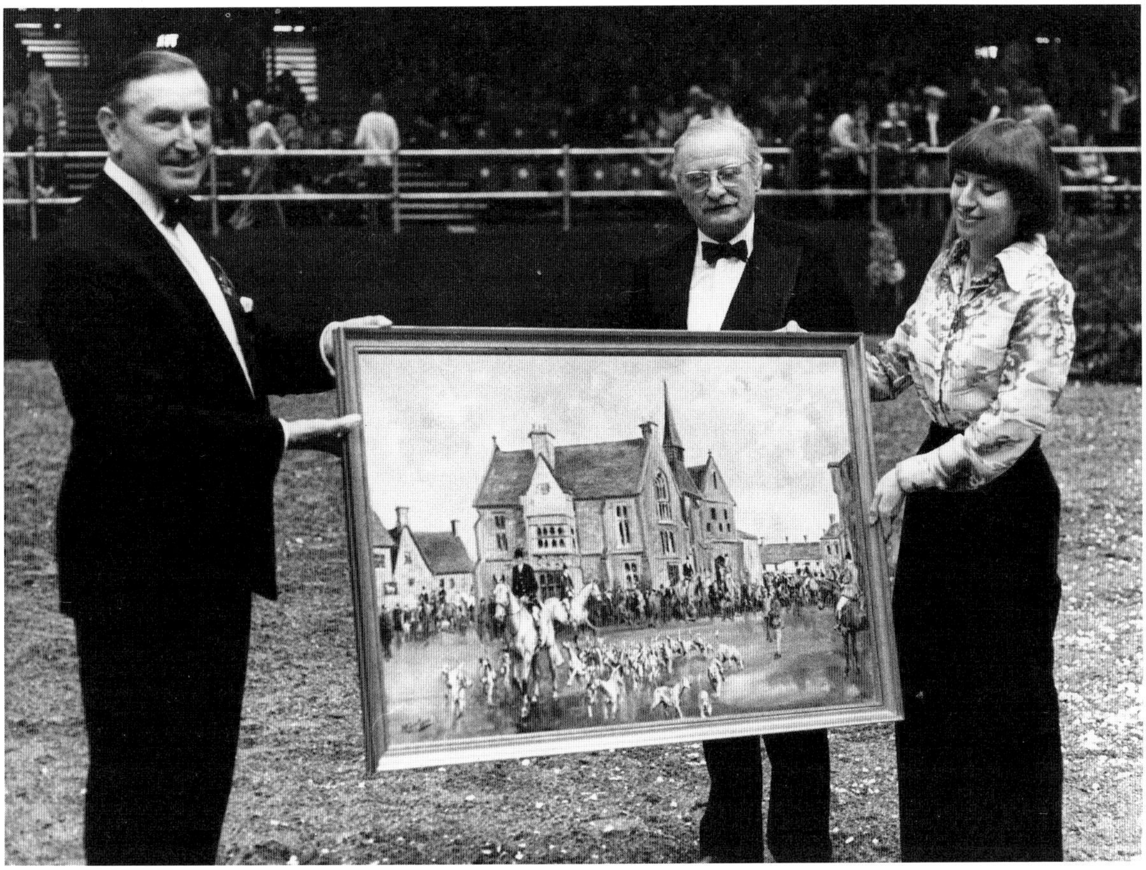

Michael was most generous with his giving to field sport and equestrian causes and in 1977 he gave the British Horse Society a 24 × 36 in (61 × 92 cm) oil painting of *The Heythrop at Stow on the Wold* with the then retiring Master, Captain Ronnie Wallace. It was raffled at shows throughout the summer at 50p a ticket. Here Michael can be seen at the Horse of the Year Show with Dorian Williams and the winner.

of effort in re-establishing himself after the war and the prodigious labours of the past twelve years had taken their toll and were undermining both his health and his ability to paint. After two score years as a professional sporting artist, Michael had the self-knowledge to accept this fact, and that his painting and health would in future be of uneven quality.

Without being unkind, one can draw an analogy with the racing folks saying 'a horse has run out of miles'. That however a successful a horse is, it can only retain its excellence for a limited period. So it was with Michael, two score or more years had passed and he realized that pneumonia and a distressing and painful infection of the inner ear would limit his capacity both to paint to the standard and produce the volume that he had previously accepted as norm.

Personal courage was a characteristic of Michael. He kept going, albeit at a reduced capacity. Two further one-man London exhibitions followed in 1976 and 1979. Each attracted little attention from the critics, even adverse comments were absent.

Stella A. Walker saw much to admire in each, though she also commented 'artists of today might well consider facial detail and not shirk it' in a reference to one of the pictures on view in the 1979 exhibition although this personal quirk was present in Michael's first published print (1936). The public were presented with an exhibition of uneven quality, a thing never heard of before in a Lyne exhibition. Good paintings such as *Stag at Bay* (*see Plate 6*) and *The 1969 Grand National: First Time Round, Becher's Brook* and *Hounds in Repose* were shown, but the exhibition also contained works that fell below the artist's normal high standards.

If this was the only problem to be faced, Michael's grit would probably have carried him through, but the situation was compounded by a further problem: *The Michael Lyne Sketchbook*. Michael had been persuaded by his coursing and publishing friend, Richard Grant Rennick, to undertake an ambitious publishing project in the form of a limited edition publication of watercolour sketches and drawings, each accompanied by a commentary by the artist. The project attracted Michael and characteristically he set to work, selecting the works to be reproduced and preparing the text. It was agreed that the book would

The dust wrapper for *The Michael Lyne Sketch Book*, published 1979.

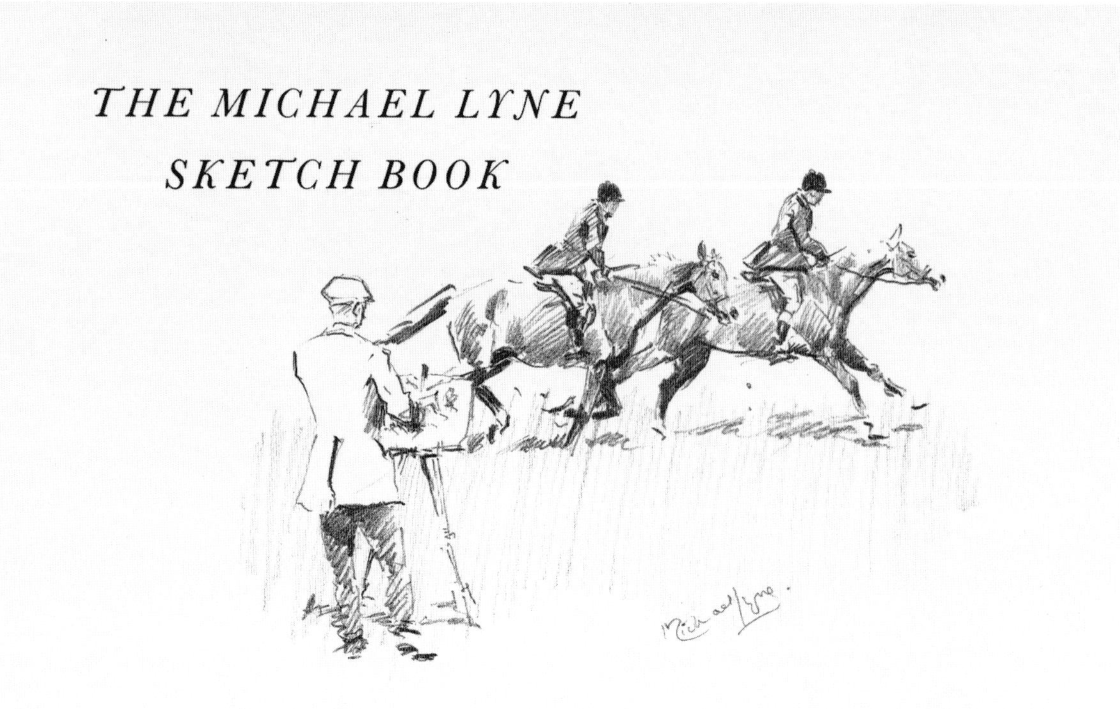

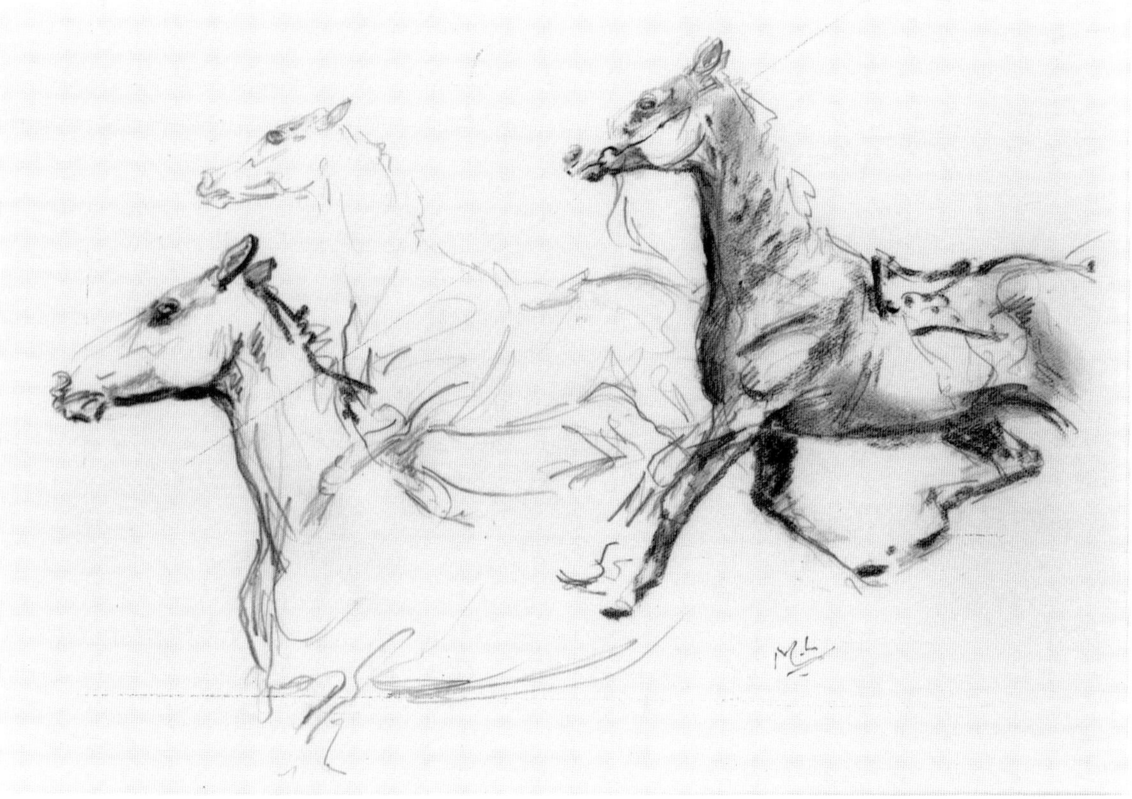

Working study for the oil painting of *The Loose Horse*. This work is typical of the artist's later drawings; visually one can see him thinking.

be launched at the 1979 Frost & Reed exhibition which would contain in addition to the customary oils, all the original material contained in the book. Michael coped with the long tedious process of proof checking and correcting, but as November 1979 approached, it became more and more apparent that the printers would not meet their deadline. Right until the private view, it was hoped that supplies would be available, but they did not materialise and the anticlimax was too much for Michael. He felt that the dual effort of preparing both the exhibition and the book, while coping with the constant fight against failing health was too much. If he had been a younger man, he would have coped, but at sixty-seven he had few reserves on which to draw. What followed was to be repeated on numerous occasions until his death. Frustration and inability to paint produced despair which led to depression from which there seemed to be no escape, for it uncovered a hitherto hidden stream of melancholy in Michael's character.

Against this background, Michael felt that he had no alternative but to retire from active painting. Frost & Reed accepted this decision, though they found it inexplicable. Michael severed his connection with London and abandoned any idea of returning to the United

States. He had no plans for the future. With the help of his wife and daughter, now married, he made what appeared at the time, to be a reasonable recovery, but it became increasingly obvious to family and friends that he would never be the same man again.

Gradually the depression lifted and Michael's general health improved, so that by late 1980 he was contemplating the future with some of his old grit and optimism. Friends rallied round and gave much support, particularly Nigel and Betty Kearsley of Burford. Nigel, an ex-regular army major, is also a good painter of horses and of that peculiar English art form 'conversation pieces'. They saw to it that Michael and Jessie had periodical short holidays by taking them on jaunts around the country and on fly-fishing trips. Michael also much enjoyed the practical therapy of advising Nigel on technical matters relating to painting. Another friend, the owner of Gay Tarquin, which Michael painted as *The Loose Horse*, made it his business each Monday during the season, to take Michael in his Land Rover and follow the Beaufort, great fun, and they both soon became well acquainted with the local pubs.

Michael decided that he would continue painting, how and when he could, such was his urge to create and communicate. He determined to refuse commission work and on a small scale concentrated on works which both attracted him and reflected his interest. The following years saw a steady stream of stylish hunting, foxhound and coursing subjects, all of them highly inventive, original and commanding immediate attention. No longer being physically capable of working long hours at his easel, Michael resumed painting in watercolour, sitting at a small table next to the easel, with his sketchbook propped up in front of him, and easy listening music playing in the background. The studio was to become a place of therapy and pleasure, rather than a dawn to dusk workroom.

Michael, having decided not to accept commission work in order to avoid the pressure of stress which it generated, did break the rule on a few occasions for old established American friends, and although he enjoyed the work, he found it both trying and exhausting. He was always relieved when the work was collected for shipment to the United States.

One of these late American commissions which gave so much pleasure but caused considerable anguish and frustration, was for the Lynes' old friend, J. Fife Symington, and was painted in 1984. Many years before Michael had painted Fife Symington's mother riding sidesaddle on the famous Symington horse, Palau, and it was her son's wish to have a joint, almost life size portrait of his parents standing at the edge of the Maryland Hunt Cup Parade ring. To enable this to be achieved, he sent to Dunfield a photograph of the couple blown up to life size, so that Michael would have a large model for the painting. The finished portrait of *Mr & Mrs Jack Symington* now hangs over the fireplace of the Jack and Arabella Symington Memorial Library in the Maryland Historical Society's building at Baltimore.

A similar commission was for the film star Gregory Peck, and was also undertaken

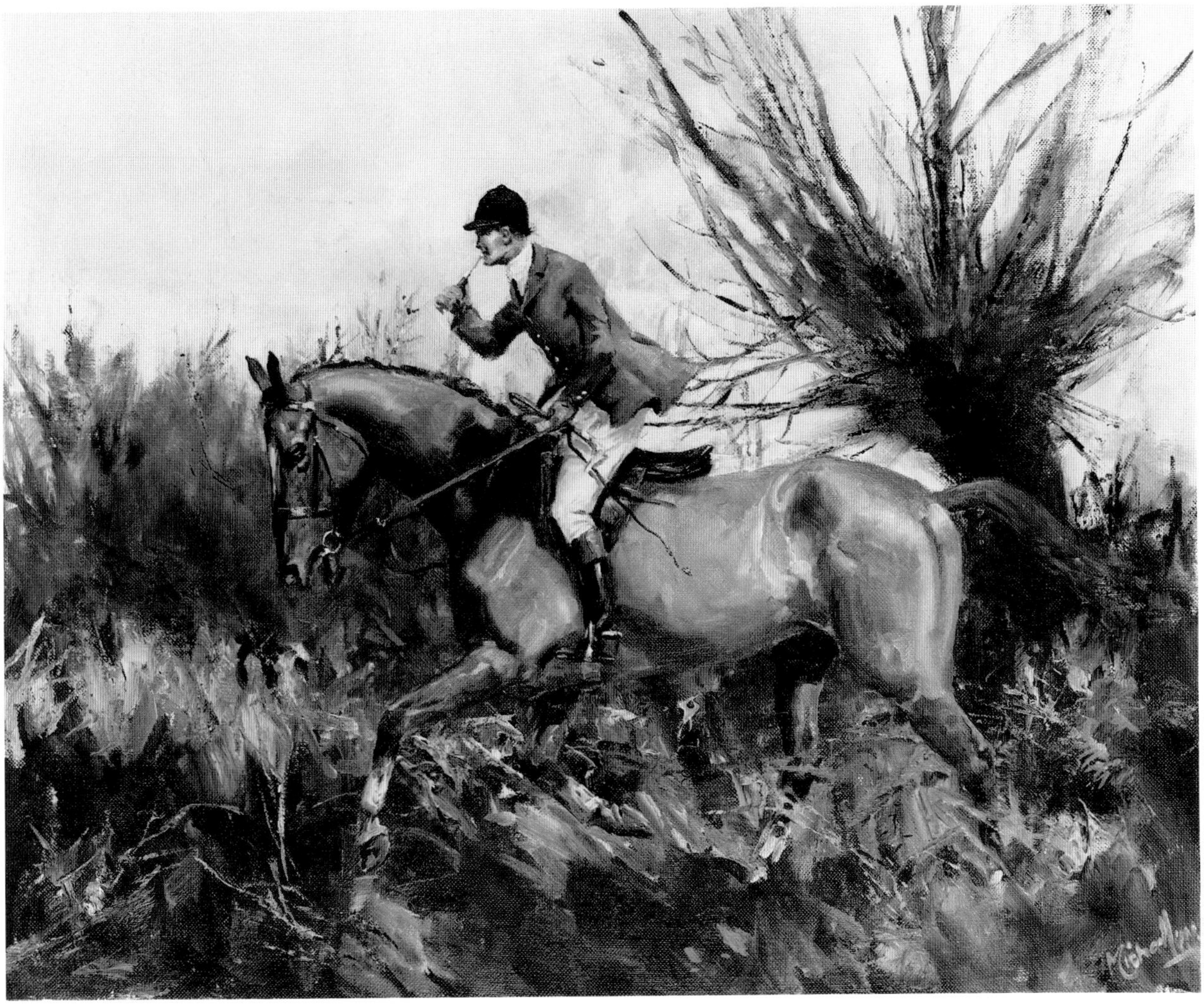

The Huntsman, 1985. Oil on canvas, 20 × 24 in (51 × 61 cm). Published by the Heale Gallery as a limited edition print.

in the same year, depicting the actor's horse Different Class with David Mould up, running in the 1968 Grand National, in which he finished third.

The American connection still continued and in 1985, Michael could write to Stella A. Walker saying 'America was and still is an outstanding seedbed for my efforts'. In 1984 the Lyne's made their final visit to the United States. The occasion was an exhibition mainly drawn from the Vorys Collection and held at the Schumacher Gallery, Capital University, Columbus, Ohio. The Lynes flew out first for a few days with their friends the Symingtons, and then travelled to Colombus. Michael and Jessie enjoyed the visit greatly, it was re-living old times, but they were glad to be back at Dunfield.

In early 1983, the Jockey Club requested Michael to paint and donate a picture of the Grand National, as part of the Aintree Appeal. Michael, who had always been most

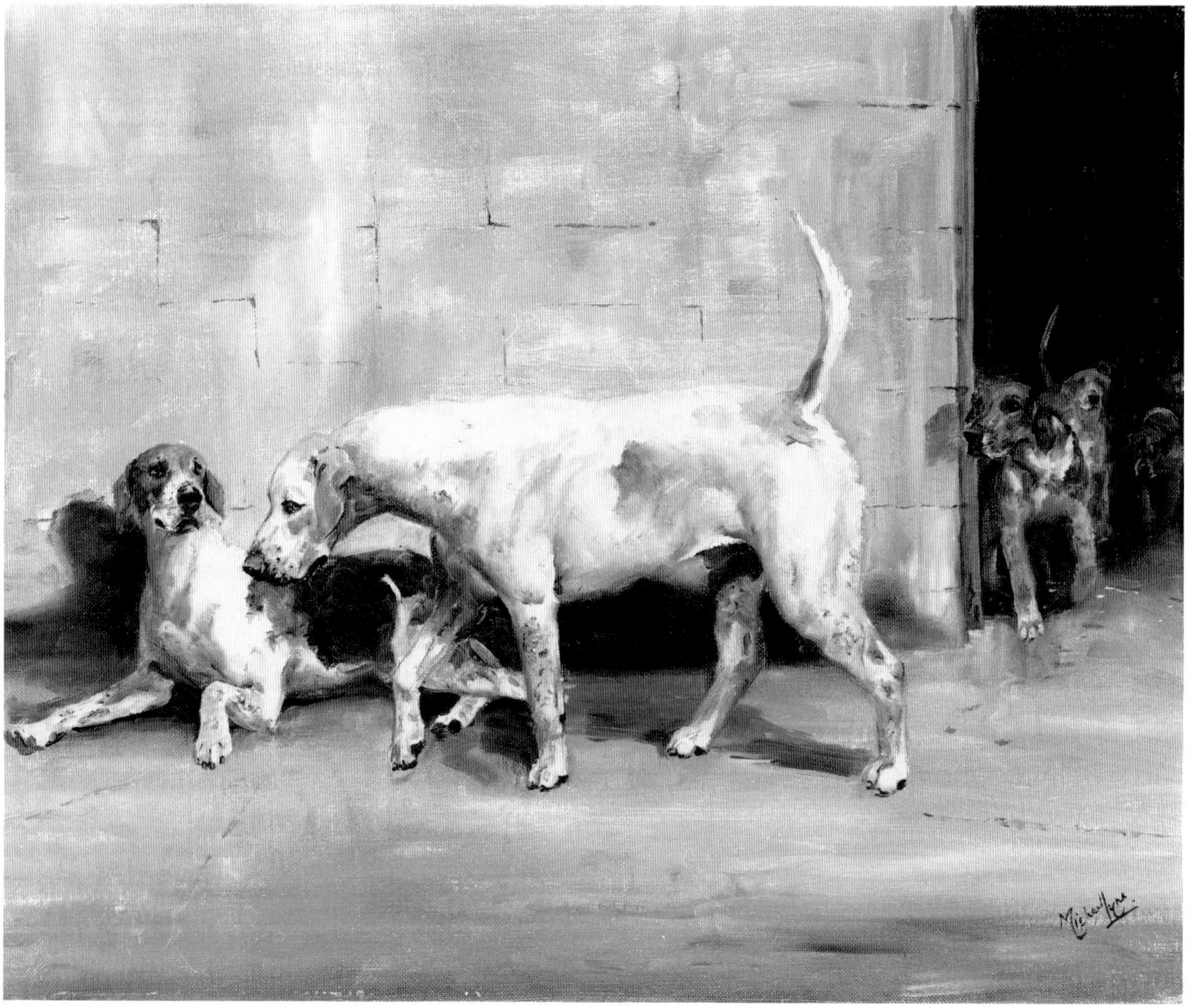

Couple of Foxhounds, 1984. Oil on canvas, 20 × 24 in (51 × 61 cm). Painted by Michael Lyne following a visit to the Stubbs Exhibition at the Tate Gallery, 1984.

generous in giving paintings to causes he supported, particularly the BFFS and the Injured Jockeys Fund, was delighted to do so. The painting was auctioned with many other superb donations at the Grand National Dinner, held at Whitbread's Porter Tun Room in Chiswell Street, City of London, in March. This was to prove Michael's last visit to London and one he enjoyed enormously. It was also the last time he saw his war time CO, Colonel Bill Whitbread. Michael was delighted, when Peter O'Sullivan, as an exceptionally skilled auctioneer, knocked down his painting, *Impressions of Aintree* to Lord Vestey, Chairman of the Appeal.

Although Michael continued painting, it was obvious to those close to him, that each year saw greater demands on his reducing energy and capability. Many who came into contact with the artist during the final years felt that he was aggressive and brusque in manner, little realising that the exterior concealed frustration and isolation. The syndrome which had become apparent in 1979 of failing physical health and melancholia had become more and more familiar. The situation was compounded by occasional remissions of the syndrome and the return of the ability to produce works of the style and quality of the score of years before, only to leave greater frustration and anger when the remission quickly departed.

A further dimension was added to the problem by increasing deafness which induced a deeply felt sense of isolation, and also by increasing respiratory problems.

Michael's final project for *The Field*, apart from two book reviews, were illustrations for a short story by Frank Barrett and illustrations for an article by Dalesman 'Horses of Another Green', both published in the 1982 Christmas edition.

The Muddy Gateway, 1985. Oil on canvas, 20 × 30 in (51 × 78 cm). Published by the Heale Gallery as a limited edition print. The subject matter is very typical of Michael Lyne's down to earth approach and constant search for new approaches to old concepts.

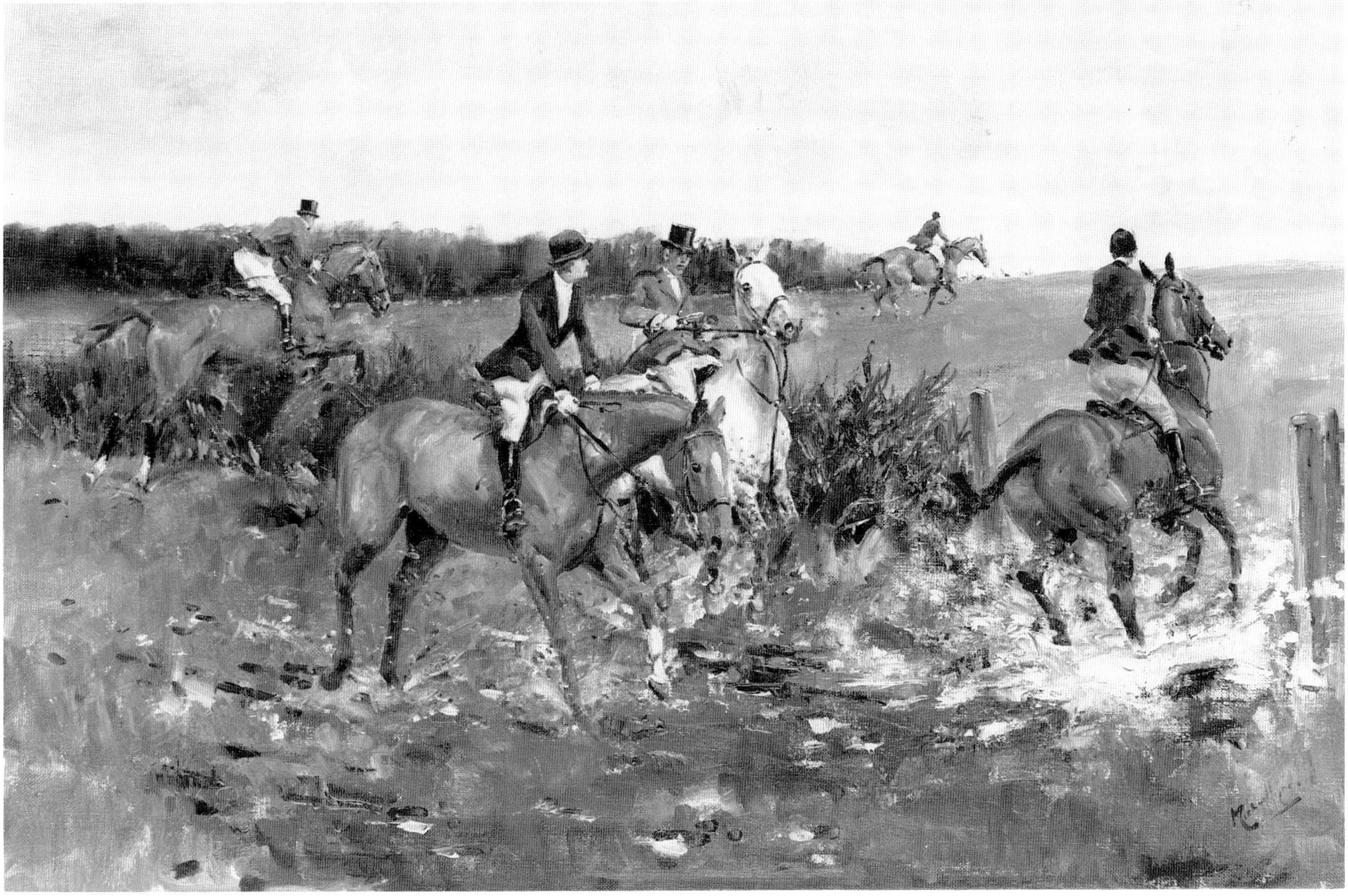

During the closing years of his life, the lack of interest in him and in his work by *Horse and Hound*, *Country Life* and *The Field* was something which Michael felt deeply and caused much pain to the old man. He could not comprehend that the style and content of magazines was changing under the ever-moving forces of modern life. Editorial preferences were now in favour of photographs and *The Field* and *Country Life* were moving away from the old spirit and humour of the country to the newer and more commercial concept of lifestyle magazines, in which field sports had but a small part to play. Michael could accept that times had changed for such magazines as *The Tatler* and that now he would no longer have a painting on its cover or a full centrefold, but he could not accept that *Country Life* and in particular *The Field*, to whom he had given so much, would ignore him.

Oil painting became laboriously slow and while the handling of paint retained almost all of its former skill, the technique and presentation became rather abrasive. Latterly, only three oils were completed, each being on the easel for an inordinate length of time. It is my view that Michael was anticipating death and made in these works valedictory statements – they were the final testament of a lifetimes work, subjects chosen with great care and created with much thought, dedication and labour.

The Fox and Hen is a clear statement of both Michael's honesty as an artist and of his deep personal interest in animals. It recalls the small boy at Upton Bishop, the despair of his nanny, going around the village with a foxbrush attached to the seat of his trousers, and convinced that he was the fox. It also demonstrates Michael's ability to record on a static canvas, the mood, atmosphere and action of a split second in time.

The second painting in the trio is *James Pigg Esq* (from the nineteenth-century Jorrocks stories by R.S. Surtees). This large portrait is, in every way, the complete antithesis of *The Fox and Hen.* A formal equestrian portrait of a huntsman, whose face shows the legacy of a thousand crashing falls, painted from a somewhat unusual angle, the spectator viewing the subject from ground level and looking up to the approaching rider and his attendant hounds. This painting shows the whimsical side of Michael's character. In life this was revealed by his unashamed enjoyment of spaghetti westerns on television, or using children's playground slides. In painting, by such pictures as *Ex Libris* or the heavy old gentleman on the grey in *Would some Pow'r the Giftie Gie Us* (Burns). Capricious notions were much enjoyed by Michael recalling the highly imaginative child of the parsonage, living in a world of his own creation. The picture occupied the easel for a very long period and Michael developed what can only be described as a 'special relationship' with it, and told me that when sitting half asleep and musing in the studio armchair, he had several conversations with Jimmy Pigg! On one occasion he went into the studio, the canvas was empty, and Jimmy was sitting in his chair. 'Ah, I wondered where you'd got to' said Michael.

The final painting of the trio is *Merry England.* 'Bay' de Courcy-Parry commented in 1938 on the feeling that Michael's landscapes had for the timeless quality of the English countryside; his paintings capturing the essential qualities of an older, kinder England, or to use Dalesman's words 'our eternal heritage, England'. Despite the vast number of changes in the intervening fifty years, Michael's view remained exactly what it had been in the 1930s, and he remained in that last golden age, almost in a time warp, capturing the pageantry and glamour of horse and hound in an Arcadia that provided a natural back-cloth for foxhunting – a countryside that could only fully realize itself by having a Field streaming across it in full cry. It is no coincidence that *Merry England* contains exactly what Dalesman commended half a century before. Michael is saying goodbye to his natural habitat, indeed the painting could be called 'Our Eternal Heritage, England'. Against a background of low hills and high fast moving cloud, the Field winds its way along a country lane, hounds and huntsmen, a reworking of the 'James Pigg' grouping, make their way to the first cover. A rear guard of car followers takes the eye into the middle distance and to a large church tower, that of Michael's own parish church of Kempsford, indicating his firm simple faith and that of which he was most proud: of being a parson's son. The Field contains several of his favourite stamp of horse: well-made grey hunters, in the foreground old pasture has given way to plough, but the farmer respects old traditions and has left adequate headlands. As the Field approaches us down the lane, we see

Merry England, 1988. Oil on canvas, 24 × 36 in (61 × 92 cm). Michael Lyne's last painting.

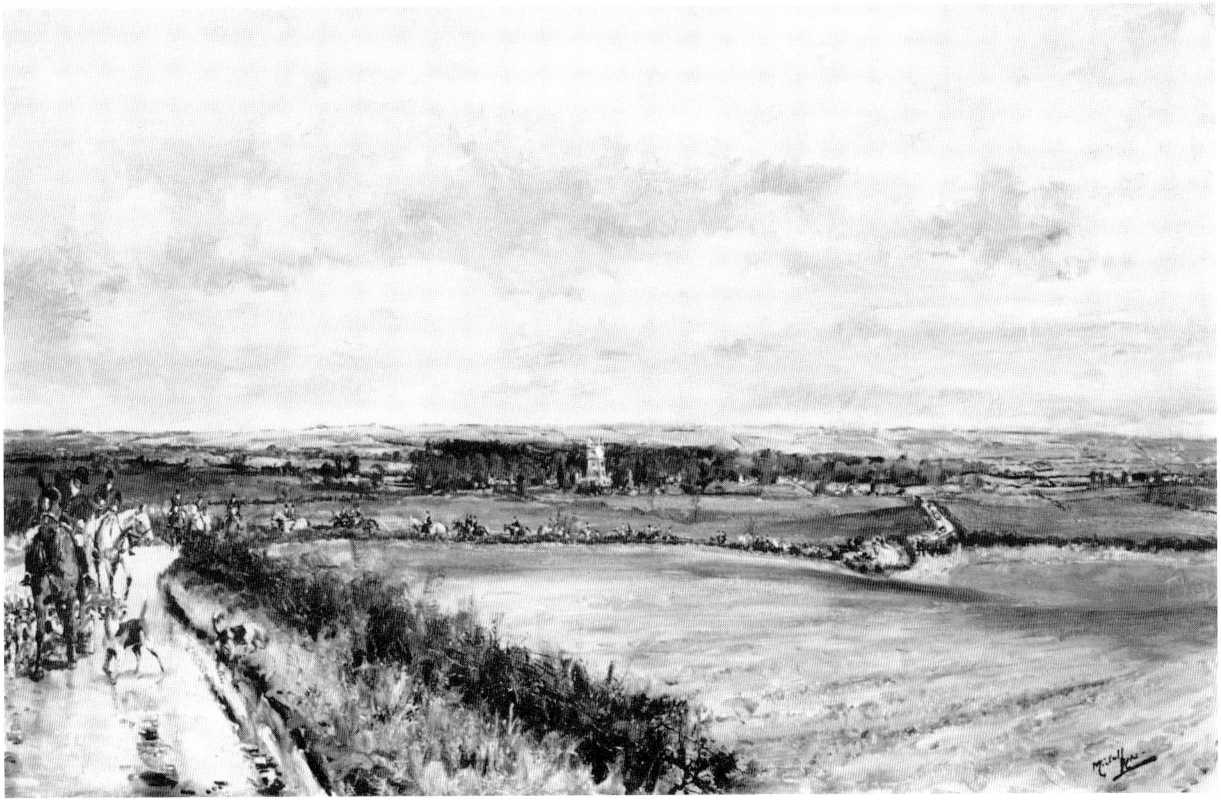

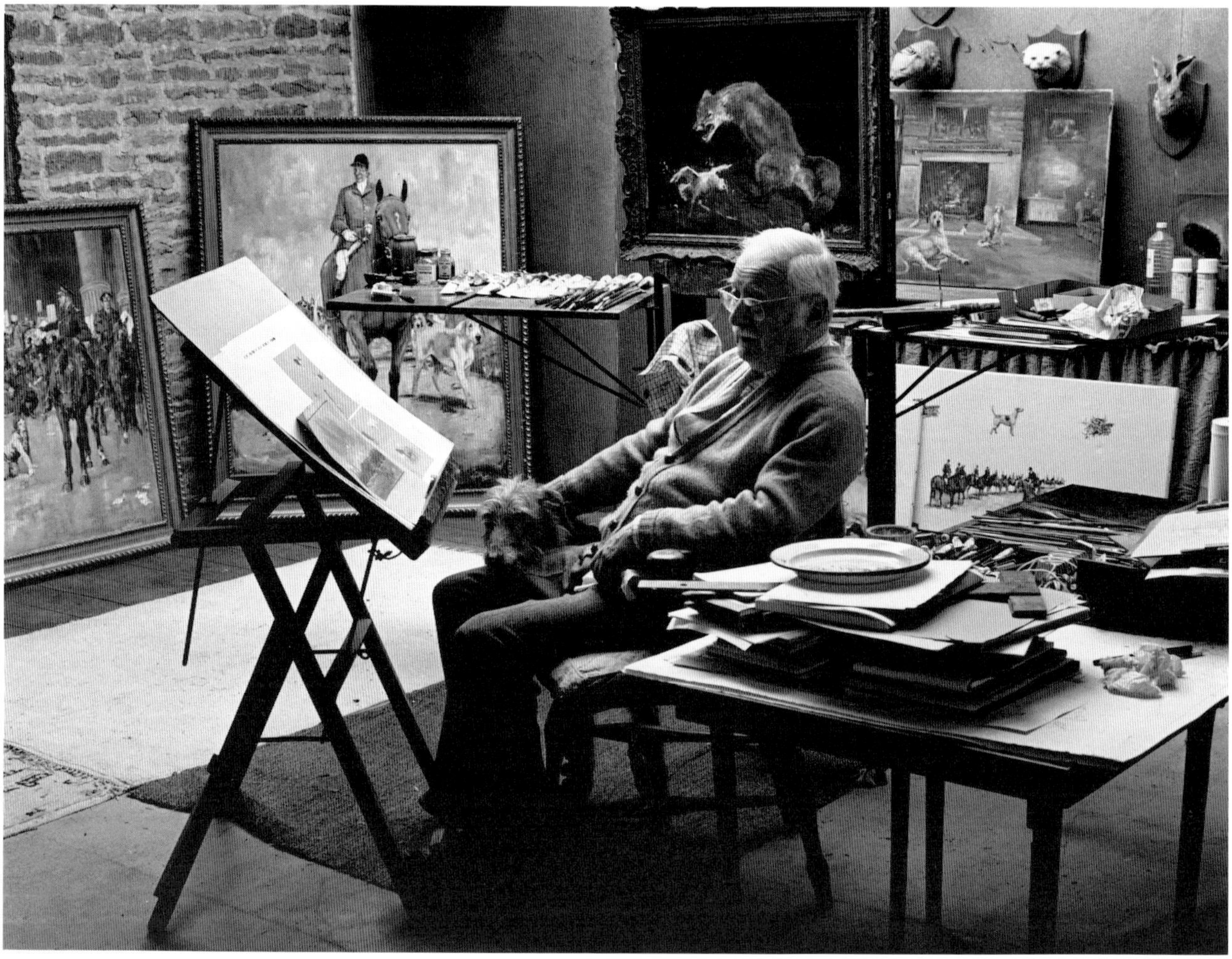

The last days: Michael Lyne in the Studio at Dunfield in the summer of 1986. In the background are two of Michael's last three paintings: *James Pigg, Esq.*, and *The Fox and Hen.* Also in the photograph is Michael's last dog, the lurcher Lupin.

how perfectly it all belongs together, the land, church, horses, hounds and huntsmen, all at ease with each other, all accepting that they formed that which was for so long, the privilege of England and to which our painter is saying his last farewell.

Gradually Michael's world shrank, he no longer followed hounds, the Salukis were not worked, nor coursing meetings attended. He gave up visiting Badminton Horse Trials. Dunfield, its dogs, studio and pond became his world, a microcosm of all that had been worth while in the past. The Kearsleys continued to ensure that Michael and Jessie had a short spring holiday and if Edward and his family were home from West Africa, they would arrange a few days on Exmoor or in the Lake District. One special event of the final years was the great Dunfield Saluki show, attended by owners from all over the United Kingdom. Both the pre-planning and the day itself meant much to Michael and gave him endless enjoyment for many months. But the deaths of his brother Richard, and 'Bay' de Courcy-Parry (aged eighty-eight), were bitter blows not easily set aside.

Plans for a large golden wedding party in the summer of 1990 were also much in Michael's mind during his last months. The planning of the retrospective exhibition which the Heale Gallery organised and which was kindly shown by the Tryon Gallery at their Cork Street premises in April 1989 was a particular source of pleasure and happiness to Michael.

The once prolific output was now reduced to a trickle of watercolour studies, and it was with great pride that Michael produced a small collection for inclusion in the retrospective exhibition. With hindsight it was very much a mind over matter situation, and it will always be a source of regret that I did not recognize it as such at the time. Shortly afterwards I received what was to be my final letter from Michael, suggesting corrections and alterations in the catalogue proofs, but giving no hint at all of distress caused by his physical decline. All the paintings and drawings for the exhibition were framed during February, for delivery to Cork Street in early March. Once the catalogue had been printed, all would be ready, and arrangements were being made for Michael and Jessie to attend the private view and opening by their old friend, Captain Ronnie Wallace, on 4 April. This all gave Michael much happiness. He died on 20 March and following a service at Kempsford Parish Church, was cremated and his ashes buried at the edge of the Dunfield water fowl pond.

Jessie, with the full support of her family, decided that the Retrospective Exhibition should continue and courageously attended the opening. As she said 'it would have been Michael's wish'.

Design for a Christmas card for Driving for the Disabled, 1987.

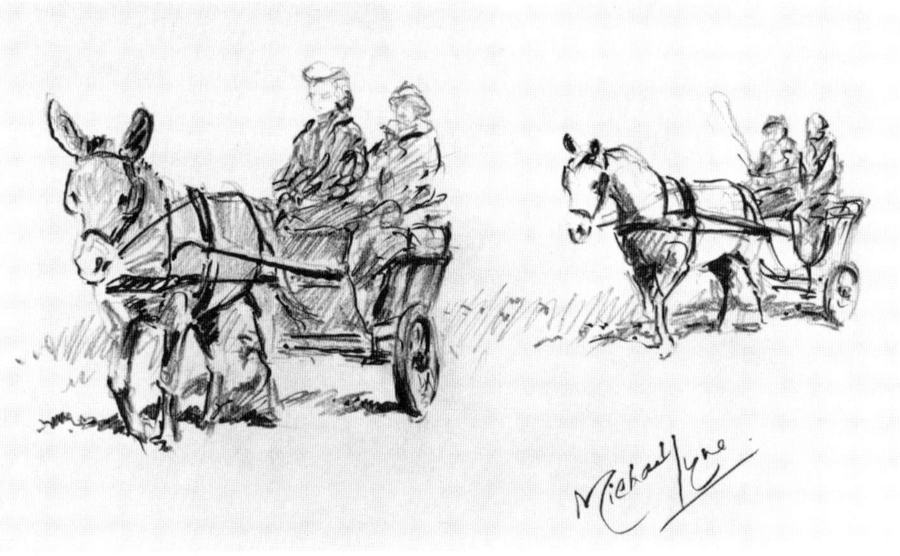

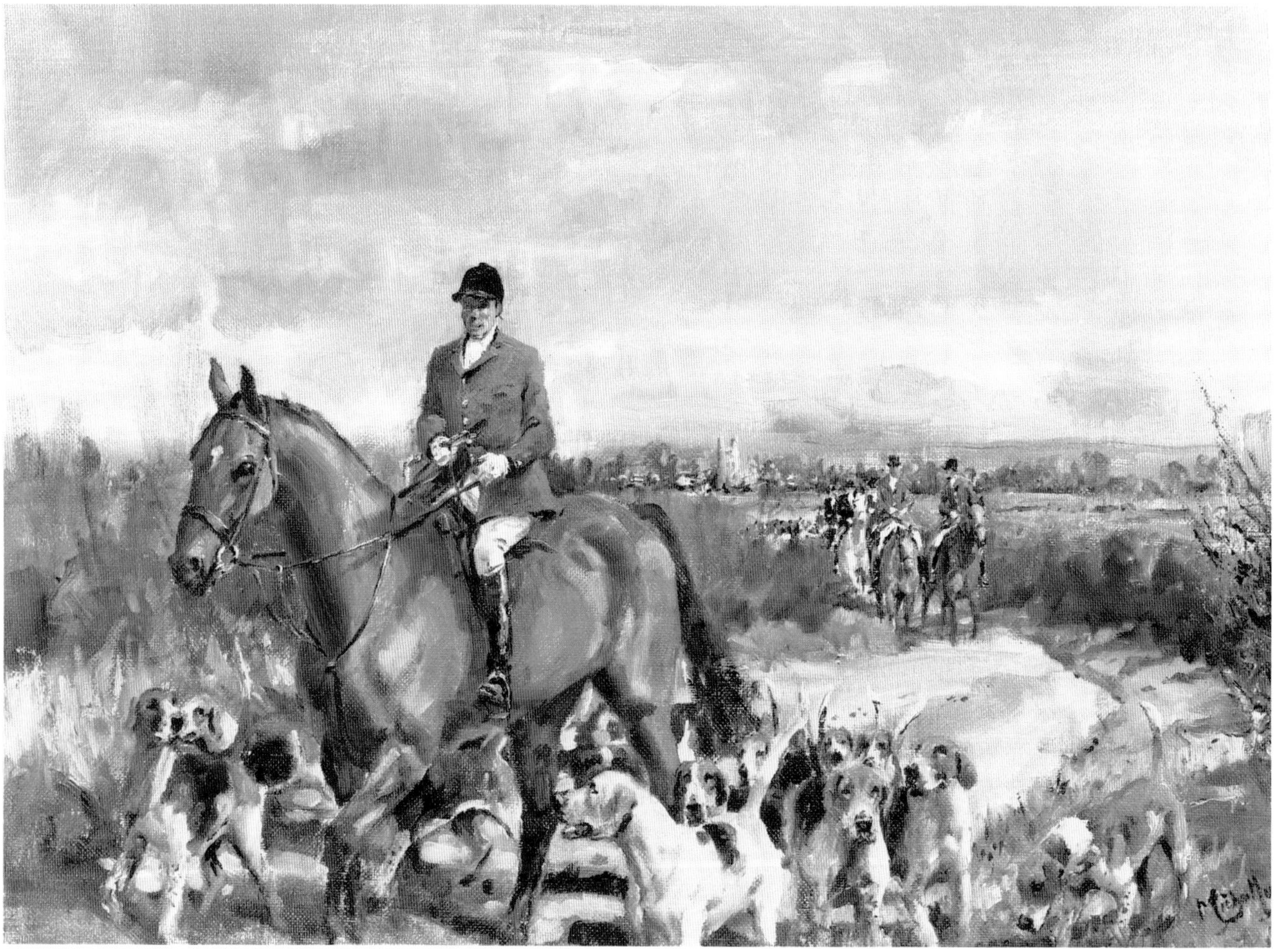

December Sunshine, 1985. Oil on canvas, 16 × 20 in (41 × 51 cm).

APPENDIX I

THE BACON FAMILY

John Bacon was born on 24 November 1740, the son of a Southwark clothworker. He was apprenticed at the age of fourteen to a Mr Crispe of Bow Churchyard in the City of London, and Lambeth, Surrey, where he had a porcelain and china factory. It was from his Master that young John learnt to model figures and proved such an apt pupil that five years later in 1759, he received the first of several premiums for a figure of 'Peace' from the Royal Society of Arts (for the encouragement of manufacturing and industry). Having completed his indentures, he would appear to have remained with his Master for some years before transferring to the employment of Mrs Coade in about 1767. Mrs Coade was the owner of a large factory in Lambeth, producing architectural sculpture and decoration in artificial stone, known as Coade Stone. The formula has long been lost, but a fine example of the factory's work stands at the southern end of Westminster Bridge in the form of a large standing lion. John Bacon carried out a number of very important commissions for the Coade Factory, and at the same time undertook commissions from Josiah Wedgwood to model motifs. During this period he entered the newly opened Royal Academy Schools on a part time basis. He received the first Gold Medal ever awarded by the Academy for sculpture; being elected Associate in 1770, two years after the Royal Academy's foundation, and a full member in 1777.

In 1778 Bacon received a further Gold Medal from the Royal Academy and attracted the attention of the Archbishop of York, who arranged for the thirty-eight-year-old sculptor to model a bust of George III for Christ Church, Oxford; the King was so delighted with it that Bacon made three additional models and in 1779 the King had Bacon appointed sculptor for the huge monument in Westminster Abbey to Pitt the Elder (Lord Chatham). Bacon never looked back and until his death a score of years later (1799), enjoyed continual success. Bacon had considerable natural talent and was largely self-taught; he knew intuitively what the public wanted and did his best to give it to them.

From the evidence of Robert Cecil's Memoir, it would appear that Bacon was greatly influenced by the Methodist Evangelical Revival led by the brothers John and Charles Wesley and George Whitfield, and was a member of an exclusive London Club, the Eclectic Society, founded in 1783 to keep key members of the Revival in touch with each other and help develop Methodist policy.

John Bacon died in 1799 and was buried in Whitefield's Tabernacle, Tottenham Court Road, which was demolished at the end of the nineteenth century and now forms the site of the American Church in London. Of the sculptor's two sons, John the younger (1777–1859) was the more successful. Thomas (1773–1832) worked in his father's studio and exhibited at the Royal Academy, but lacked both talent and the perception of public taste. After his father's death he assisted his younger brother, John, to complete the unfinished work in the studio, but shortly after 1800 all trace of him was lost.

John Bacon the Younger was both trained by his father and the Royal Academy Schools. At the age of sixteen, he won a Silver Medal, followed by a Gold Medal at the age of twenty for a statue of Cassandra and in 1799, on his father's death, he took over the business. With the large volume of works in hand he held, in 1803, the first ever public commercial exhibition of sculpture. For almost thirty years John the Younger enjoyed a successful and prosperous professional life, but changes in taste and fashion, forced him into retirement at the early age of fifty-three.

John Bacon the Elder's enthusiasm for religion was inherited by his grandsons Francis and John. Francis Bacon became the Rector of Wymondham, near Oakham, Rutland, and John Bacon the first incumbent of the remote Berkshire parish of Lambourn Woodlands. The Revd Francis Bacon's son, Francis, became a Lieutenant of the Royal Marine Artillery but resigned his commission to design and market a hammerless breach loader shotgun, to be produced in Birmingham and sold through a chain of agents. In its original form it was designed with a single barrel, possibly with the view to its being used as a service rifle. Subsequently it became a 'Siamese Twin' and was marketed as a sporting shotgun. This gun enjoyed a short vogue in the very early 1870s, but disappeared after 1874 – gun experts consider that Lieutenant Bacon made a very creditable effort to popularise an unconventional shotgun and helped prepare the way for the next stage of the sporting gun development. Throughout his life, Michael Lyne always shot with his inherited 'Bacon Patented' shotgun.

John Bacon, the third, with his young Jewish bride, moved to his Berkshire parish in 1837, where they remained for twenty-five years, raising a family of four sons: Maunsell John and Harry Vivian, both to become clergymen, John Mackenzie making something of a reputation as a pioneer in scientific aeronautics and Francis, a successful architect, who lived in Earlstone, Burghclere, and was the maternal grandfather of Michael Lyne. The Revd John Bacon's wife was born in London during 1811 and lived to be over one hundred years of age, retaining all her faculties and being able to read and write, without the aid of spectacles, until her death during the First World War. A delightful photograph exists of this very old lady, nursing her great-grandchild, John Lyne, with Richard and Mary Lyne in the background, and depicting one hundred and eighty-one years of family life, and whilst this may not in any way be a record, it is a remarkable demonstration of the strength and continuity that was once the backbone of England (see page 21). Mary Lyne, today Mrs Mary Winnington-Ingram, is extraordinarily proud of her great-grandmother and drew the writer's attention to the view of George Bernard Shaw, the

Irish Playwright, who said with his usual sagacity that 'all creative people should have a Jewish great-grandmother'. Michael Lyne, too, benefited from this advice; for it was from his great-grandmother that he inherited the spontaneous and voluptuous sense of colour so apparent in many of his oil paintings.

With the wonders of genetics and in true family tradition, Francis Bacon of Burghclere's youngest daughter, Cicely Joan (Mrs Richard Arundell Lyne) inherited the practical and artistic qualities of her family, becoming a talented botanical artist who exhibited regularly at the Royal Society of Painters in Watercolours, and also an amateur photographer of distinction, illustrating several books. By the standards of the time, she was both very well equipped and produced work of an extremely high quality, winning many prizes. One of his mother's sisters, Christiana M. Bacon hunted with the Vine, under the Mastership of Sir Nelson Rycroft, for many seasons and having given up riding, followed hounds in a chauffeur-driven car – often tense with excitement. A brother was a keen shot and fisherman and wrote *Enchanted Days with Rod and Gun*.

Michael commented that none of his immediate ancestors, other than his aunt and uncle, had any interest in animals. He felt there is a pre-ordained life pattern formulated for all of us, and to struggle against it can only lead to disaster. So convinced was he of his own calling that the lack of sporting antecedents was of little consequence, though he valued the Bacon connection highly.

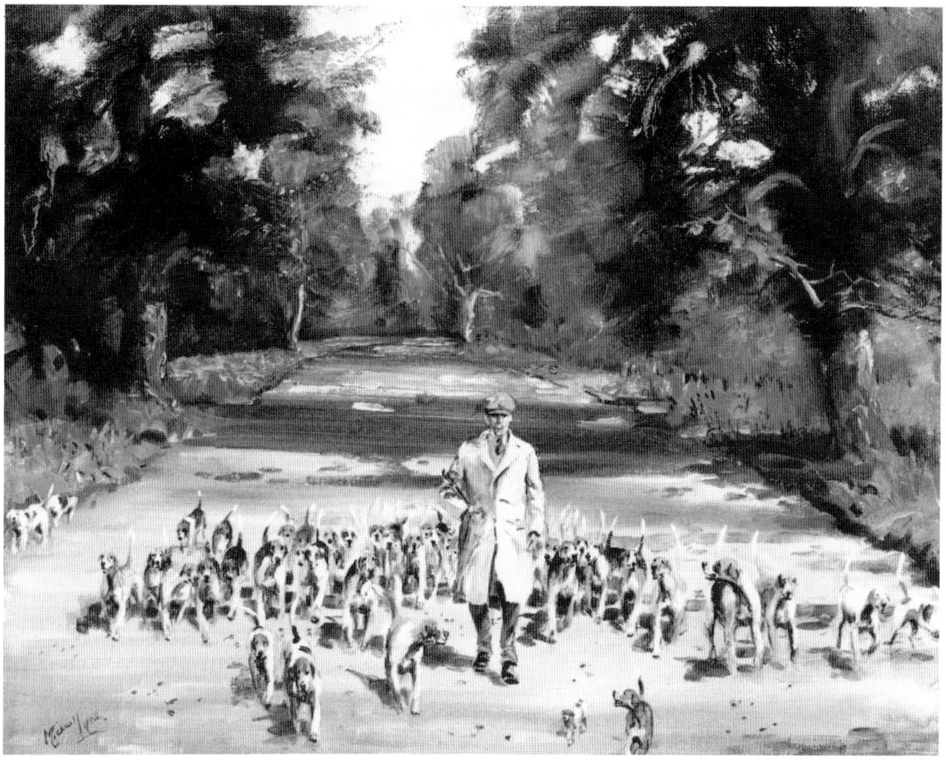

Walking Out, 1979. Oil on canvas, 20 x 24 in (51 x 61 cm). The picture was commenced at the Kildare Kennels, Jigginstown, Naas and completed at the VWH Kennels, Meysey Hampton, Cirencester. In the foreground is the diminutive Jack Russell 'Poker' which Michael acquired from the Kildare Huntsman. Exhibited in the 1979 Frost & Reed Exhibition, the picture was published by the Heale Gallery as a limited edition print.

APPENDIX II

ONE-MAN LONDON EXHIBITIONS

Arthur Ackermann & Sons Ltd
157 New Bond Street, W1

1938 Hunting watercolours relating to illustrations in the Artist's *Horses, Hounds and Country* including: The United, North Cotswold, Warwickshire, Beaufort, Berkeley, Pytchley and the Quorn

Arthur Ackermann & Son Ltd
3 Old Bond Street, W1

1946 61 Watercolours: 54 Hunting; 4 Guernsey Cattle; 3 Nature Studies. Packs included: Quorn, Fernie, Pytchley, Woodland Pytchley, Warwickshire, North Warwickshire, Beaufort, Heythrop, Berkeley, North Cotswold, Ledbury, the D & S and Lady Curre's

1947 35 Watercolours: 27 Hunting, 4 1947 Grand National, 3 Nature Studies and 1 Coursing Study. Packs included: The Belvoir, Cottesmore, Whaddon Chase, Ledbury, VWH, North Cotswold, Beaufort and the Ludlow

1951 35 Watercolours: 28 Hunting, 2 Ascot, Pond at Dunfield, 2 Coursing and 2 Nature Studies. For the first time American packs were included (Middleburg, Millbrook and Piedmont) in addition to 10 British packs

Frost & Reed Ltd
41 New Bond Street, W1

1964 Oils and Watercolours: Foxhunting, Beagling, Flat and National Hunt Racing and Coursing
Major works: *VWH at Water Eaton Vale* (*see p. 115*); *The Cottesmore*; *The Pytchley*; *1964 Cheltenham Gold Cup – Mill House and Arkle backing down to the start and returning to the stables*

1965 23 Oils and 70 Watercolours: Foxhunting, Flat and National Hunt Racing, Coursing and Hound Studies. The watercolours were working sketches for paintings of British and American packs.
Major works: *The VWH Crossing the Thames at Kempsford* (*see Plate 13*); *1965 Grand National: Canal Turn* (*see Plate 10*)

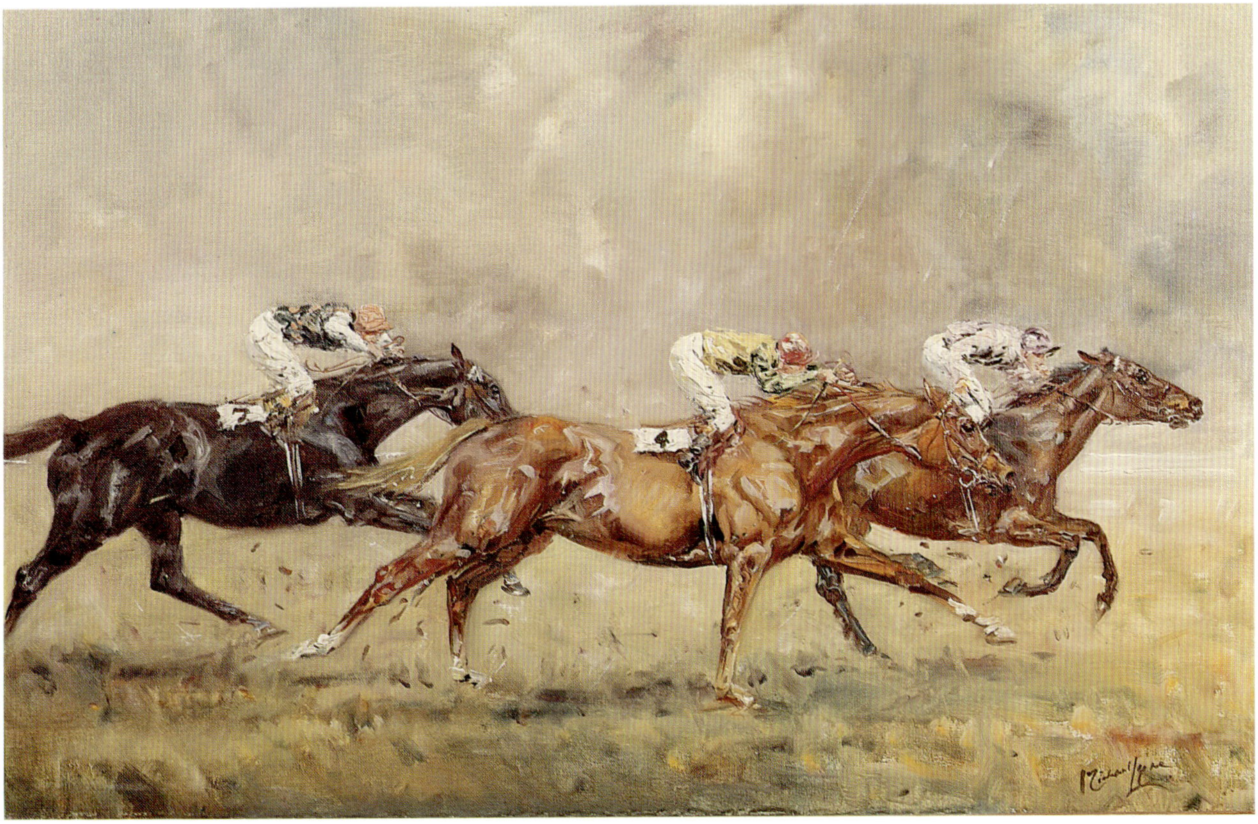

(*above*) *The Last Ounce*, 1969 and (*below*) *Photograph for Second and Third*. Both signed, oil on canvas, 24 × 36 in (61 × 92 cm).

PLATE 15

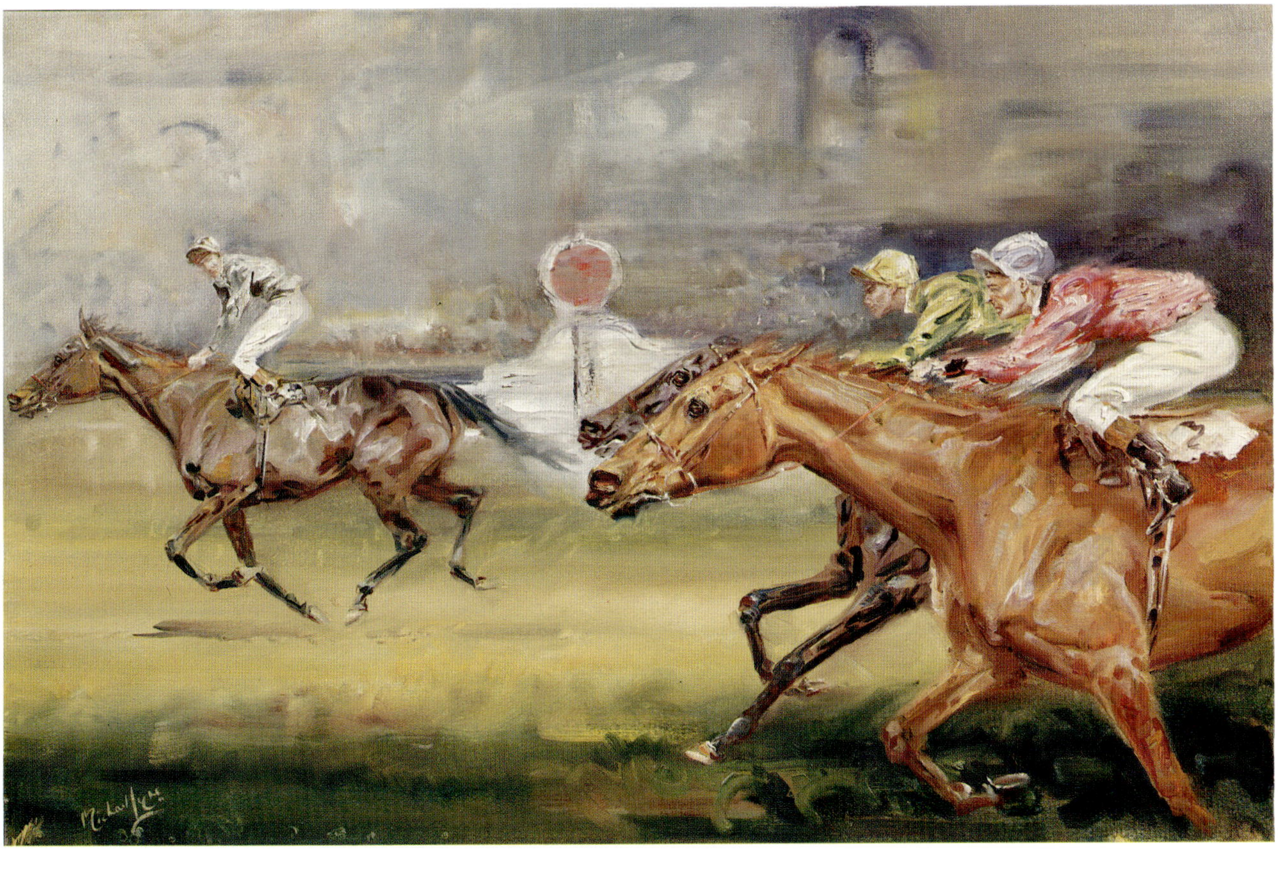

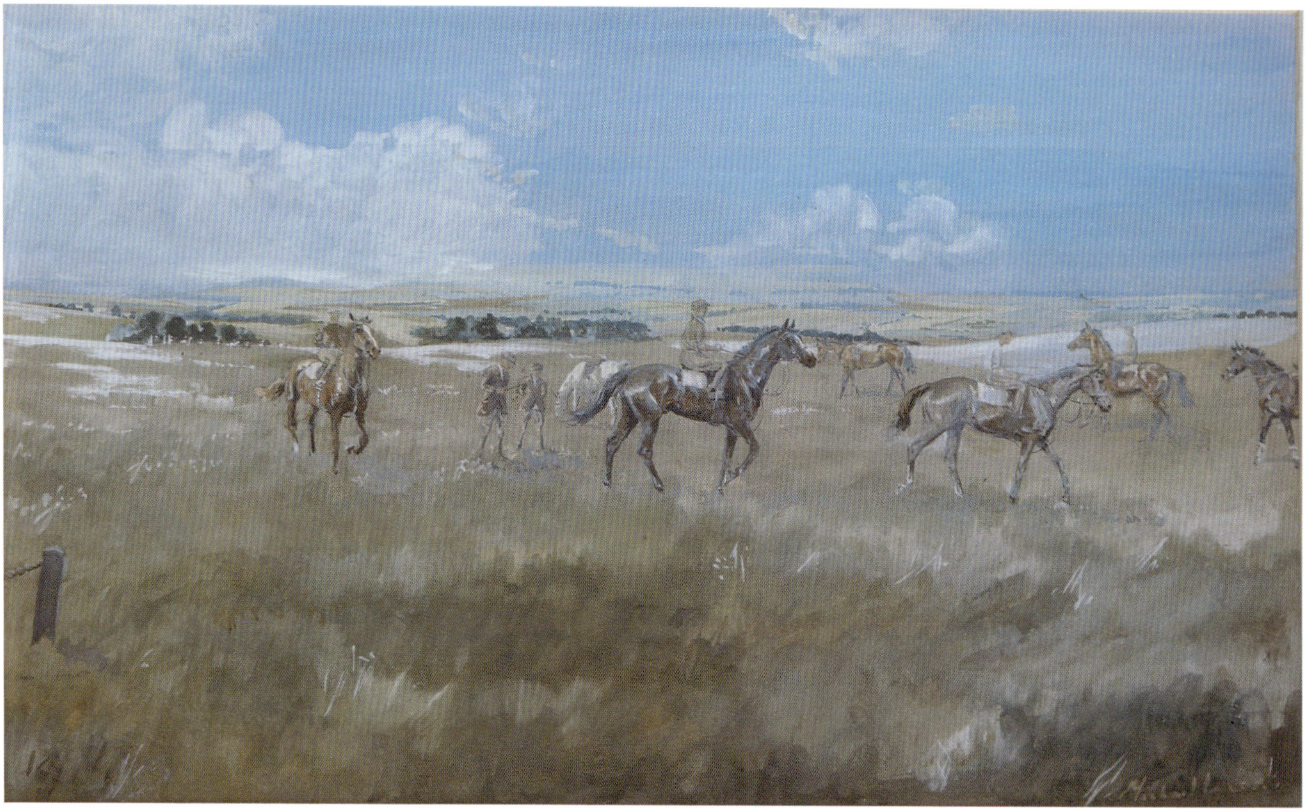

(above) Racehorses being exercised on Cleeve Hill, above Cheltenham, 1935. Signed and dated, watercolour, 8.5 × 12.75 in (22 × 32 cm). A fine example of Michael Lyne's early work. *(below) The Cotswold Hunt, a Lawn Meet at Sudgrove House*, 1975. Signed, oil on canvas, 24 × 36 in (61 × 92 cm). Pat and Sam Koechlin-Smythe can be seen bringing refreshments to the hunt.

PLATE 16

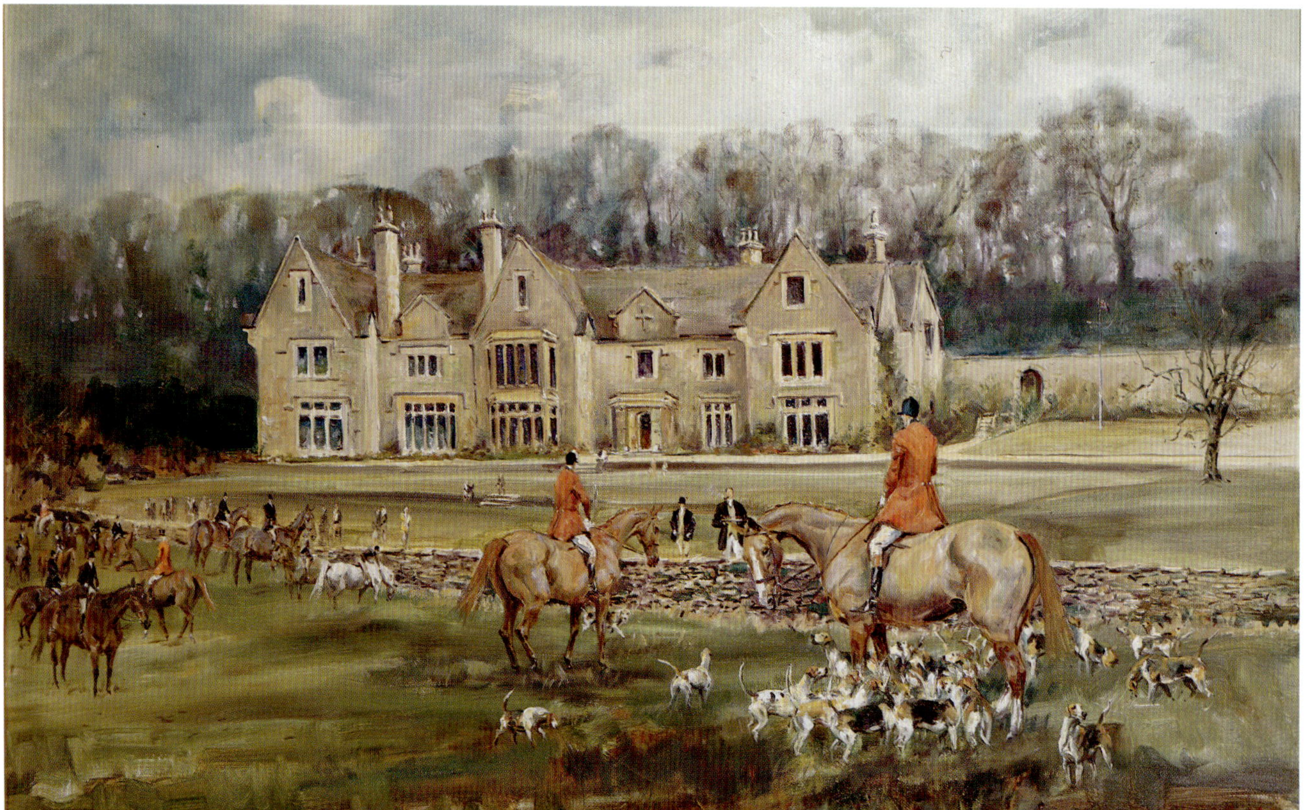

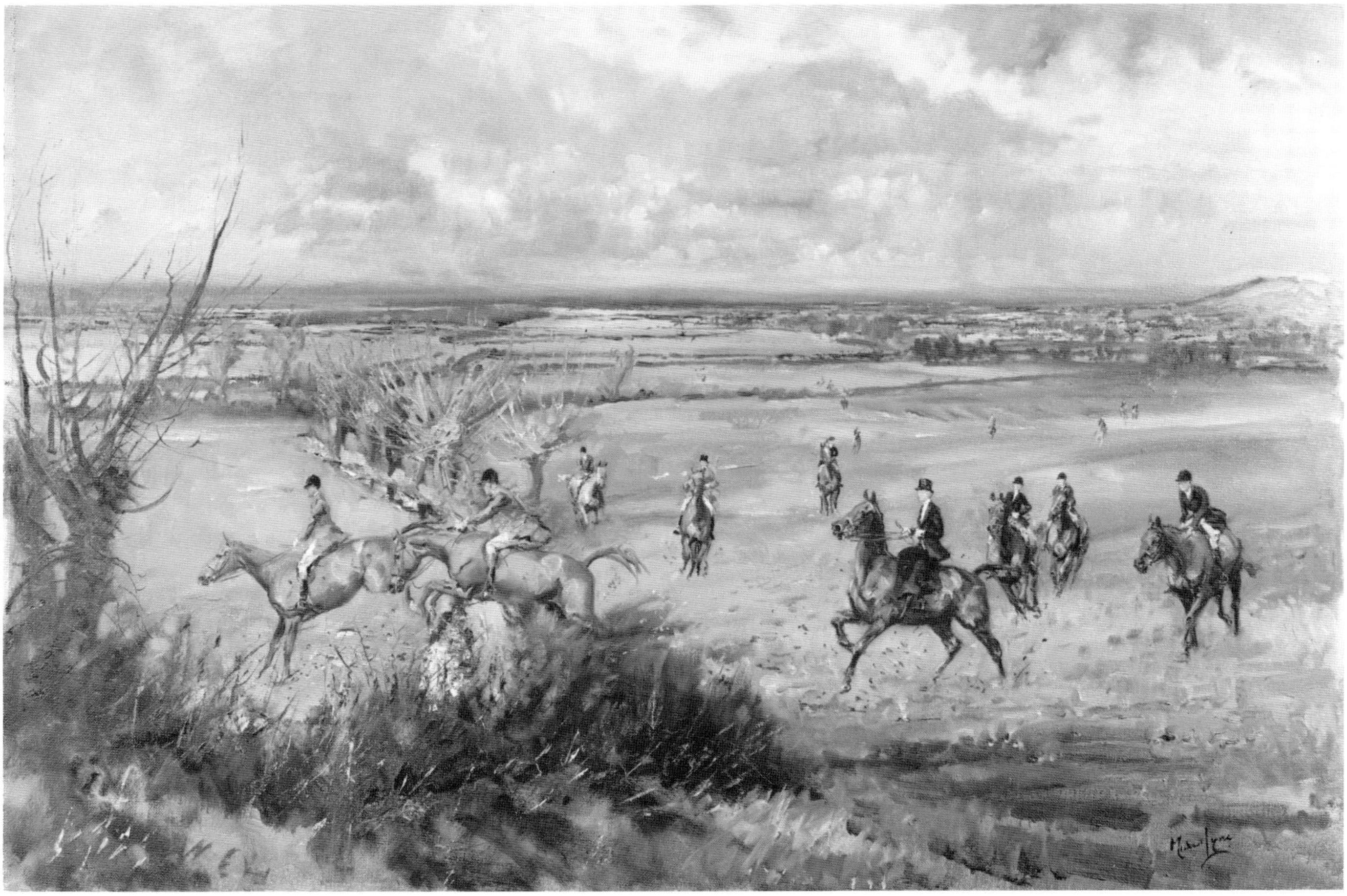

The VWH at Water Eaton Vale. Oil on canvas, 24 × 36 in (61 × 92 cm). It was included in the 1964 Frost & Reed Exhibition. Stella A. Walker, in *Horse & Hound*, commented that the painting illustrated how well Michael Lyne understood the job in hand.

1967 38 Oil Paintings: Foxhunting, Staghunting, Flat and National Hunt Racing; Coursing and Hound Studies
Major works: *Kennel Fight*; *1967 Grand National: the Twenty-third Fence (see Plate 10)*; *Staghunting: the Lay-On*; *The Old Berks on the White Horse*; *The Dumfriesshire*

Frost & Reed at The Christopher Wade Galley
28 Bruton Street, W1

1969 49 Oil Paintings: Foxhunting, Staghunting, Flat and National Hunt Racing, Stalking, Coursing and Hound Studies
Major works: *I Think It's Going to Clear*; *The Huntsman (see Plate 12)*; *The Whipper In*; *The Quorn near Wymeswold*; *The Quorn from Ella's Gorse; Stag at Bay (see Plate 6)*; *VWH at Ampney St Mary*; *Arabians Racing at Busetta (see Plate 11)*; *VIP*; *Marking to Ground (see p. 89)*

M. Jean Bocquillon's Buckhounds in the Forest of Compiègne. Oil on canvas, 30 × 20 in (76 × 51 cm). It was exhibited at Frost & Reed in 1976.

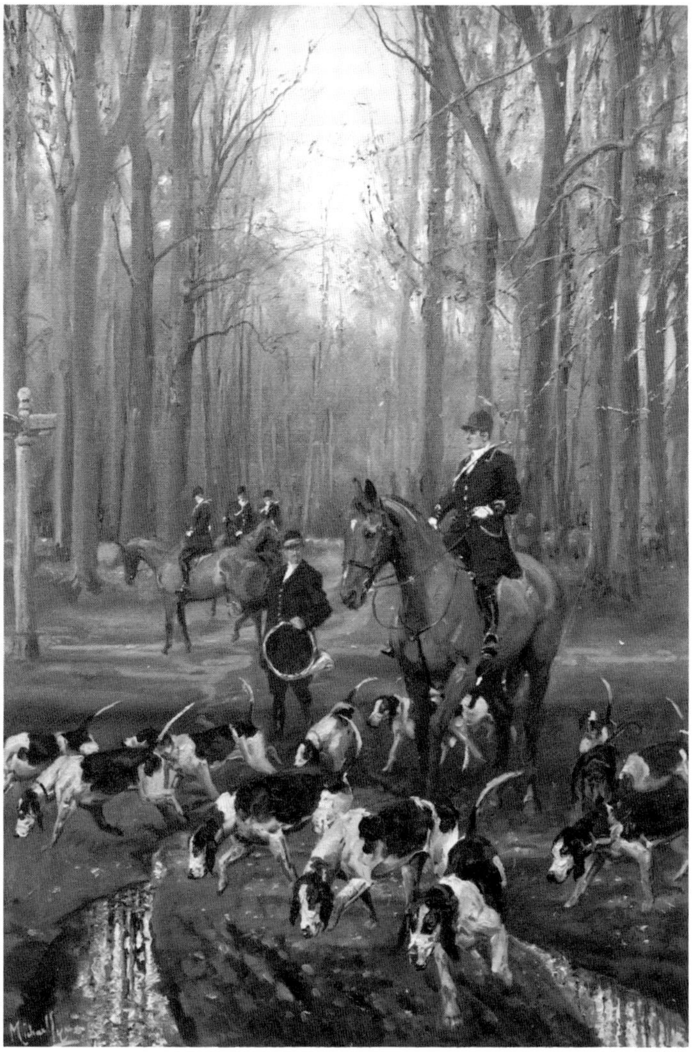

1971 Selection of Oil Paintings: Hunting, Racing and Field Sports – including four paintings shown in the British Pavilion at the World Exhibition of Hunting, Budapest
Major works: *The Warwickshire near Compton Wynyates* and *The Warwickshire at Compton Wynyates*

1975 Selection of Oil Paintings: Foxhunting, Staghunting, Flat and National Hunt Racing, Stalking, Hound Studies and an Aerial View.
Major works: *The North Cotswold at Trafalgar*; *The Heythrop at Redesdale*; *The Scarteen*; *Rest for the Weary* (*see Plate 3*); *Summertime*; *Aerial View*; *The Hunt*

1976 19 Oil Paintings: Foxhunting, French Staghunting, Arab and National Hunt Racing, Stalking, Four-in-Hand Driving
Major works: *Buckhounds in the Forest of Compiègne* (*see p. 114*); *M. de Rothschild's Staghounds – The End* (*see Plate 5*); *The Belvoir at Hough on the Hill*; *A Ploughing Match*; *Stalking – Black Corries*

1979 31 Oil Paintings: Foxhunting, Staghunting, Flat and National Hunt Racing, Stalking, Coursing (Bronze Group), together with the original watercolours and drawings from *The Michael Lyne Sketchbook*
Major works: *Walking Out* (*see p. 111*); *Out to Grass* (*see p. 75*); *1969 Grand National: First Time Round Becher's Brook*; Coursing Group of a Brace of Greyhounds and a Hare (Bronze edition of 10) (*see p. 95*)

The Tryon Gallery
23/24 Cork Street, W1

1989 Retrospective Exhibition organised by The Heale Gallery, Curry Rivel, Somerset. 8 Oil Paintings, 58 Water Colours and 32 Drawings covering the 51 years 1938 – 1988 and every aspect of the Painter's art

OTHER ONE-MAN EXHIBITIONS

Provincial

1972 Liverpool – Adelphi Hotel – Grand National (organised by Frost & Reed)
1981 Stowe School – Game Fair (organised by Heale Gallery)
Dublin – Combridge and Son (organised by Heale Gallery)
1983 Bath – Cleveland Gallery (organised by Heale Gallery)

United States

1950 Scott & Fowles – New York
1958 Kennedy Galleries – New York
1972 National Museum of Sport – New York (organised by Frost & Reed)
& 1974
1984 Schumacher Gallery, Capital University – Columbus, Ohio (paintings from the Vory's Collection supplied by the Heale Gallery, England)
1986 Red Fox Gallery – Middleburg, Virginia
& 1990

APPENDIX III

SIGNED LIMITED EDITION PRINTS

Year	Title	No.	Publisher	Size (in)	(cm)
1938	*The Cotswold at Hawling*	250	E. & S.	7.5 × 10.5	19 × 27
	The Cotswold at Notgrove	250	E. & S.	7.5 × 10.5	19 × 27
	The North Cotswold at Lyne's Barn	250	E. & S.	7.5 × 10.5	19 × 27
	North Ledbury	250	E. & S.	7.5 × 10.5	19 × 27
	The Ledbury	250	E. & S.	7.5 × 10.5	19 × 27
	The Ledbury at Downend	250	E. & S.	7.5 × 10.5	19 × 27
1939	*The United: Dalesman and his Hounds at the Anchor Inn*	200	E. & S.	15 × 13	38 × 33
1946	*The Beaufort Away From Bowl Down Wood, Leighterton*		A.B.	13 × 20	33 × 51
1954	*The Beaufort at Worcester Lodge*	300	F. & R.	15 × 21	38 × 53
	The Cotswold near Shipton Oliffe	300	F. & R.	15 × 21	38 × 53
1956	*The Heythrop at Upper Slaughter*	300	F. & R.	15 × 21	38 × 53
	The Royal Agricultural College Beagles at Jarvis Quarry	300	F. & R.	15 × 21	38 × 53
	The Whaddon Chase at Waterloo	300	F. & R.	15 × 21	38 × 53
1960	*Rokeby Farm, Virginia*	150	F. & R.	15 × 21	38 × 53
1964	*The VWH Point to Point – Impression*	200	F. & R.	16 × 21	41 × 53
1967	*Ex Libris*	500	F. & R.	15.5 × 23.75	39 × 60
	Grand National – The Canal Turn, 1965	700	F. & R.	19 × 25	48 × 64
1971	*Away*	500	F. & R.	23 × 35	58 × 89
	VIP	500	F. & R. (Venture Prints)	26 × 20	66 × 51
1972	*Hurdle Race*	500	F. & R.	24 × 36	61 × 92
1975	*Goodwood, They're Off*	500	F. & R.	24 × 36	61 × 92
	The Belvoir Running into Goadby Gorse	500	F. & R.	24 × 30	61 × 76
	The Belvoir Running away from Goadby Gorse	500	F. & R.	24 × 30	61 × 76
1979	*The Wynnstay: Caught on Top*	750	W.A.S.	12 × 20	30 × 51

Year	Title	No.	Publisher	Size (in)	(cm)
1981	*The Loose Horse*	200	H.G.	15 × 19	38 × 48
1982	*Walking Out*	300	H.G.	14 × 16	36 × 41
	Studies of Foxes	300	H.G.	13 × 20	33 × 51
1983	*Irish Bank*	300	H.G.	8 × 11	20 × 28
	The Heythrop at Blenheim	300	H.G.	7 × 13	18 × 33
	The Beaufort at Worcester Lodge	300	H.G.	7 × 13	18 × 33
	Crawley and Horsham Brandon '80 – Peterborough Champion 1983	200	H.G. & C. & H.H.	9.75 × 12	25 × 31
	Hounds Jumping Over a Brook	100	S.& N.S.B.	9 × 13.5	23 × 34
1984	Set of Four Coursing Studies: *The Slipper*; *The Run Up*; *First Turn*; *The Judge*	500	B.F.S.S.	10 × 15	26 × 38
1985	*The Huntsman*	399	H.G.	14 × 16.5	36 × 42
	The Muddy Gateway	399	H.G.	13.5 × 21	34 × 53

The Beaufort at Badminton, The 10th Duke's 70th Birthday Meet, 1970. Watercolour, 7 × 12 in (18 × 30 cm), published as a limited edition print of 100 by Heale Gallery in 1987.

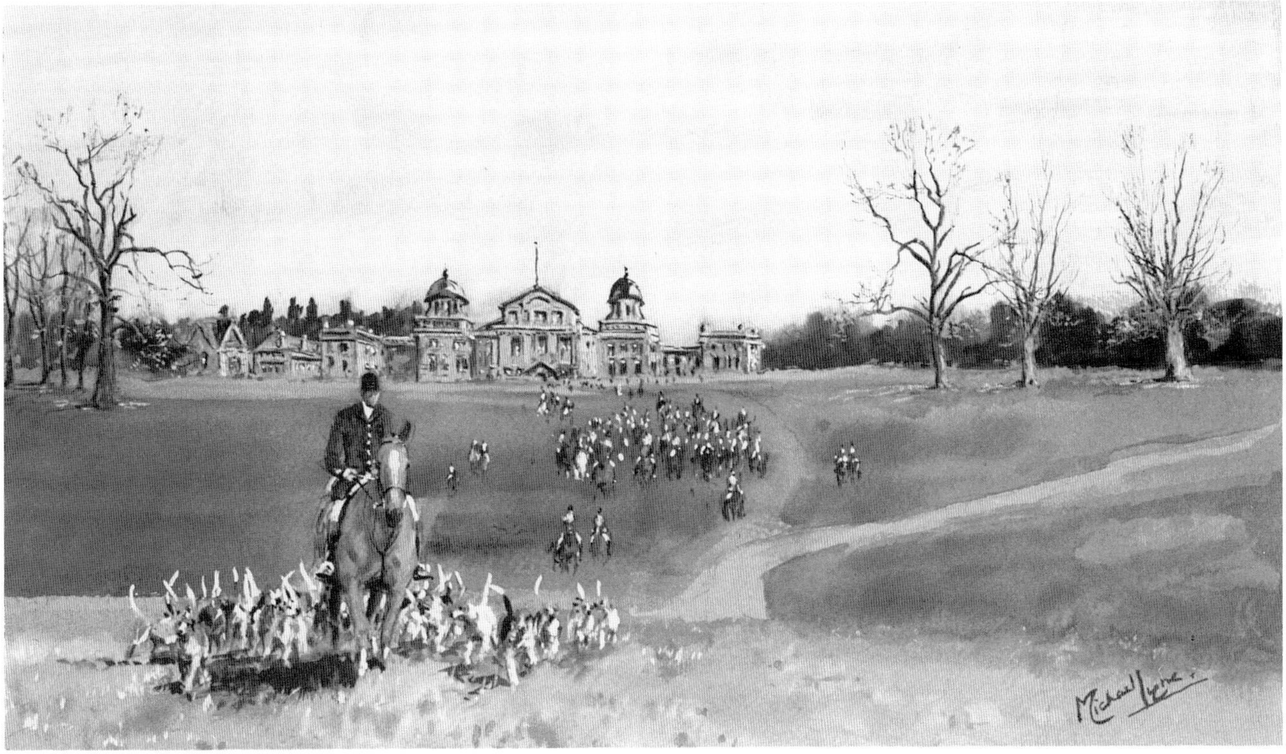

Year	Title	No.	Publisher	Size (in)	(cm)
1987	*The Beaufort at Badminton*	100	H.G.	7 × 12	18 × 30
	Hounds on a Line	100	S.& N.S.B.	9 × 13.5	23 × 34

Key

E. & S.	Eyre and Spottiswood
F. & R.	Frost & Reed
W.A.S.	Wynnstay Arts Society
H.G.	Heale Gallery
C. & H.H.	The Crawley & Horsham Hunt
S. & N.S.B.	Surrey & North Sussex Beagles
B.F.S.S.	The British Field Sports Society
A.B.	Alfred Bell

Dimensions: Height × width

UNLIMITED EDITION PRINTS

Medici Society

The Devon & Somerset Staghounds crossing a stream, 1936, 10.75 × 16.5 in, 27 × 42 cm
The Ledbury crossing a road, 1936, 9 × 11.5 in, 23 × 29 cm

Frost & Reed

In 1979 Frost & Reed (Venture Prints) issued two titles in an unlimited edition:
i) *By the Way*, 24 × 30 in, 61 × 76 cm
ii) *Grand National: First Time Round Becher's Brook*, 1969, 24 × 30 in, 61 × 76 cm
Frost & Reed also included unlimited sections in the following limited edition titles:
i) 1971 – *Away*
ii) 1972 – *Hurdle Race*

Heale Gallery

The Loose Horse, 1981, was an edition of 950 of which only 200 were signed.

The British Field Sports Society

The Society has published three black and white broadsheets of Michael Lyne's drawings:
i) *Coursing*
ii) *Beagling*
iii) *Foxhunting*
Each is approximately 15 × 24 in (38 × 61 cm) in size; the artist signed many copies in aid of the Society's funds.

APPENDIX IV

BOOKS WRITTEN AND ILLUSTRATED BY MICHAEL LYNE

1938 *Horses, Hounds and Country,* Eyre & Spottiswood, London
Studies from a Sportsman's Note Book
Coloured frontispiece. 3 coloured plates, 47 black and white illus. 4to, 95 pp

1939 *Hunting, Here and There,* Eyre & Spottiswood, London
Text and illustrations destroyed by enemy action, 1940

1973 *From Litter to Later On,* Standfast Press, Gloucestershire
The story of a litter of puppies.
Coloured frontispiece, 1 double page coloured plate, 47 black and white illus. 4to, 90 pp

1974 *A Parson's Son,* J.A. Allen, London
Autobiographical introduction to a selection of articles previously published in *The Field* and *Country Life.*
Signed, limited edition of 750 copies. Coloured frontispiece, 12 coloured plates. 28 black and white illustrations. Oblong folio, 150 pp

1979 *The Michael Lyne Sketchbook,* Standfast Press, Gloucestershire.
Pages from the Artist's Sketchbook with supporting text.
Signed limited edition of 550 copies. 21 coloured plates, numerous pencil sketches and monochrome plates. Oblong folio, 114 pp

In addition to his books, Michael Lyne was a regular contributor to *The Field* and *Country Life* for over thirty-five years.

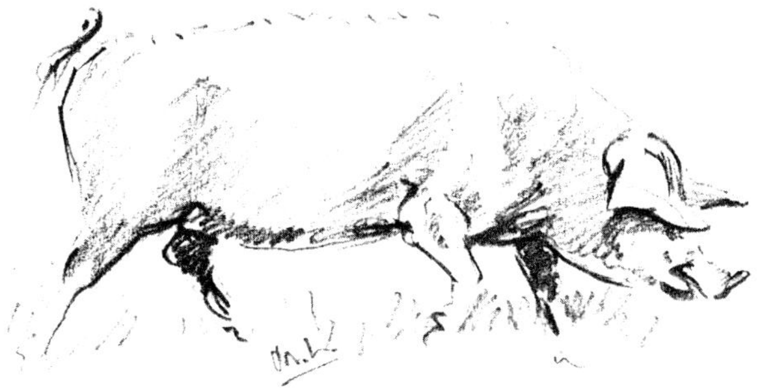

APPENDIX V

BOOKS ILLUSTRATED BY MICHAEL LYNE

Alcorn, Robert H., *Riding High,* 1953, 254 pp

Baron, Henry, *Martin Claims Damages,* A Sporting Romance, 1937, 266 pp

Bishop, Tim, *Horses, Hounds and the Odd Stag*, 1979, 44 ills including 1 in colour, 81 pp

Burrows, George T., *Gentleman Charles*, A History of Foxhunting, 1951, 50 illus and pencil drawings, 240 pp

Fairhurst, Jill, *Vicky*, The Story of a Domesticated Vixen, 1964, 91 pp

The Field, Foxhunting Guide, 15 pp

Goldschmidt, Sidney G., *Skilled Horsemanship*, 1937, 136 pp

Goeldner, Christian T., *The Thoroughbred Field Hunter*, 1977, 127 pp

Hooper, Maurice, *Special Training for Modern Shooters*

Lynch, Stanilaus, *Rhymes of an Irish Huntsman*, 1937, 60 pp

Moore, Daphne, *In Nimrod's Footsteps*, Some reflections on hunting on a shoestring, 1974, 208 pp

Morris, Pamela Macgregor, *Blue Rosette*, 1950, 303 pp

Neale, Douglas, *Nearly All Hunting*, Twenty-five couple of Sporting and almost sporting essays, 1950, 200 pp

Newsham, Stuart, *The Hunting Diaries of Stanley Barker*, 1981

Parry, C.N. de Courcy (Dalesman), *Here Lies My Story*, 1964, repr. 1966, 272 pp

Peel, Hazel Mary, *Easter the Showjumper*, 1964, 180 pp

Percy, Cyril Heber, *Hym*, The life story of a famous fox, 1959, 107 pp

Percy, Cyril Heber, *Us Four*, A Biography of 4 Brothers, 1963, 124 pp

Percy, Cyril Heber, *While Others Sleep*, The story of a poacher, 1962, 133 pp

Pitt, Frances, *Hounds, Horses and Hunting*, 1948, 272 pp

Rennick, Richard Grant (Ed), *Coursing: the pursuit of game with gazehounds*, 1976, 303 pp

Reynolds, James, *Keep a Silver Dollar*, 1960

Self, Margaret Cabell (Ed), *A Treasury of Horse Stories*, 1953, 340 pp

Self, Margaret Cabell (Ed), *A Second Treasury of Horse Stories*, 1954, 232 pp

Spooner, Glenda, *Royal Crusader*, The autobiography of a horse, 1948, 222 pp

Standford, John Keith, *The Horsemasters*, 1975

Summerhays, R.S. & Stella A. Walker, *The Controversial Horse*, 1966, 224 pp

Walker, Stella A. (Compiler), *Enamoured of an Ass*, A Donkey Anthology, 1977, 196 pp

Wathen, D., *Harehunters All*, One hundred articles on beagles and harehunters, Privately printed limited edition
Williams, Dorian, *Lost*, 1974, Repr. 1983, 102 pp
Wynmalen, Henry, *The Horse in Action*, 1954, New Edn 1973, 58 pp
Wynmalen, Henry, *Riding for Children*, 1949, 31 pp

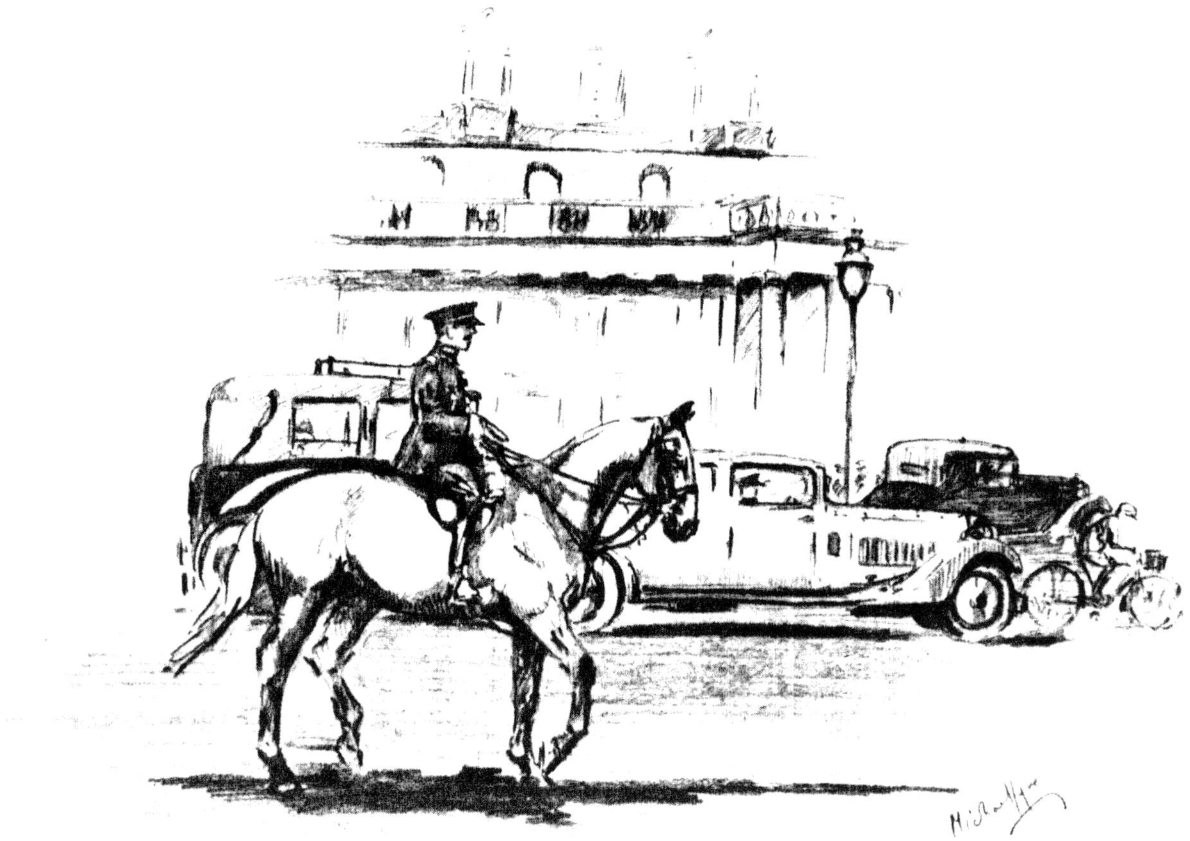

Our well-mannered Police horses

From *Skilled Horsemanship*, 1937.

APPENDIX VI

THE ARTIST'S CHARACTER

Rather than attempt what would, at its best, be a pretentious assessment of the artist's character, included in this appendix are extracts from three letters which I received, in response to my appeal for information about Michael, in an attempt to define the essential person from completely different standpoints.

The first is from his eldest grandson, Henry, the other from friends in the United States and England.

'To call Michael Lyne just an artist would be a misinterpretation of his character. For he was not only an artist but to me Grandfather.

'He was at home with people who loved the countryside; unfortunately I am not that way inclined so could never talk about dogs or wildfowl without asking him what 'exactly' was the difference between Salukis and Lurchers or Mallard and Herons.

'Grandfather always encouraged me in his second love, rugby, so that relating the events of a match to him would be exciting as he always had his own ideas of what to do.

'His determination and arrogance was often contagious, for his utterance about yet another "bloody jogger" as we passed one on the road was just an ambiguous way of saying that he wouldn't mind being in the jogger's shoes.

'I now refer to runners as "bloody joggers" as if it was second nature.'

Henry Lyne, age 14 (written at 30,000 feet flying from London to Accra), Autumn 1989

'One of the greatest pleasures I have enjoyed during my lifetime has been foxhunting in England, North America and Ireland. It has always been a challenge for me to find a sporting artist whose expertise combined the essence of an English or American foxhunting landscape with the ability to place in that landscape horses and hounds with exactness of conformation and movement. Michael Lyne, an old friend, who first visited me in Maryland in 1952, is that artist par excellence. Besides being a master of color with the above attributes, Michael's versatility included a flair for painting the creatures of nature: ducks, dogs, foxes and birds, with very charming likenesses and easy brush strokes. It is hard for us to say which are greater heritages left to the world of sporting art – Michael's watercolors or his oils.

'He was a devoted family man, of simple tastes and charming manner, who loved nothing better than a day on his grey horse with the VWH. His paintings will always reflect happy personal memories from all those who are fortunate to own them and will charm the casual observer in the years to come.'

J. Fife Symington, Baltimore, Maryland, November 1989

'When at school before the war, I admired Michael Lyne's watercolours immensely and cut out the prints from *The Field* to stick in my albums. After soldiering in the late sixties,

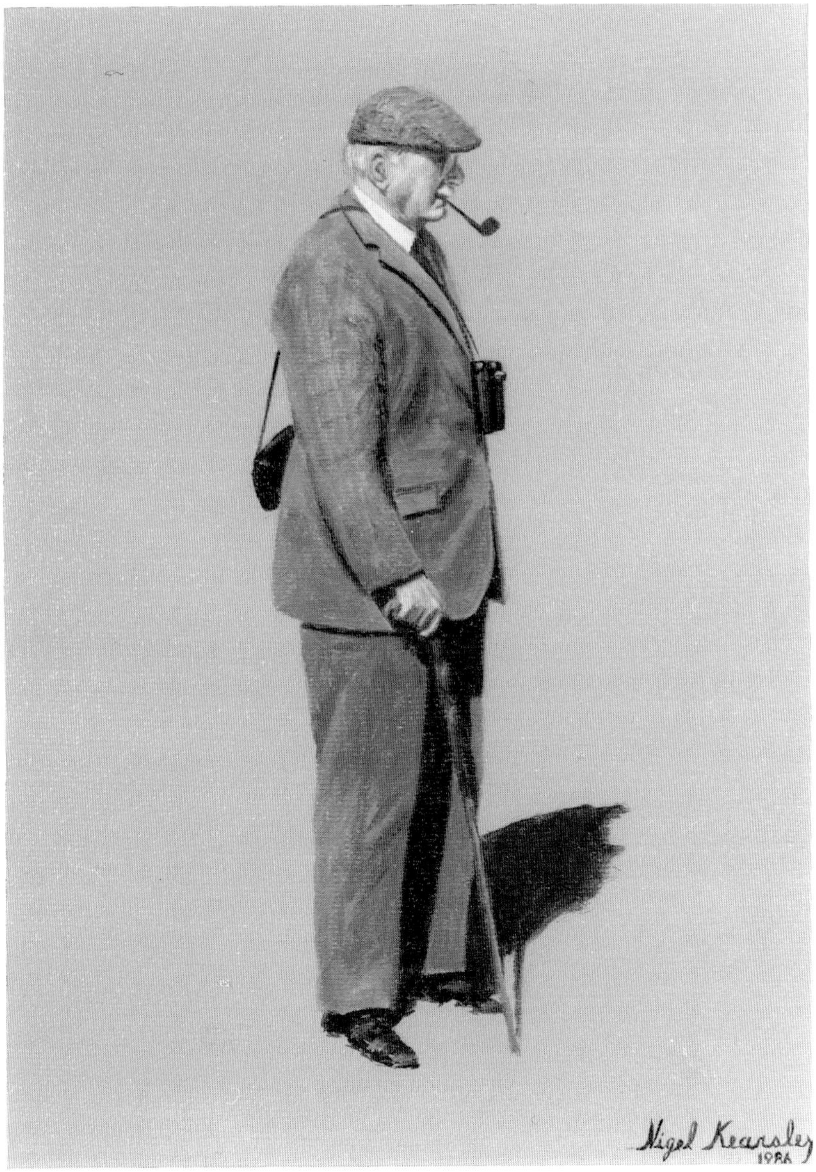

Nigel Kearsley's portrait of Michael on Exmoor, Spring 1986.

I decided to start painting and set out to meet Michael by going to one of his exhibitions at Frost & Reed. I asked a senior director if he could put me in touch with Michael. "I'm afraid that is impossible," he said, "he lives in the depths of the country and does not like to be disturbed." I was crestfallen!

'My wife and I then moved to Gloucestershire: to my joy I found that Michael lived nearby and we met. This led to a wonderful twenty years of friendship when we were constantly in touch and during which he taught me all I now know about painting.

'He kindly mentions me in *The Michael Lyne Sketchbook* and of our happy days fishing together.

'I am always thrilled by his sense of colour, his draughtsmanship and the life and drama in his work. He always used a tiny palette, rarely mixing his paints, but dipping his brush into the pure colour when applying it. Any mixing was then done on the canvas and this, I feel, was his special technique. His methods as a tutor were unusual. "Don't ask me what colours I use in a chestnut horse – I never know myself!" He always advised me especially in times of stress. One day I had made a mess of the foreground of a big hunting picture and took it, in a state of misery, to Michael at 10 am. He emerged with a large glass of whisky. "Drink this," he said. "Go home – scrape out that foreground and do it again with a palette knife." It was the best picture I have ever painted!

'In latter years my wife and I have taken Michael and Jessie on a holiday each year, visiting Exmoor, Wales, Shropshire and Hereford which included his old home at Ross-on-Wye and a Monastery at Llanthony founded by one of his ancestors.

'His colourful reminiscences of the old days always fascinated us.

'Michael, a brilliant artist, was so lovable in his appreciation of country life, his modesty about his own skills, and his devotion to Jessie and his family. No look at the life and work of Michael Lyne is complete without remembering his devotion to Jessie and hers to him. Whilst wandering around the countryside looking up old hunting haunts he would turn and say quite unexpectedly, "My best thing in life has always been Jessie you know, my life and painting and the inspiration for it would have been so different otherwise – maybe not at all."

'We miss a valued old friend.'

Nigel Kearsley, Burford, Oxon.

INDEX